**LET
OUR
CHILDREN
GO!**

LET OUR CHILDREN GO!

BY TED PATRICK
WITH TOM DULACK

Thomas Congdon Books

E. P. DUTTON & CO., INC. I NEW YORK I 1976

Published simultaneously in Canada by
Clarke, Irwin & Company Limited, Toronto and Vancouver
ISBN: 0-525-14450-1

Library of Congress Cataloging in Publication Data

Patrick, Ted.
  Let our children go!

  1. Sects—Controversial literature. 2. Youth—Religious life.
3. Patrick, Ted. I. Dulack, Tom, 1935–   joint author. II. Title.
BP603.P37   1976   200′.1′9 [B]   75-45298

FOREWORD
by Tom Dulack

When the idea of my collaborating on this book was first proposed to me, I didn't know who Ted Patrick was. It had to be explained to me that he is a former civil servant from California whose life's mission is to rescue young people who have fallen prey to pseudo-religious cults—and to counter cult indoctrination by a process called deprogramming. At first I was dubious, but I eventually agreed to the collaboration. It seemed challenging and intriguing to me, and since I'd recently published a novel dealing with the psychology of religious phenomena, I felt the subject was one I could approach with the sort of critical and objective point of view that would be important to a book like this.

I'd been interviewing Patrick night and day for about a week before I saw my first deprogramming. By that time I'd heard a considerable portion of his story, and I was unsure about a great deal of it. But the first time I met a boy who had been "abducted" by his parents and brought to Patrick, my skepticism was overwhelmed.

The boy indeed looked like a zombie. He seemed encased in a mental bell jar no one could penetrate. He would not eat or drink. He would not answer questions. He wouldn't talk at all. He kept drifting off into a sort of trance, and when, to discourage this, Patrick and the boy's parents would try to put him on his feet and walk him around, he would collapse as though he were made of rags.

Eventually Patrick broke him. The emotion of the moment, when the boy began to weep and embraced his parents, was so high as to be embarrassing to me. To be a witness to these convulsions of family feeling was almost appalling. I came away wondering what it was I'd actually experienced.

After that it grew progressively harder to remain skeptical of Patrick. I sat in on several more deprogrammings, and they deepened my sense of the ugly mystery attaching to the psychological incarceration of these children by the cults. I also came increasingly to realize that in these deprogrammings, families were being reconstituted. Under the unique pressures of these bizarre situations, blood relatives declared things to one another they would otherwise probably never have uttered in all of their lives. I saw one eighteen-year-old clutching his twenty-year-old brother by the shoulders and shaking him and crying, "Don't you understand, I love you! I want you back! I want my brother back!" For someone like me, who had not exchanged a spontaneous syllable of explicit affection with his own brother in thirty years, this kind of moment was, to say the least, disturbing and impressive.

Friends keep asking me, "What really happens in a deprogramming? How does Patrick do it?" I can only reply, based on my experience with him, that he does what he says he does—beyond question. He really does expunge the effects of a young person's indoctrination. How he does it is something else. It has to do, I think, with the peculiar force of his personality.

It's not easy to convey the strange atmosphere of a deprogramming, the fierce intensity of the battle between Patrick and one of the cult victims. Patrick sits there for eighteen hours at a time with scarcely an interruption, knee to knee with his subject, and seems to impose his will on him. Wearing the subject down physically is no doubt part of it. There is, however, something more than simply exhausting the antagonist. It is almost as if Patrick transfers some kind of psychic energy from himself to whomever he's deprogramming, a spiritual transfusion with Patrick as the donor.

When he is not deprogramming (which isn't often) nothing about Patrick would suggest a man who has the ability to alter people's lives. He likes soul music and rock; he likes good food and is proud of his cooking. He likes to dance, he's a good singer, a devoted family man. In public he can come across as a bit dogmatic; in private he's modest, soft-spoken, humorous, and shrewd.

Patrick is a black, fundamentalist Christian; I am white, a

lapsed Roman Catholic. He admires Ronald Reagan; I campaigned for Eugene McCarthy and would do it again. He is a high school dropout; I teach English literature in a university. We are very different people. Nevertheless, if either of my own daughters got caught up in one of the cults discussed in this book, or one of the many that are not discussed, I would not hesitate to invade the cult with several large and brutal friends, forcibly remove her, and pay any amount of money to persuade Patrick to drop whatever he was doing and come deprogram her. And I would not rest easily until he arrived.

It is my voice that introduces each of the chapters that follow. Every story is factual, but although each episode concerns real people and real cases, names have been changed, where indicated, to protect the privacy of certain persons who have not previously been exposed to the public eye.

**LET
OUR
CHILDREN
GO!**

PROLOGUE

At 6:05 A.M., May 29, 1975, TWA flight 507 from Los Angeles touched down at John F. Kennedy International Airport in New York. Weary from the long transcontinental voyage, jet-lagged, having eaten only a grapefruit for breakfast an hour before, a nineteen-year-old boy disembarked from the plane and walked on stiff legs through the arrival area looking for his parents. Though he had been a dean's list student for a year and a half at his New England university, he was now a dropout. His name was not Bernie Weber, but he will be called that.

There were a few other young men his age in the terminal sleepily checking backpacks through the ticket counters, lounging over coffee cups in the restaurants, or dozing in sculpted plastic chairs. Most were bearded, with long hair tied back with sweat bands and bandanas, and they wore scruffy jeans and sandals. In contrast, Bernie Weber was close-trimmed, clean-shaven, wearing a green sport jacket on the lapel of which was pinned a red and white badge with a design like a spider web identifying him as a member of the Unification Church, and as a disciple of a Korean evangelist named Sun Myung Moon.

Bernie Weber had traveled from the Unification center in Los Angeles ostensibly to attend the marriage of a cousin and to see his grandfather from Israel who was visiting New York. The real reason for his journey across the country, however, was to withdraw nearly one thousand dollars from his bank account in order to donate it to the Unification Church.

Bernie's parents had not yet arrived to meet him. And so, with his cheap borrowed suitcase at his feet, the boy opened a paperback volume entitled *Unification Thought* and applied himself to understanding its contents.

> Logos has the polarities of Sung Sang and Hyung Sang, and positivity and negativity. Then what are the concrete contents of the polarity of the Logos? Its Sung Sang is reason and its

Hyung Sang is law (principles). The unified body created through the action of give-and-take between the Sung Sang (Inner Sung Sang) and the Hyung Sang (Inner Hyung Sang) is Logos.

His eyes watered; it was hard to concentrate. He did not know what he was reading. But so much the better, he assured himself. The more difficult it was, the more meritorious his struggle to understand. Nevertheless, he was tired. He had not slept on the plane, and he had a headache, and he was hungry. He wanted to go to a restaurant and drink a glass of orange juice, eat a doughnut. But he knew that was Satan talking to him, Satan tempting him. It was Satan tempting him to sit down too, and Satan interfering with his powers of concentration, confusing him, obscuring the truth of what he was trying to read, with burning eyes, in his blue and white primer. He would remain standing, and he would pray, to Sun Myung Moon, the Father, the Master, his Messiah. And deal Satan a blow.

"We're going to smash Satan today!" the other members of his family had screamed in chorus back in L.A. *"Abaji! Mansei!"* Sending him off, as they sent everyone off on missions, in the manner of Kamikaze pilots shouting *"Banzai!"* Arms thrust straight up above their heads. *"Mansei! Mansei! Mansei!"* Victory for the Father for ten thousand years. The Father, Sun Myung Moon, to whom Bernie Weber now, in JFK, early in the morning, prayed fervently to fortify him against the temptation to sit down and drink a glass of orange juice.

Then his parents were there, Harold and Valerie Weber, and his mother was kissing him, a handsome woman, smiling an artificial smile, trying hard to keep the anxiety from spilling over. She was intent on obeying the black man's instructions not to alarm her son or arouse his suspicions—as intent as was Bernie himself on deceiving her into thinking that he had come home to attend a wedding.

For a brief moment as she kissed him, and as he shook hands with his father—a slight, balding real estate broker from Paterson, New Jersey—he experienced a kind of emotional churning deep inside, like a motor that has lain idle for months turning over sluggishly once or twice, and he knew a moment of doubt, even fear, mixed with sorrow, regret and love as he smelled his mother's cologne and gripped his father's hand. But he suppressed the feeling; that was Satan too, and these middle-aged people whose name he shared were of Satan (though perhaps all unwittingly), just as everything outside of Moon was Satan. And a kind of glaze came across his eyes, and he turned away with a fixed vacant smile which caused Valerie Weber to turn away too, in order to conceal the despair she knew was in her face.

They walked out of the terminal, the boy between his parents, all of them speaking in stiff, grotesquely polite little bursts of irrelevancy, as though they were all utter strangers condemned to each other's company for an indefinite period of time.

Out in the airport parking lot, two members of the black man's team were waiting. The one giving the orders was a thin, stoop-shouldered Vietnam veteran who will be called Joe Franklin. Franklin had a young cousin who, like Bernie Weber, joined up with Sun Myung Moon and told his parents he hated them. Now his cousin was back in school and living with his family again. The other person in the parking lot was Franklin's back-up, a deceptively sleepy-looking eighteen-year-old named Kevin. Kevin himself was recently rescued from a small and barbaric cult of garbage-eaters in the Southwest. Now they were both waiting, sitting in a rented blue Plymouth that was parked next to the Webers' Impala station wagon.

"That's them, Kevin," Franklin said, pointing toward the approaching Webers. "You drive out the exit first and pay for both cars. Then go straight out to the Van Wyck and over the Whitestone Bridge. We'll be right behind you."

"Ted says the kid might know some karate."

"Don't worry about it. He won't pull no damn karate on me. Besides, the way they work those kids and starve 'em, he's in no condition to fight." Franklin put out his cigarette in the ashtray and nodded out the window to Jeff Weber, Bernie's younger brother, seated a few feet away in the back of the Webers' Impala.

Bernie and his parents drew nearer. Bernie seemed to suspect nothing. His brother Jeff, following instructions, opened the rear door but did not get out. Bernie handed in his suitcase, and, as his parents got into the front seat, he slid in beside his brother. He did not notice Joe Franklin stepping out of the adjacent Plymouth and walking briskly around to the station wagon, coming up behind him just as he was climbing in. Bernie reached out to close the door, but the handle was snatched from his grasp as Franklin yanked the door open and jumped into the seat next to him.

"Hi, Bernie," he said, smiling, offering his hand. "I'm Joe."

He locked the door, and the station wagon, with Harold Weber at the wheel, moved out behind the Plymouth, which had pulled ahead. It was accomplished just like that.

"Pleased to meet you," said Bernie. And for a long time he did not dare to say anything else. He was squeezed between his brother and the stranger and he knew he was in trouble— very serious trouble, the kind of trouble they'd warned him about at the center, endlessly explaining what he should do in case it happened. And now it had happened, and they were taking him some place to torture him in an attempt to "deprogram" him.

Ignoring the attempts of the others to make cheerful small talk, he withdrew into himself, as he was conditioned to do, and stared sightlessly straight ahead, preparing himself for the impending ordeal. He prayed that he would be strong enough to resist them. He was wary but confident. Of course. Master would protect him. The truth would be his shield.

At eight-thirty that morning, in a house in Wallingford,

Connecticut, the black man was awakened by the sound of the door chimes and he knew the Webers had arrived. He'd slept poorly in the warm, airless bedroom, but he could not open a window—all the windows in the house had been nailed shut the night before. It was a standard security measure—they all tried to go out the windows at the first opportunity.

He was in no hurry to rise. Joe Franklin could work on Bernie for a while. He preferred not to confront the victim until the young person became accustomed to the idea of his detention, and realized that they were not going to injure him, that they were only going to talk. In the past, when the black man appeared too early into the deprogramming, victims tended to panic; the cults lectured about him—"Black Lightning" they called him—instilling an unreasoning fear of him in the kids, and on more than one occasion when he'd walked into the room the young person had lost his head, tried to bolt.

So he would let Joe have the first crack at Bernie. Joe was pretty good, but he talked too much, and tended to preach, which was a waste of breath in the beginning, when the victim's mind was still closed. At this stage, the mind was like a bottle with its cap screwed on tight. Nothing could go in. You had to unscrew that cap first, by asking questions, forcing him to start thinking again, inducing him to talk.

He lay in bed and thought about all there was to do that day in addition to deprogramming Bernie Weber. Two weeks before he had been convicted on a charge of false imprisonment, in Orange County, California, a very conservative part of the country. It was like being tried in darkest Mississippi. Worse. Sentencing was next week, an appeal had to be filed and the lawyer was hassling him for money. But there was no money; he was virtually broke.

And Denver. He was appealing last year's Denver conviction, also for false imprisonment, and the California case could be construed as a violation of his probation. A jail term loomed. And then the assistant U.S. Attorney in Seattle was threatening to appeal the Seattle acquittal in that Church of Armageddon case.

Such appeals had happened only a few times in our history, and he wondered if there had been any communication between Seattle and the Denver D.A. It seemed likely.

The black man lay there and thought about how he could not afford to defend himself. And if he went to jail, what would Ruth Ann and the children do? How would they live? And who would carry on the work while he was out of circulation?

Well, that was next week. Something would either turn up, or it wouldn't. It seemed out of his hands. More pressing was to coordinate the travel schedules of some twenty-four helpers in the next few days. The Goski family wanted help with the four members of their family who belonged to the Brother Julius cult here in Connecticut. The plan was to snatch all four simultaneously. Dangerous and complicated, requiring split-second planning and flawless execution. It would be best to send them to New Jersey, to the place in the mountains. He would need at least twenty people for that. Then there was the girl in Boston in the Children of God. They were snatching her this morning. He would send her to Westchester; Joe could drive over that night and begin deprogramming her while he worked on Weber. And maybe Winnie, yes, fly Winnie back East from Kansas where she was completing her rehabilitation and have her assist Joe. Once the kids were out, they all wanted to help others get out, and it strengthened them to see what they had looked like, to hear a kid from another cult parroting the exact same Scriptural quotations, responding the same way they had responded, in the same words, to the same questions, no matter which cult they had belonged to.

Bill would be flying into New York from Dayton. John and Bob would be driving to Boston. A plane ticket for Winnie to LaGuardia. And he had to send somebody up to Syracuse to find that doctor's daughter who, like Bernie Weber, had been ensnared by Moon. And call the lawyer in California. And the reporter who wanted to come out today to interview him.

From the sounds of the voices he could tell that they'd taken Bernie down into the basement. It was safe for him to get up, have some breakfast, and get busy. The worst thing about going to jail would be the emptiness of the days, the absence of activity, movement, work, twenty hours a day, organizing, traveling, freeing up the gear-locked brains of the young and innocent victims of Sun Myung Moon and the Children of God.

"Let's get rolling," he said out loud. "Let's move on out!" And he padded into the bathroom.

There isn't much in the basement—a long heavy cream-colored couch against one wall, and a couple of green plastic bucket chairs brought down from the kitchen. A salt-and-pepper shag carpet wall to wall. A washer and drier combination in one corner. A wrought iron spiral staircase descending from the living room, and people coming and going sound like jailers as their shoes strike the metal. Three narrow oblong windows, locked, up near the ceiling, are overgrown with weeds and uncut lawn: you would have to stand on a chair to unlock them and even then you couldn't squeeze your body through. In spite of the carpet and the panelling on the walls, it is dank, humid, with a basement smell.

Bernie Weber is sitting on the edge of the couch, his ankles crossed primly, his hands folded between his knees, his spine rigid, trying to fathom the strategy of his abductors, tense, watchful behind his dilated eyes, fearful, wondering from what direction the first blow will come.

So far Bernie has said nothing. All the talking has been done by the heavy-lidded man with a drooping moustache, large white teeth, and prominent Italianate nose—Joe Franklin —who is sitting opposite Bernie in one of the green kitchen chairs. His manner is relaxed, low-keyed, congenial. But Bernie sees him as the Devil incarnate. He listens to Franklin for only a short while before deciding that he will not speak. They'd cautioned him in Los Angeles, "If you're kidnapped, don't say anything, not a word. We'll find you, we'll get you out, and we'll bring charges and put them all in jail." So he won't speak, he won't cooperate in any way. He will resist them with every fiber of his being, however long it takes.

"You see," Franklin is saying, smoking, smiling, his teeth

white below the moustache, "you think Moon is the Messiah, don't you? Of course you do. They programmed you to believe that. I've heard 'em do it. I've infiltrated Unification centers all over the country. But Moon ain't no Messiah. You know what Moon is?" he questioned easily, pleasantly. "Moon is a pimp. He's a pimp, that's all, and you're nothing but a male prostitute. You've given yourself to him body and soul, and you go out in the streets and sell yourself and bring the money back to him. You ain't selling plastic flowers and Cracker Jack. You're selling yourself, and you're giving the money to that pimp."

The boy's unblinking eyes do not flicker from Franklin's face. But he is nonetheless aware of his mother sitting on a cushion to the left of his feet, gazing up from the floor at him, and he cannot believe she will permit this man to call him a prostitute. He waits for her to object, but she says nothing, nor does his father, also seated on the floor, cross-legged, on the other side. That they do not object is proof to him of their iniquity; what he has been told at the center is true: he has only one family, the Unification Church, and only one parent, Sun Myung Moon, to whom he now begins to pray.

"How much money did you bring in every day selling those damned flowers? Three hundred? Four? I know kids that sold six hundred in one day." Swiveling in his chair, Franklin addresses Valerie Weber. "I went out selling one day, I didn't even know what I was doing, and I brought in nearly two hundred bucks. It's a racket, is all it is." Swiveling back. "That ain't no church. It's just one big rip-off, and the guy doing the ripping off is Moon. Tell me, Bernie—where do you think that money you raised went to? Huh? You told those poor old ladies on the street corner and in the parking lots that the money was for drug reform and prison reform and this and that and everything else. But you knew that was a lie, didn't you? They told you it was okay to lie because everyone outside of Unification Church is of the Devil, and it's okay to lie to the Devil. But where do *you* think the money went?"

The boy is not listening. He is summoning up a mental pic-

ture of the Master, the Father—the flat round face, the high
cheekbones, the dark shadows of his slanted eyes, the beloved
features he has contemplated for long hours on end, as they
all did, until he felt faint and dizzy with the pure ecstasy of
what was revealed to him in the depths of the photograph of
this man who had come as the Third Adam to save the world.
To block out the blasphemies spewing like smoke from the
mouth of the diabolic man sitting across from him, he concen-
trates on the words of the Master: *You may again want to ask
me, 'With what authority do you say these things?' I spoke with
Jesus Christ in the spirit world. And I also spoke with John
the Baptist. This is my authority . . . If you believe the Bible
you must believe what I am saying.*

"You see," Franklin explains to the parents, who sit there
as attentive and innocent as freshmen in a lecture hall the first
week of school, "he can't answer, 'cause he can't think anymore. He's been brainwashed. They tell him not to think, because thinking's of the Devil. Moon says, 'I am your brain.'
Doesn't he, Bernie? Moon's taken his brain away, his power
to think. But we're gonna give it back to him."

And the boy, aware of his parents, seeing them without looking at them—this Jewish boy, Bar-Mitzvahed in Isreal, raised
in a Zionist atmosphere—presses another button in his mind,
and the Master's words return as from a computer: *The cruci-
fixion of Jesus was a result of the faithlessness of the Jewish
people.* Everything that has happened to him on this dreadful
morning has confirmed all he was taught since joining the Unification Church ten months ago.

Upstairs he hears voices, footsteps, the clink and clatter of
silverware and dishes, water running in the sink. He wonders
if Ted Patrick is in the house. Black Lightning. Will he be
struck? He doesn't care. If he has to die for Sun Myung Moon,
he will. He is prepared to die. It will be a privilege to die.

He puts himself into a kind of trance in which time seems
to cease. In fact three hours go by, during which he does not
speak, and does not move, ankles crossed, hands folded, spine

arched, in a posture of intense militancy, a curious smile distorting his features, like a grimace, or the drawing back of the lips from a corpse's teeth when rigor mortis sets in.

"The way they get them is by on-the-spot hypnosis. Once they get them, they brainwash them. The technique is the same as the North Koreans used on our prisoners of war," says Ted Patrick.

The reporter nods and writes in her pad. The black man lounges against the kitchen sink eating a ham and cheese sandwich and drinking a glass of orange juice. He is wearing light blue bellbottomed jeans, high-heeled patent leather shoes, and a short sleeved white turtleneck. At a first meeting he does not inspire either awe or confidence. He is five feet eight inches tall, forty-five years old, has a small pot belly, wears owlish horn-rimmed glasses. He also suffers from a speech impediment that converts th's to f's or v's. Upon meeting him, many parents despair of his ever rescuing and deprogramming their child. Their shock and incredulity soon dissipate, however. He is, ultimately, a powerful and persuasive man.

"They don't let a kid sleep, they don't let him eat. They hit him with tape recordings of Scripture, lectures, discussions, workshops—night and day. They wear him down, wear him out. Pretty soon he believes anything. Some kids go out fundraising three days after they join."

"What about freedom of religion?" the reporter asks.

"Moon's got nothing to do with religion!" he replies emphatically. "Moon's a crook, plain and simple. They're all crooks. You name 'em. Hare Krishna. The Divine Light Mission. Guru Maharaj Ji. The New Testament Missionary Fellowship. Brother Julius. Love Israel. The Children of God. Not a brown penny's worth of difference between any of 'em. I've taken 'em all on. Deprogrammed hundreds of kids from all those cults."

He places several phone calls concerning his legal problems and travel arrangements for assistants scattered all over the country. At one point he takes a call and says, "I don't want to talk on this phone. Might be tapped. I'll call you later from a phone booth." The impression is created that the house is under siege.

The mother, father, and brother Jeff, along with Kevin, clomp up and down the circular stairs bringing reports of what's happening with Bernie, which is nothing. "He hasn't moved, he's not saying anything."

Patrick gazes out the kitchen window at the knee high grass in the backyard and drums his fingers on the Formica countertop. "Think I'll let Joe have him a while longer," he murmurs. "Tell Kevin to get some sleep. Has to be somebody awake all night with him."

Moments later, sipping coffee, he remarks to the reporter, "See, he's a robot right now." She does not take this down; she merely looks at him, quizzically, skeptically. "I tell the parents, 'You're not dealing with your son at this point. You're dealing with a zombie. You have to do whatever's necessary to get him back.' "

It is hot and humid outside, stifling inside. The Webers have brought a week's supply of food—cold cuts, loaves of bread, bottles of soda, milk, paper plates, and napkins—along with sleeping bags, blankets, pillows. The sink and counter begin to fill up with dirty dishes.

Everyone speaks in muted voices, and the people are as tense and anxious as relatives waiting in a hospital lounge for news of a loved one on whom surgery is being performed.

"He's lost thirty pounds since he joined ten months ago," Mrs. Weber informs the reporter who listens sympathetically. Mrs. Weber is frying hamburgers, taking refuge from her fears in managing the kitchen.

"It's been ten long months of nightmare," confirms her husband. "This thing has turned our lives upside down."

"Hiring this man was the biggest decision we've ever had to make," his wife adds. "You take cream and sugar? We tried everything, talked to everybody—lawyers, psychiatrists, the police. We finally went to our rabbi and he said, 'If you don't hire him to get your boy,' " she gestures at the black man who is again conferring on the phone near the kitchen door, " 'you'll never see Bernie again. There's no other way.' "

"I don't believe he's going to break," Jeff Weber says. "He's strong. Strong and stubborn. Once he gets his mind set on something, he won't budge."

"Oh, he'll budge," Patrick says, overhearing as he hangs up. He looks at the tops of his patent leather shoes for a moment, then repeats, "He'll budge, all right."

At two, he decides to go down.

After six hours some of the recalcitrance has drained from Bernie's posture; his shoulders are slumped now, his spine slack, though his ankles remain crossed and his hands are folded as before. Lying on the floor is his notebook, which Joe Franklin has expropriated. In the notebook, the boy had written:

> Feeling:
>   where am *I*?
> So completely lost
>   and very far away
> Oh God, have they buried me?
>   and do I dare dig beneath
> storms and tempests beyond
>   consciousness
> becoming one   or
>   split into pieces
> what's the glue

Though Bernie doesn't realize it, those words in the journal reveal a lot about his treatment at the hands of Reverend Moon. "Brainwashing" is by now a vague, almost devalued word, but the process itself most definitely still exists. Dr. Robert J. Lifton of Yale, an authority on North Korean thought reform, prefers to describe the process as one of "ego destruction"—and that is clearly what Bernie is suffering from. Now it's up to Patrick to find the glue and help put the pieces back together.

Descending, his stacked heels clanging on the iron, the black man crosses the room with a briefcase in one hand, smiles, and says quietly, "Hello, Bernie. I'm Ted Patrick."

Bernie Weber has been expecting a gorilla. From the tales he's heard about Patrick, he has imagined a black giant, a nigger-thug-rapist, some hallucination of an interior lineman for the L.A. Rams, a raw-meat eater.

Now, seeing him, meeting him, Bernie is almost moved to laugh with giddy relief. "This is Ted Patrick?" he thinks. "I can handle him." He looks so innocuous, a pot-bellied absurd little man. In his relief, however, he fails to take into account the hard swelling ledge of shoulders outlined beneath the tight white turtleneck, and the arms with muscles as clearly defined as strips of lath beneath the flesh, the substructure of a former middleweight boxer's conditioned physique. And, of course, he cannot guess that his adversary, having deprogrammed scores of people just like him, knows, and will continue to know every step the rest of the way, almost exactly what Bernie is thinking.

Because Patrick likes to work alone, the others—the reporter, Kevin, Bernie's family—at a signal from Joe Franklin rise and leave. They seem touched with a confusion of piety, solemnity, reverence, and a portion of guilt, as they withdraw, on tiptoe, eyes downcast, like mourners escaping from a wake.

Seated in front of the boy, so close that their knees almost touch, their eyes locked, Patrick gets right into it, disdaining preliminaries.

"You think you are a Christian. You think you are doing the Lord's work. You think you worship the Lord. But you don't worship the Lord. You worship Moon. Did the Lord ever tell you to hate your father and mother? Joe Franklin told me that when he asked you, 'Do you love Moon more than your own father,' you said, 'Yes.' You love Moon more than your own father and mother who birthed you into this world and gave you everything. Where does it say in the Bible that you should hate your father and mother? Where does it say that? And where does it say in the Bible that you should spend all your life, twenty hours a day, out on the streets cheating little old ladies, lying to them, robbing them of their money? Where does it say that? Christ told the rich man to give away everything he owned. But He didn't say, 'Give it to Me.' And he certainly didn't say, 'Give it to Moon.' "

He talks quietly, slowly, almost inaudibly. As he talks, he works with a felt-tip pen on a photograph of Sun Myung Moon that he has taken from his briefcase. He draws a pair of horns on Moon's head, then a moustache, pointed ears, making a caricature of the Devil out of the image the boy has been conditioned to love and revere.

"Why would you give up your God-given mind, Bernie? God gave you that mind, a good mind, a brilliant mind. You are a brilliant boy, and you have everything going for you. Why would you give up that God-given mind to worship Moon? You're not doing the Lord's work. You worship this son of a bitch. See him?" He holds up the vandalized picture. The boy refuses to look. Patrick moves it to within a few inches of his eyes; he still refuses to look—the rigor mortis smile is on his face again. "There's your god. There's the son of a bitch. Recognize him? That's who you worship. Satan the snake."

Patrick pauses, rocks back in the chair, deliberately rips the picture into confetti and tosses the pieces into the boy's lap. "There's your god. Satan the snake. You know, Moon doesn't speak English." His voice is filled with sorrowful contempt. "You think God can't speak English if He wanted to? Moon says he's God. But he can't speak English. Why's that, Bernie? Think about it. Why?" He waits. "Why?" There's a prolonged silence. Patrick is in no hurry. He rocks back and forth. "You're not going to talk. That's okay. You want to smile at me. Well, I'll smile right back at you. We'll smile together. I've got nothing else to do. I can stay here three, four months. Even longer. Nobody's going anywhere."

This registers on Bernie. He does not realize that the average deprogramming requires no more than three days. That five days is exceptional. That eleven days is the record. If he knew that, he might be able to make the physical and psychological adjustments necessary to withstand Patrick. But he doesn't know, and hearing Patrick talk about four months or more, he swallows, cringes, thinks, "There's no way I can hold out for four months." And makes up his mind that he will fast. "I'll fast for seven days," he tells himself. "Then they'll have to take me to a hospital. Once I'm out of here, I can call one of the centers. Escape."

His back is aching from the concentrated effort of physical resistance. It has been seven hours since he arrived, and he's tired. He shifts his position, crosses his legs, the confetti drizzles from his lap to the floor.

"God is a God of love. But Moon doesn't teach you anything except to hate. Hate your mother and father. Hate your brother. Hate food. Hate sex. Hate your school. Hate your government. Your face is just filled with hate. That's Satan the snake speaking. That's not God. Satan the snake preaches hatred. Hatred is of the Devil. But your parents love you. Your brother loves you. They would do anything for you. What's the Fourth Commandment? Come on, Bernie, you know the Fourth Commandment? According to Moon, the Fourth Commandment is Hate thy Father and Mother. But that's not what God says . . ."

Like many of the other cults, the Unification Church employs the Bible as a point of departure for its doctrine. The vast majority of recruits are not schooled in the Bible, and thus are relatively easy prey to misinterpretations. Patrick knows it well, however, and he exploits his knowledge. Moon argues that the Bible has to be read selectively, that portions of it must be accepted as literal truth, while other portions cannot be taken that way. Patrick says, "It's either all true, or none of it is." And just as a recruit is victimized by becoming entangled in the webs and knots of Scripture, until he is totally confused, Patrick confuses him afresh, reversing the process, forcing him to make the mental journey back through that terrible labyrinth, bringing him back out the way he went.

"All we want you to do is think for yourself again, Bernie. To use your God-given mind. Now look. How can Moon be the Messiah if he was born of woman? How can he be the

Second Coming of Christ? The Bible says Christ was born of a Virgin. We know Moon wasn't born of no Virgin."

Reaching for the large white Bible in his briefcase, he opens it and leafs through the pages. "Let's just see what the Bible says about the Second Coming. Here it is. You want to read it? No? Okay, I'll read it."

"We didn't know anything about this Unification Church in the beginning." Valerie Weber is plastering together ham sandwiches in the kitchen. In the rear bedroom Joe Franklin, who will have to relieve Patrick during the night, is sleeping. Kevin, who has not slept for more than an hour at a time in three days, is lying face down on the floor in the living room. "At first," Mrs. Weber continues, "I suppose we didn't want to know the truth. We kept telling ourselves that it was all right, that it must be okay. We kept believing all the lies Bernie was writing to us about the good work they were doing. But then the signs began to become unmistakable. The letters he wrote, the way he sounded on the telephone. It wasn't Bernie. It was some weird stranger. Then he started trying to proselytize Jeff, and his little sister, who's only thirteen. That's when I knew we had to get help. But wherever we turned—the police, the FBI, the courts—it was the same old story. There was no help— except Ted Patrick."

She does not regret the decision to spend fifteen hundred dollars to try to rescue her son. She has been confirmed in that decision by an NBC television special broadcast a few weeks earlier, a documentary on the Unification Church, which caused a furor and provoked an unusually heavy viewer response. The Webers managed to obtain a videotape of the show.

"All of a sudden," she continues, "everybody was talking about cults. It seemed like everyone you spoke to knew someone who had a child in a cult." Nevertheless, she is apprehensive. So is her husband. "I just wish I had Ted's confidence," he remarks, shaking his head. "I'm not sure he can bring Bernie out of this."

Jeff, a serious, curly-haired, open-faced athletic teenager

who has been reading a copy of *Helter Skelter* he found in one of the bedrooms, drinks from a Pepsi bottle and says flatly, "I don't think he'll ever break. He's stubborn as a mule."

At five o'clock, Patrick asks Bernie's father to run the video-tape of the NBC documentary. Everyone goes down to watch it on the portable TV in the basement. Bernie Weber looks a little less glassy by this time. Without realizing it, he has altered his defensive strategy, choosing now to pose as a caricature of the attentive student, listening too intently to Patrick, mocking him by his appearance of excessive zeal to understand the black man's arguments. And now he is even talking a little; has conceded that his tactic of silence was not working, and was unworkable—especially if he was to remain there for four months. What he has not admitted to himself is that by altering his strategy, he has made a concession: Patrick is scoring.

There are other signs he is weakening. He has removed his jacket, removed his shoes, and sits far back on the couch now. And from time to time the muscles in his thin, tanned face relax, and the eyes actually seem to be receiving impressions, perhaps a clue that his mind is absorbing impressions too. Because he can't stand hearing Patrick read, he has been reading aloud from the Bible. But as yet he has not engaged Patrick in any debate.

The documentary comes on. He watches with apparent interest and curiosity. In L.A. they were not permitted to watch it. There is Moon, shrieking, his face distorted, on the stage in Madison Square Garden, and the voice of the interpreter: "Master speaks . . . 'We can control the government . . . we can smash the world!' " Strutting up and down in a white robe, karate-chopping the air with his arms, stamping, shouting, arms thrusting up above his head, shouting again and again, *"Mansei! Mansei! Mansei!"* And the throng responding, echoing his *Mansei*'s as from a single collective throat. And there are images of young people like himself, neat, clipped, combed, in jackets and ties and sports coats, the girls in prim knee-length skirts, their faces and smiles more plastic than the flowers they are hustling on street corners, in parking lots, at train stations, in shopping centers. And a grim shot of the railroad tracks in upstate New York on which a frenzied disciple lay down, stretching his neck across the tracks, and was decapitated by an onrushing locomotive. Testimony from parents. Testimony from deprogrammed young people—deprogrammed by Ted Patrick. It is a heavy, appalling, horrifying presentation, and everyone in the basement is sickened by it, and angered.

"You're never going back," Harold Weber vows to his son when it's over. "If we have to stay here forever with you, you are never going back to that bunch." His son looks thoughtful, gazes at the narrow windows through which the late afternoon sun enters weakly through the weeds, does not reply.

It is nearly midnight. Plates smeared with spaghetti sauce clutter the kitchen table. The linoleum is dirty, greasy, slippery. Bags of rubbish are piled next to the bolted kitchen door. Everyone feels sullied. From the basement, Patrick's indefatigable voice can be heard, along with Bernie's indistinct replies. They are arguing now, Patrick interrogating, Bernie defending himself. From time to time Patrick plays a tape recording of someone he has deprogrammed from the Moon cult, trying to illustrate for Bernie how he has been duped. Valerie Weber slumbers on the living room couch. Joe Franklin, just awakened, wanders into the kitchen and rummages in the refrigerator, staring into the shelves for long moments as though regarding himself in a mirror. Kevin, red-eyed, roams from room to room, grumbling, searching vainly for a comfortable corner to settle into. He finally chooses an upholstered chair, and curls up in it. Harold Weber and Jeff sit cross-legged on the floor at the top of the stairs, straining to hear what is transpiring below.

In the dining room, the reporter muses over a black book, resembling a Bible, entitled *Divine Principle*. It is incomprehensible. It reminds her of *Mein Kampf*. It is Sun Myung Moon's variation on, and answer to, and substitute for, Holy Scripture.

"Course nobody can understand the damn thing," Joe Franklin drawls. "That's the whole idea. Bernie's never read it. They give them a study guide. It's all just a pile of junk."

The premises of the book are convoluted. *Divine Principle* seems to be based on the interconnected theories that Christ was not God; that His mission on earth was not to die on the cross, but to breed a new race of men, free of sin; that His mission was aborted by his murder, and that Sun Myung Moon is the New Messiah sent to complete the mission Christ failed to accomplish.

"Hell, even that ain't original," Franklin snorts. "We got a copy of a legal document from some group in Korea called the Monastery of Israel. You know, Moon is always saying Divine Principle was revealed to him by God. But these dudes in the Monastery of Israel are suing him because they say they wrote all that shit down thirty, forty years before Moon ever published *Divine Principle*. He stole it from them, word for word." He is disgusted, cynical, tired. He chews on a piece of cheese without appetite.

"What were you before you got into all this?"

"A Catholic."

"What are you now?"

"A Christian. What are you?"

"Nothing," says the reporter with a yawn.

"That's okay," replies Franklin. "Better to be nothing than to belong to one of these damn cults."

By three in the morning everyone is asleep except Patrick, Bernie, and Franklin. For twelve hours Patrick has not left his chair except once, to answer an important phone call and use the bathroom. He has eaten a sandwich brought down to him, drunk a can of Hawaiian Punch, and smoked a White Owl cigar. Bernie Weber has neither eaten nor drunk anything in the more than eighteen hours he has been in the house. He has gone to the bathroom once, around noon, where he inspected the window and found it nailed shut.

Without being aware that he was being forced into yet another tactic of retreat, he has begun to argue with Patrick. He has been quoting *Divine Principle* in rebuttal to Patrick's attacks. But every paragraph and concept of *Divine Principle* he has employed has been refuted by Patrick, quoting from the Bible. Also, watching Patrick eagerly consume his sandwich, Bernie has altered his resolve to fast for seven days. "I can never last seven days," he thought "I'll fast three days. "It has furthermore become progressively difficult to pray to Sun Myung Moon. He is exhausted and confused. Moon, Christ, St. Matthew, Divine Principle, Luke, the Old Testament, Abraham, Adam, Logos, Genesis, Revelations, blood guilt, indemnity, Jews, Christians, cults, are all exploding in his head like kernels in a popper. Two days ago it was all so simple, clear, scientific even—the lines of logic direct. He wonders why he can't get back to that, and feels he could if they'd only leave him alone, stop badgering him, give him time to sort out his thoughts, let him sleep and purge his brain. He forgets that he got involved in the Unification Church the same way—that *they* wouldn't let him alone either, badgered him, wouldn't let him sleep.

At four, Franklin comes down to relieve Patrick, who curls up on some cushions near the washing machine and is asleep instantly. Franklin takes the chair opposite Bernie and smiles. "How we doin'?" he inquires pleasantly. "Ted tells me you're coming along just fine. You hungry? You want something to eat? Drink?"

Setting his teeth, Bernie shakes his head. But he is thinking, "Maybe I'll fast just for two days."

The sun strikes the empty platter and the empty cup, the pristine white paper napkin and the untouched silverware. His mother, father and brother have all eaten breakfast. He has declined.

They finally let him sleep for four hours on the couch ("That's about one more hour than they let him sleep when he was getting into the cult," Franklin says), and when he wakes up he asks if he can take a shower. Now, bathed but not refreshed by the cold water any more than by the sleep he's had he sits at the head of the dining room table, facing his family without expression, his spine not touching the back of his chair.

It is already another hot day. Ted Patrick is on the telephone in one of the bedrooms. Kevin is sleeping in the basement on the couch. The reporter is toasting an English muffin in the kitchen. Joe Franklin sits in a leather chair in a corner of the living room where Bernie can't see him, smokes Winchesters and watches and listens to the family attentively.

No visible change is evident in the boy from the previous morning. He seems as remote, closed-off, isolated as before. But significant modifications have taken place in his brain. His mind is turbulent. Again and again and again during the night, Patrick had stung him with questions he was unable to answer. He found himself repeating over and over, "You don't understand. There's no point in trying to make you understand. You're distorting the truth. The answer to that is in *Divine Principle.*" Sensitive finally to the inadequacy of these responses, he was baffled that he could not bring to bear on this black and devious heretic the hitherto absolutely lucid truths of his religion. Then too, amazingly enough, this man Patrick seemed to know *Divine Principle* better than he did. Patrick made him feel tongue-tied and ashamed. How little he had really studied *Divine Principle* in all those months. *Don't worry about it,* Patrick had quoted his leaders mockingly. *If you don't get it now, you'll get it by and by.* Which, though he'd denied it, was exactly what they had told him. He'd attended lectures and study groups and workshops about *Divine Principle,* but his firsthand knowledge of that crucial work was not substantial. And when he'd expressed doubts, when he'd been puzzled or confused, his leaders had assured him that *Divine Principle* was "deep." He couldn't expect to grasp it immediately. And when his doubts persisted, he was informed that Satan was invading him.

Compounding his ignorance of *Divine Principle* was his ignorance of the Bible. It seemed, incredibly enough, that he didn't *know* anything. It was humiliating how expert Patrick was, how easily he caught him up in contradictions, half truths, clumsy errors. Bernie had read extensively in Schopenhauer and Hesse. Compared to him, Patrick was a crude and vulgar semi-literate. Yet he understood the Bible and *Divine Principle* so thoroughly that Bernie was reduced to mumbling revolting inanities like, "The spirit has its own vocabulary," to explain passages in Moon's doctrine that amounted, on close inspection, to approximate gibberish.

In addition to his theological confusion, he is now profoundly uncertain about the nature of this man whom he has worshiped for nearly a year. The question this morning is less whether Moon is indeed the Messiah than whether he is even a holy, if mortal, man. Patrick had shown him newspaper and magazine stories revealing that Moon was living in lavish splendor in a million dollar estate in Barrytown, New York, while his followers slept on floors and ate peanut butter, half froze to death selling plastic flowers, died of malnutrition and committed suicide in front of trains. And what *did* happen to the money they raised? Bernie knew it did not go for philanthropic purposes. Not much of it even went to convert disbelievers or unify the various Christian faiths as Moon maintained; that work was done by kids like him, for free. *Where does the money go? Where does the money go?* they kept pounding away at him. And he couldn't answer. A pimp, a crook, a con man. And he, Bernie Weber, a male prostitute.

"He's like a brick wall," his mother had exclaimed earlier while he was showering. But the twenty-four hours of hammering have produced a network of fissures behind the plaster on the wall. Indeed, as he sits at the table with his family, the plaster is about all that is holding the bricks together.

His father is reading aloud the letters Bernie had written from California, starting with those sent when he first joined the cult the previous August. He is reading them in sequence, to demonstrate in Bernie's own words the changes that have come over him, progressively, in those ten months.

In the aggregate the letters amount to a case history documenting a process of reverse evolution, as though a moth were to revert to a grub. In August, the letters are replete with warm, even heated expressions of love for the family, legitimate uncertainties about his identity and purpose in life, spiritual ache and psychological upheaval. As the months pass, the tone shifts, the content detours from self-analysis and concern for the family on the East Coast, and is confined to describing his new "family" and defining the theology he has embraced. Personality, elasticity, a spirit of sober philosophical inquiry all give way to hysterical dogmatism. A congealing of his thought processes becomes apparent. Where before there were questions, now there are only simplistic declarations about the nature of God and man, and then diatribes. Finally, in the spring, whole sections of the letters are being ripped piecemeal from the blue and white book called *Unification Thought*. No trace survives in the most recent letters of the mind and personality of the boy named Bernie Weber who had left home ten months earlier.

The father reads them all, his voice cracking; he is weeping, strangling on the emotions this dismal journal provokes in him. It is torture for him to go on, but he does, blowing his nose, wiping his eyes, interrupting himself with passionate appeals to his expressionless son to "think, realize, try to understand what these mean, what they've done to you!"

His brother Jeff is crying too, unashamedly, and Bernie, though he does not show it, is moved. The letters do not account for his emotion; he doesn't remember writing most of them, and now doesn't understand most of what he said. He is moved rather by the tears and anguish of his father, and his brother weeping. His mother's eyes are dry. She could not have reached him anyway; a mother's devotion can be discounted. It is Jeff and his father who astound him. Had he ever seen Jeff weep? It is phenomenal. And they are weeping for him! Why? Can they care that much? Moon said they were of the Devil. Is it possible they are bent on deceiving him? Can those tears be fraudulent? God is Love, Ted Patrick has been insisting. Love. How many times yesterday did he hear that? And now this: what can this be if not love?

Their weeping makes him miserable. It is appalling. "What

have I done to them to make them feel this way? How have I injured them?" Ted Patrick said he has forgotten how to think. That isn't exactly true. He may have stopped thinking, but he still knows how. What he's forgotten, he suddenly realizes, is how to *feel*. It is all at once so lucid. He is like a baby, and he perceives their love for him in an entirely novel way, in a way he has not understood since he was five years old, when it was possible to embrace his parents, when it was not shameful to kiss his brother or to weep as they are weeping now. "Why can they weep like that, with no shame or embarrassment or self-consciousness, what gives them that permission? And why can't I?"

There is a pause at the table as Harold Weber tries to gain some control over himself. He holds the last letter in his hands, folding it back and forth along the crease; it's as limp as a handkerchief from all the times it's been handled, coming apart at the seams.

"And this one," he says at last. "The one you sent to your grandfather in Israel. Were you trying to kill him? Were you trying to kill that man, your own grandfather, who doesn't have a mean bone in his body? Who loves you more than life itself. And you send him *this* letter?"

He begins to read. The letter consists mainly of quotes from *Divine Principle* and *Unification Thought* strung together with incoherent expressions of fealty to Sun Myung Moon and invitations to the Zionist grandfather to read the enclosed literature with the idea of joining him in the propagation of this new and wonderful faith.

"How could you?" his father keeps asking. "What were you thinking? How *could* you, Bernie?"

Gazing at the plate, counting the flowers in the pattern, the boy tries to remember writing the letter. Did he write it, or did one of the leaders write it for him? Indeed, how *could* he have said things like that?

His father breaks down, begins to cough. Bernie raises his face to look at him, but he can't see for the tears in his own eyes.

His father is sitting with his head in his hands, his shoulders heaving. "I don't know what's happened to you, I don't know what they've done to you, I don't understand anything except that they've almost killed you, and almost killed us, and that can't be right. I don't care what God you worship, I know that can't be right, and if I have to stay here for six months to get you out, I'm prepared to stay here for six months, if it means my job, my career, if it means my life, I'm prepared to do it!"

And Joe Franklin is leaning in the doorway, arms crossed, having waited patiently for just this moment, these familiar signs of the crumbling of the boy's resistance, and he says softly, "I'm gonna ask you one more time, Bernie. Who do you love more? That pimp—or your father?"

Bernie hesitates for a moment. Then the words come out haltingly, wrenchingly, "My father. I love my father."

And he rises from his chair and comes around the corner of the table and half kneels, half sprawls against his father, his face pressed awkwardly against Harold Weber's chest, and they cry together in each other's arms.

"Good," says Patrick a while later. "That's good. It'll go fast from now on. The cap's unscrewed. He's not deprogrammed yet, but that's a major turning point."

It takes nine more hours of talking in the basement before Patrick can declare with certainty, "He's out of it." The fear and guilt the cult has programmed Bernie with do not vanish instantaneously. Reflex action is still a prominent element in his psychology, and will continue to be for a few weeks. He will go to a home in Ohio for "rehabilitation" (a euphemism for a vacation). "We try to keep him occupied. Riding a bike, going swimming, good food, lots of sleep. Let him meet other kids who were deprogrammed so they can compare notes. Keep him away from the Bible. Keep him away from the telephone so he won't call the cult."

The reporter, exhausted but impressed (though in a few days she will file a critical story for her newspaper) wants to know why, if he's really deprogrammed, he would want to call the cult.

Patrick lights a White Owl. "They float, that's why." It's his term for backsliding. "It's been so long since he's thought for himself, it's not easy. It's like a car that's been sitting in the garage for ten months. The battery will be dead. To start the car, you have to use a jumper cable. After it starts, if you turn the key off, it'll go dead again. But if you let the engine run long enough, the battery will recharge itself and be like new. The mind works the same way. In a few days, he'll be fine."

The phone rings, and a minute later Patrick is immersed in plans for the snatch of the Goski Big Four which has been postponed for a few days. Brother Julius is in the hospital in Meriden, nobody knows why.

Two weeks later, Bernie Weber, cheerful, open, friendly, intelligent, twelve pounds heavier, is also on the phone. He is talking from his parents' house to a member of the Unification Church in Syracuse who has been snatched. "Look," he argues earnestly, "I know what you're going through. I was in there myself. In the L.A. center. It's all a swindle. Moon is a con man. A crook! Look, just ask yourself, where does all that money we raised go to? What's it used for? Why do we have to sleep on floors and go hungry and work around the clock while Moon's living in a mansion in Barrytown? Think about it. Think! They've taken your mind away."

CHAPTER ONE

TED PATRICK: I never planned to be a deprogrammer. It's not a job I applied for, and in the beginning I never imagined I'd be in it for four years, deprogramming and arranging for the deprogramming of over one thousand Americans, rescuing them from religious cults. It's not a job I want to continue to do. But until now [the fall of 1975] no one else has been willing to step forward and rectify a dangerous situation in this country which I believe poses threats and challenges to the core of our way of life. Until someone does, I feel I have no choice except to continue in my work.

In the summer of 1971 I was Governor Ronald Reagan's Special Representative for Community Relations in San Diego and Imperial counties in southern California. It was an interesting and demanding job which cast me in the role of a sort of ombudsman, fielding complaints, answering questions, cutting through bureaucratic red tape at every level of the government, trying to provide services in general for a very far-reaching constituency from every class, every race, every walk of life. In my three years in that position, I'd worked hard to make myself visible and available. When the cult troubles began to surface, it was logical enough for distraught and frightened parents to come to my office with requests for assistance.

At the time I was absolutely not aware of the existence of any cults, let alone those that were evil in their nature and purposes. I don't think many people were, anywhere in the country. This, in spite of the fact that by the summer of 1971 the cult movement in America was widespread, well-entrenched, and mushrooming rapidly.

The first actual step of my involvement in fighting the cults was an incident involving my son Michael, who was then fourteen, at Mission Beach in San Diego on the Fourth of July. I had rented a suite in the Bahia Hotel across from the beach, as I did every Fourth of July; the nature of my work kept me away from home for long stretches of time, and the weekend at the Bahia each summer had come to be a special time for me and my family.

There were fireworks that night at Belmont Park and my children and my nephews and their friends all wanted to go. I gave them permission. I also gave them careful instructions about being back at the hotel immediately after the fireworks were over.

My son Michael and one of my nephews, however, did not return with the others after the fireworks display. After waiting a reasonable amount of time, my guests and my relatives divided up into teams of two and three and we went out looking for them. We didn't find them. Three hours later, around half past midnight, extremely worried by then, I called the police department.

As I was dialing, Michael and my nephew walked in. Naturally their mothers fussed about them, and our relief was mixed with anger over their disobedience, which had disrupted the party. I was struck, however, by the look on my son's face. The first thought that passed through my mind was, "He's been smoking grass!" He looked vacant, somehow—glazed, drifting.

"Where the heck you been?" I started in on him. "We've been out all over town looking for you. What did I tell you about getting back here on time?"

Michael shook his head, as if he were trying to clear it.

"What's wrong, you been drinking?" I asked him, continuing to bluster a little but puzzled now.

"I don't know," he said finally, speaking very low, his eyes still not focusing. "We *were* on our way back to the hotel. We saw the fireworks and we were coming back, and then . . ."

"Some people stopped us," my nephew put in. He looked nervous and upset but not as vague and "spacey" as Michael.

Michael nodded. "They had Bibles and guitars. One of them asked us, 'Do you believe in God? Do you know Christ died on the cross for our sins? Do you have Christ in your hearts?' "

"We didn't want to talk to them, they were creepy. But, I don't know, there was something about them, we couldn't leave."

"They said," Michael went on, "that they had a family. They said the name of the family was Children of God. They wanted us to come home with them, to join them."

"No more work, remember?" my nephew prodded Michael. "They said that. And we wouldn't ever be sick anymore. We wouldn't have any problems."

Michael nodded; gradually his eyes seemed to clear a little. "Yeah, problem-free. And we wouldn't have to go to church anymore, or school even, because those things are of the Devil."

"Of the Devil!" my nephew supported him. "That's what they said. And they said our parents were of Satan."

And then Michael told me, "Every time we tried to leave, they grabbed us by the arms, made us look into their eyes. I never saw eyes like that before. It made me dizzy to look at them."

My brothers and sisters didn't take the incident seriously. The boys' story sounded like a farfetched lie invented to cover up their delinquency in returning to the hotel.

"You ought to be a book writer," my sister-in-law scolded, "with the imagination you've got."

But then my boy handed over to me some pamphlets they'd given him. It was the first propaganda literature I had ever seen from the group calling themselves the Children of God.

"It doesn't make any sense," I said, glancing at the pamphlets. "All kinds of crazy stuff about what's wrong with the country."

"Maybe it's a Communist-front thing," my wife suggested.

"Maybe," I agreed. "I'll send it all up to the Attorney General's office in the morning, see if they have anything on them."

But by morning the pamphlets had somehow gotten lost, and I ended up putting the whole matter out of my mind.

It wasn't until a week later, on July 12, that a woman I'll call Mrs. Samuel Jackson walked into my office to file a complaint about the disappearance of her son the night of the Fourth of July. He had last been seen near Mission Beach, in company with a group of young people carrying Bibles and guitars.

The lady was very upset. "On the morning of the Fourth,

Billy told us he was going to have breakfast with some friends. Afterwards they were going surfing near Mission Beach. He said he had a date that night and asked his father if he could use the car. Well, he never came home."

The Jacksons weren't alarmed until after dark, when they began receiving phone calls from some of the friends Billy had supposedly been with that day. The boys didn't know where he was. The Jacksons then telephoned the girl Billy had said he had the date with. She was irritated because Billy had never shown up or called to break the date.

"At midnight we called the police and the sheriff's department," Mrs. Jackson explained. "I told them I wanted to report a missing person. But the police wouldn't accept the report because Billy is only nineteen. 'That makes him a runaway,' they told me. 'We can't do anything about runaways.' So then I called the FBI. They told me to call the local police. It was a runaround."

In the days following, the Jacksons and Billy's friends checked hospitals, called acquaintances, scoured other beaches where he might have gone surfing, appealed again and again to law enforcement agencies. "But there was no sign of him. It was as if he'd been swallowed up, like he'd simply vanished from the face of the earth."

Then, on the ninth, five days after his disappearance, young Jackson telephoned. He was calling from a commune belonging to the Children of God. "I'm not coming home." he declared, "because my problem is in my home. You and Dad are living in sin and if you don't repent you are going to burn in hell. I've found a new family, a real family, a spiritual family."

Mrs. Jackson could hear other voices in the background which seemed to be advising him what to say. She claimed that Billy did not sound like himself. "He sounded like he was drugged, like he was a zombie reading a script."

Then someone else came onto the phone describing himself as an Elder. "We are a Christian family," he said, " and we are called the Children of God. Your son is nineteen years old, he is here of his own free will, and there's nothing you can do about it. He has found God, is serving the Lord, and is free from Satan once and for all." Then the Elder hunger up. She did not speak to Billy again.

Mrs. Jackson had come to me because no one else in the government and law enforcement agencies she appealed to seemed at all interested in her plight. To be honest, I'm not sure I would have taken much interest in her story either if it hadn't been for the incident involving my own son. Listening to her, I at last realized what had happened to Michael. The stories were identical. At any rate, that morning, watching this lady weeping in my office, I made up my mind that I would at least do some telephoning of my own to see what I could discover about the operations of these Children of God.

I started with churches and youth groups. I drew blanks. It was the same with the law enforcement agencies. Nothing. I was on the phone all day, neglecting my other work. The more blanks I drew, the more determined I was to locate someone who knew something about this group. They printed pamphlets. They accosted youngsters on the streets. They had a commune. It must be possible to track them down.

Finally, I telephoned a place called the Crisis Center, out at Ocean Beach, which was in the business of helping dropouts and other kids with problems. A volunteer at the Center said that indeed they were familiar with the Children of God. "They've ripped off a lot of our kids in the past couple weeks."

"I need names, addresses," I said. "I want to launch a full-scale investigation."

The Crisis Center had the names of six people who had reported having trouble with the sect, and I began calling them. I hit pay dirt right off the bat.

I'll call her Mrs. Betty Spahn. She had, as she put it, lost a child to the Children of God and, like Mrs. Jackson, had been unable to get help from any of the governmental agencies she'd appealed to. "Thank God somebody is finally going to do something about that bunch."

"I'd like to get together with you and tape an interview as soon as possible," I said.

"Tomorrow, Mr. Patrick. Come on over tomorrow night, around eight. There are four other families I know who are involved in this too. I'll have them come and you can interview them too. Maybe they'll know others that I don't know with kids inside."

From that point on, the thing just snowballed. Each of the four groups of parents I talked to the next night at the Spahn home knew a couple of other families with children in the cult. Their stories were all identical: the child vanished without a trace, surfaced a week later with a phone call in which he re-nounced (and in cases denounced) his parents, sounded like a zombie (a word that came up spontaneously from the begin-ning), seemed to be reading from a script, and so on.

In two days time I had received news of twenty-six families with parallel experiences. By the end of the week, I had names of fifty-two families, all with children who had disappeared into the Children of God. It took me two weeks to interview all of them.

What they told me amazed and disturbed me. I had the un-easy feeling that, large as this group of parents I'd contacted was, it was only the tip of an iceberg. These complaints about the Children of God fell within the realm of my duties as the Governor's Special Representative for Community Affairs. I did not hesitate to inform my superiors in Sacramento that I was going to be devoting a lot of time in the next few weeks to pursuing an investigation of the cult. It was part of my job to investigate, make a judgment, and get action. The higher-ups in Sacramento—especially my immediate superior Bob Keyes—were interested, concerned and sympathetic, and encouraged me to do what needed to be done.

What needed to be done, I decided, was for me to secure firsthand, eyewitness information on the Children of God op-eration. So I made up my mind to join the cult.

It was about seven o'clock on a Sunday evening toward the end of July that I arrived at Mission Beach, which, everything considered, seemed a logical place to make contact with the Children of God. By this time I was aware that they did what they called their "witnessing" at Mission Beach, the adjoining amusement park, and surrounding areas just about every weekend. There are a series of beautiful beaches along the coast of Southern California which are ideal staging grounds for cults like the Children of God for two reasons: (1) every weekend the beaches are thronged with upwards of 100,000 people and, (2) most of the people are very young and, therefore, very susceptible to hustles and con games.

For all the interviews I'd done since the morning Mrs. Jackson had entered my office, for all the information I'd gathered on the cult, I really didn't know what I would do or say to make them believe that I was a sincere convert, when and if I found them. I was also a little worried about what infiltrating the cult would entail, especially since my wife and children had no idea I was going to do this. I admit too that as I strolled through the park across from Mission Beach, seeing all the weekend picnickers, the kids on the slides and swings, listening to the music from the merry-go-round, enjoying the beautiful summer evening coming down on the Pacific, I really would not have been too disappointed if I had failed to make contact with the Children of God. It was something I was determined to do, but not necessarily something I wanted to do.

At any rate I didn't have much time for this kind of debating with myself, because as I crossed from in front of the Bahia Hotel and headed for the beach, I saw a big blue bus in the parking lot. That bus had been described to me any number of times, but even if it hadn't, the white lettering on its side said CHILDREN OF GOD.

About twenty yards from the bus, four nicely dressed young men, their arms filled with newspapers, were talking earnestly to a blonde girl in a yellow bikini. The boys appeared to be about twenty, with short hair, clean shaven, wearing coats and ties. The girl looked to be sixteen or so. She had a box of popcorn in her hand and a purse slung over her shoulder. The boys had her surrounded and whenever she took a few steps as though to break away from them, they all shifted around and surrounded her again so she really couldn't move.

"That's them," I thought, and I wandered over and pretended

to get interested in what the boys were saying. "Don't you realize that Christ died on the cross for *you?* Don't you realize that? Don't you care? Don't you want to serve the Lord?"

The girl was embarrassed, shifting from one bare foot to the other, shrugging her shoulders, nibbling on popcorn. Finally she said, "Look, I'm engaged to be married. My fiancé is over there on the beach. He's going to wonder what's happened to me. Do you mind?"

"Excuse me," I interrupted with an innocent smile. "I heard what you were saying about the Lord. I think maybe you're just the people I've been looking for."

A couple of the boys seized on this, delighted, which gave the girl an opening to leave. She did, but the other two followed her; I couldn't help wondering what kind of reception they were going to get from her boyfriend.

"Do you believe that Christ died for your sins?" one of the boys said. They came up tight on me, close, and while they talked they kept touching me lightly and staring at me with eyes that resembled Michael's the night of the Fourth of July—dilated pupils, empty, staring, as if they were stoned.

"I've been searching for the Lord," I said. "But I didn't know where to find him." And I made up a story about the misery of my life.

"Praise Jesus!" one of the boys said. "We love you, brother. Praise the Lord. Do you want to serve the Lord one hundred percent?"

"One hundred percent," I nodded.

"Hallelujah!" they said. "Praise Jesus!"

And they invited me over to the bus to talk further about becoming a convert to the Children of God.

When I entered the bus, it contained about fourteen other people, mostly young, between the ages of sixteen and twenty-five, about equally divided between boys and girls. I was the oldest person there and the only black one, but neither of those details seemed to be important. I learned later on that almost every cult has a sprinkling of over-thirty's, and a sprinkling of blacks, so a black forty-one-year-old convert was unusual, but acceptable enough.

Some of the seats had been removed to make room for a table and chairs. They were serving coffee and sandwiches, but I'd heard that there was at least a possibility that the Children of God secured their converts by drugging them, so I refused both the food and drink.

Two young men, not the same ones I'd talked to outside, began discussing the Bible with me. "Did you know that in Luke 14:26 it says, 'If any man come to me, and hate not his father and mother, and wife, and children, and brethren, and sisters, yea and his own life also, he cannot be my disciple.'? You agree with that, Ted?"

"Sure I agree with it," I'd say. And they'd do their "Praise the Lord" and "Hallelujah" bits again.

They introduced me to some of their "literature." The pamphlets reminded me of the "eight-pagers" that used to circulate on the streets when I was a kid in Chattanooga—the little crude cartoon books showing Blondie and Dagwood, for example, or the Katzenjammer Kids. The eight-pagers, of course, were also pornographic, and the pamphlets the kids gave me in the bus were far from that, but I would have to say that intellectually they were worse. The three of us used one of them to pray from together. The prayer went like this:

Dear Lord, please forgive me for being bad and naughty and deserving a good spanking! Thank you so much for sending Jesus your Son to take my spanking for me. I now receive him as my savior and as your son and ask you to come into my heart and make me be good and love you.

That pamphlet, incidentally, was called, "You Gotta Be a Baby."

The whole thing was like a Sunday-school class for first-graders. And yet all around me were young adults who looked healthy and intelligent. I guessed that many of them were college students, yet here they were lapping up this kind of drivel with deep emotion and enthusiasm. I couldn't figure it out. We all should have been holding our sides with laughter. Instead we were shouting, "Praise Jesus!" and, "I love you, brother, I love you!" and "Hallelujah!" I think it was then that I first began to credit the theories I'd heard from some of the parents that their children had been hypnotized. How else to explain all this? But it would have to be a sort of "on-the-spot" hypnosis, and at that time I didn't know whether or not this was possible. Since then, the accounts given by many former cult members have convinced me that it is.

At any rate, we prayed and read and talked and "Hallelujah-ed" for about forty-five minutes. I pretended to go along with the program and eventually they asked me if I wanted to go to their house in Santee, a suburb of San Diego, for a workshop and discussion session. I promptly agreed.

By this time more people had boarded the bus, and I was surprised to see the girl in the yellow bikini and a young man whom I took to be the boyfriend she'd mentioned. The girl had changed into a T-shirt and white shorts and her boyfriend, a tall, bearded fellow who looked to be about twenty-two years old, was wearing a denim work shirt and blue jeans. The girl looked very confused and frightened, but her boyfriend was already, apparently, somehow spaced out. The wide staring eyes, the empty face. I wondered again how anyone, however susceptible, could get himself hooked so quickly unless a form of instantaneous hypnotism was involved. The couple were separated at once, the boy being taken to the rear of the bus and the girl kept up front near me. Once she was alone, three people, two girls and a boy, started working on her as they had worked on me, only more so, since obviously she was going to be as difficult as I had been easy. At one point she looked at me with a pleading expression in her eyes, as if to say "Help, get us out of here!" but I made myself give her a zombie grin and chorused along with the others, "Praise the Lord!"

It was almost dark, around nine o'clock, when the bus pulled out of the parking lot and headed for Santee. During the forty-five minute ride, we sang songs and read the Bible and talked about our private lives with our so-called counselors who were very interested to know how much money we had in the bank, what kind of cars we owned, what our love life was like, and so forth.

I was hungry and thirsty, but I was still afraid that the sandwiches and coffee might be drugged, so I hung on, resisting the temptation to try some, figuring I could get some water out of a tap when we reached Santee.

It was too dark when we arrived to see very much, but I took a good look around the next day. It was a low, frame, three-bedroom house set on about four acres well back from the road on a slope of land that moved uphill to a stand of trees thick enough to be called a woods. To the right of the house, which was fronted along the road by a wooden fence, were five huge army tents. To the left and to the rear was a field filled with automobiles, buses, motorcycles, jeeps. These had all been "contributed" to the cult by converts, and were being sold to dealers as quickly as possible. I estimated the value of these automotive contributions to be in excess of fifty thousand dollars. Thirty or so converts had arrived with me in the bus; I quickly figured that if half of them owned cars and gave them to the cult, and say 100 converts were made each weekend (which was a serious underestimation, as it turned out), then in automobiles alone the cult was taking in two hundred thousand dollars a month.

But there was other merchandise too. One of the army tents was stocked like an electronics store. Dozens of television sets, stereos, speaker systems, amplifiers, cameras, binoculars—all given up for Jesus by converts to the cult—were piled up, worth, I guessed, about another fifty thousand dollars or so. Just seeing and appreciating the size and scope of that second-hand retail operation convinced me that whatever the Children of God's real business was, it had nothing to do with religion and a hell of a lot to do with turning a rapid buck. I think it would have convinced anyone.

When we arrived that first night our bus was met by a bunch of members who came running out of the house singing and shouting: "Thank you Jesus, Praise God for you." They hugged us and cried, "We love you, brother, we love you, sister! God bless you. God bless you, brother!" There was every outward appearance of sincerity and enthusiasm, and several people on our bus were clearly impressed and pleased by this greeting. But to me it seemed without depth or real feeling—it looked like an act, like a performance according to a script. And the script wasn't very convincing and neither were the actors.

We went into the house, into a large living room empty of furniture except for a few tables piled up with the group's literature. The walls were hung with Scriptural quotations and pictures of Fred Jordan and David Berg, the organizers of Children of God. The room was crowded and hot. About forty or fifty young people were sitting on the floor listening to a lecture by one of the so-called Elders of the commune. I sat down in a corner and listened. It was incredible. It amounted to a "Hate your parents" class of indoctrination.

"Your parents are the enemy!" the Elder shouted. "You have to surrender your whole life to God, you have to give him everything, I mean everything, one hundred percent. Not eighty, not ninety, but one hundred percent! And that means giving up your parents too. He that's not with us is against us—and that's your parents. 'He that loveth his father, mother, sister, and brother more than Me is not worthy of me.' That's what the Bible says. Do you believe the Bible? Do you believe the Bible is the inspired word of God who sent His only beloved son to die on the cross for you? If you believe it, then you believe you gotta hate your father and your mother because they're evil, because they're of Satan, because they *are* Satan."

For a black boy raised in the South who over the years had heard some of the best when it came to conning people from the pulpit, this was pretty feeble stuff. But not many of the middle-class white kids in the room had any experience at all with real evangelical preaching, and they gobbled it up like it was the Holy Ghost talking to them.

This went on for about an hour, and then when he was finished we were separated into small groups in different rooms of the house and I was presented with an application form filled with very personal questions. "Do your parents own a home? Do you live by yourself? Do you have a family? Do you have a job? How much do you make? Do you have a car? Is it in your name? Is it paid for? Do you have a bank account? How much is in it? Is there any other name on it besides yours? Do you own any furniture? Do you know any influential people with money?"

Their concern with a prospective convert's financial situation is so transparent you would think it would alert the slowest, least perceptive person to what was going on. Or at least make them pause and think. But the indoctrination is cleverly orchestrated, and while you are being queried directly about your financial status, you are at the same time listening to tape recordings of Bible verses, being exhorted by one member to pray and praise the Lord, and being hugged by another member who tells you he loves you, brother—so it is all very confusing and one does not use his powers of concentration or critical ability in a normal way. It's a sort of mental and psychological blitzing. They confuse and harass you quite effectively so that you often don't really know what you are doing or saying.

And if you do hesitate even for a moment, or express some doubt, or ask a potentially embarrassing question, as various people did at Santee, they step up the attack. "That's Satan speaking in you. You don't want to sign? You're not willing to give up your car for the Lord? He died on the cross for you. And you won't give him a lousy car in return? What did the Lord say to the rich man? Forsake all and follow me. You think you can get to heaven in your Oldsmobile? The world's going to end, brother—and it's going to end soon. And we're the only ones going to be saved, that's right, the Children of God. We are the chosen people and you gotta do what Moses Berg tells you to do without thinking about it, if you want to be saved. You want to be saved, don't you? Well, you're not going to be saved unless you do what Moses tells you. 'Cause he's been appointed and anointed by God and God speaks through him, and you have to take that on faith and give up worrying about understanding. You forsake understanding too because your mind is Satan, and thinking is the machinery of the Devil."

On and on like that and pretty soon the convert would meekly sign away his Oldsmobile and his bank account and everything else, including his right to think and all his family ties, without a whimper.

I was never left alone, not for a minute, not even to go to the toilet. After I signed the application—admitting to possession of a car, some stereo equipment, and several musical instruments—I went back to the living room and sat down on the floor again to listen to another lecture and to hear more tapes. Other buses had arrived and the crowd inside the house had doubled in the hour and a half or so since I'd been there. It was a hot, hot night, and everyone was sweating. The place smelled like a sty. It was airless, and I was getting tired and very thirsty. But when I would mention to one of the leaders assigned to me that I would like a glass of water, he would reply, "You're hearing the living word of God. Isn't that more important than a glass of water?"

I've been in the service, and I was a middleweight boxer for a while, and my life has not been what you would call easy. So I figured I was in better physical condition, simply tougher and better able to withstand the heat and weariness and hunger and thirst than the other people, the kids, who looked soft and pampered and vulnerable. I tried to imagine what kind of hell they were going through, what kind of pressures motivated by the desire to eat, drink, and sleep might be at work forcing them to sign anything, to agree to anything. I recalled tales of brainwashing sessions reported by American prisoners of war coming home from Korea and resolved that when I got out of there I would look up some of the literature on the subject of mind control and brainwashing, because what I was witnessing sounded pretty much like what I'd read about in the papers in the fifties.

Another Elder stood up before us and began reading a so-called MO-letter. Like everything else in this cult, the MO-letter is so fantastic it's not easy to describe. MO is an abbreviation of "Moses," which is what David Berg, the leader of the group, calls himself. The letters are actually little mimeographed magazines in which Berg talks to his followers about everything that's on his mind. Much of what he writes makes no sense at all; MO-letters often sound like the ravings of a seriously demented man. To his disciples, however, they represent something close to the inspired word of God, and that night in Santee we were subjected to readings from them, and tape recordings of them, all night long. I've since obtained copies of the letters read to us that night. Here's a sample:

> God has broken up the marriages of almost our entire top leadership at some time or another, with one or two exceptions who are apart from their partners most of the time anyway. I've certainly seen a lot of good fruit in these, since this had happened, and also it has borne good fruit amongst the kids. Is breaking up families anything *new* with God? God is in the business of breaking up families—little private families! *If you have not forsaken your husband and wife for the Lord at sometime or other, you have not forsaken all!*

And another example, typical of the MO-letters and reflecting the kind of mind that operates the Children of God cult.

> I'm picking 'em off in the way that hurts them most! I'm picking off their children for the Lord. When they get to the point they don't deserve us anymore, God may let 'em slaughter us. The parents have filled 'em so full of houses and cars and education and all that shit—it's like making them eat their father's dung! And now the kids want to kill 'em for it! You can hardly blame 'em! I've felt like that myself sometimes! May God deliver me from being around these Systemites! I'd hate to think of what I might do if I'd had a tommy-gun sometimes—I might have been tempted to mow them down! I would have made a hell of a Communist!
>
> It's time for the rape of America, but they're trying to respect her! She doesn't deserve respect: *She's an old Whore!*
> *She thinks she owns the pimps, but the pimps own her!* But if they sink *with* her, she does own them see? *But if they're smart pimps, they'll cut her off* and let her *die. But we already told her she's going to die!* She's mad at us! And now *we have*

*to tell her pimps to let her go, 'cause they're just going to lose
money 'cause she's going to die!*

*She's an old whore! She's old and ugly and diseased and
proud and pompous! She's so selfish! She's cruel and destructive, and all her little European money pimps better dump her,
or they'll go down with her!*

To be fair to the kids in Santee that night, I must say that
the madness of these MO-letters was not as evident then as it
is when you see the words printed on the page. It's quite another
situation when the Elder is spouting these words at you, or tapes
of Berg screaming them at you are being played at a high
decibel count, and you are being badgered continually by a
group of Elders who never leave your side—they work in shifts,
so they are always fresh and wide awake. They preach Scripture
to you even as you urinate, so that the Bible and God and
Moses Berg and love of country and hatred of the system and
guilt over your family problems and your sexuality all get
mixed up and are exaggerated by your lack of sleep, your
hunger and thirst.

For those who have never undergone an experience like this,
I would compare the effect of the whole program to being in a
club where rock music is being played very loud and you
happen to be seated near one of the speakers. You are deafened,
you can't think or even really hear, but you can *feel* the rhythms
of the bass and percussion inside your bones—the marrow of
your bones begins to vibrate, your blood begins to jive. You are
swinging! Everybody knows that. Well, make the transfer of
that mental and physical condition; add the fact that instead
of hearing music, you are being flooded with political and sexual
and Scriptural vibrations; extend the time to forty consecutive
hours or so; starve yourself; dehydrate yourself; and then try
to imagine your frame of mind at the end of those forty hours.
That would be a rough approximation of the effect of the program that weekend at Santee.

We were not allowed to sleep that Sunday night. The programming, the indoctrination, the brainwashing never let up.

There was very little variation in what the Elders told us, in what tapes they played. It was just the same thing, repeated endlessly.

Around dawn, we were told that we would have breakfast as soon as everyone had memorized three Bible verses. That wasn't a problem for me; I could have recited 300 Bible verses if I wanted to. But nobody could eat until everybody had done that, and you can imagine what it's like trying to memorize anything after more than twelve hours of the sort of ordeal those kids had been put through. It must have been around nine Monday morning before we finally ate. We went outside and were served tin plates with a small portion of oatmeal mixed with powdered milk and water. It was nasty stuff, but we were all so hungry we were grateful for it. Grateful to get out of that stinking house too, and into the fresh air, though even that was spoiled by the fact that we could not escape the tape recorders and the programmers. We listened to Scripture while we sat on the grass eating, and we heard more MO-letters and more repetitious denunciations of the society.

At first you get frantic for silence—just five minutes of peace and privacy. Then your senses begin to get numb—you grow accustomed to the constant noise. You also, as you get tired, stop really registering what they tell you. You don't hear individual words anymore, just a stream of babbling and shriek- ing. I guess that's when the programming starts becoming effective—when the conscious mind stops functioning out of weariness and all that propaganda begins to seep into your un- conscious.

It was a hot sunny morning. About 100 degrees and heating up. The sun practically blinded you and beat on your head like a hammer.

I saw kids who were members painting one of the buses and getting it ready to go out on missions. Tapes were playing while they worked. Other kids were fixing some boards on the porch of the house; they were chanting Scriptural verses. Female members, who were in charge of keeping in order the "respect- able clothes" members wore while proselytizing, were working inside, singing hymns as they sewed on buttons and pressed the boys' shirts. (By the way, I have yet to discover a cult in which females are not employed as a servant class. I wish some of those girls had been in charge of what we had to eat. But apparently the Elders cared more about how their members looked than how well they were fed.)

Study groups were scattered all over the grounds; in the tents, on the hillside, in the pasture down behind where the cars were parked—about fifty or sixty kids to a group, each with its own leader preaching and lecturing. Lots of buses had rolled in during the night and the total attendance that morning I estimated at between 250 and 300.

Our leaders concentrated on the family issue, urging us to hate our parents, reading from the MO-letters: "They live like animals. What do they do? They eat and drink, sleep and fuck, shit and piss—they suck the asshole of the System, that's all they do. Fuck them! They're not your family. There's only one family. *This* is your family. And you don't leave. Leaving here and going back to that is like a dog returning to his vomit, it's like going back and eating your own shit! Moses is your Father—there's no salvation except through him. You leave here you'll have blood on your hands. You leave here you'll be struck by lightning. You go back to that shit-filth flesh-family and you'll all be killed!

"Listen to what Moses says about your vomit-stinking parents. This is what he says: 'You, my dear parents are the greatest rebels against God . . . to hell with your devilish system. May God damn your unbelieving hearts. God is going to destroy you and save us . . . for truly this is a wicked and adulterous and rebellious generation which I shall destroy and I say God damn you all to Hell!' That's God talking, God talking through Moses, and you'd better listen to him."

Along with the other craziness they sandbagged us with that day was the information that every now and then Moses Berg goes up to Heaven and stays there chatting with God for two or three weeks at a time! Remember, these were mostly college kids, with, I discovered later, above-average I.Q.'s. After being informed that David Berg periodically goes up to Heaven body and soul for a vacation with God, they clapped their hands and shouted, "Praise the Lord!"

We sat outside all day, breaking only once to do a sort of dance, all in a circle, arms around each other's shoulders, and singing, everybody working himself up into a frenzy. Here's a sample of the kind of songs we sung:

> Down, down, the sun's going down,
> The axe is laid to the tree.
> Proud America she spins around,
> She shall be brought to her knees.
> Look at the way they raised us.
> Look at the way they raised us.
> They think their money has amazed us.
> America's sinking fast in the sand.
>
> The system is fucked and it's getting me down.
> Oh, Lord, I can't stand it.
> The system is fucked and it's getting me down.
> Oh, Lord, I can't stand it.

We ate again at seven that evening. Oatmeal. It was horrible and so was the stew they served us in the tin army-style mess kits. I gathered that they obtained the bulk of their food from the garbage bins of local supermarkets. It certainly tasted like it. Loudspeakers hung in trees continued to blare Scriptural texts and MO-letters all during this meal.

Then there was more brainwashing, group discussions, lectures, memorizing selected Bible verses. The kids weren't even moving much anymore, they were so fatigued. They just stared straight ahead with blank faces, sitting there, swaying back and forth. I saw the young couple who were engaged to be married, the girl in the yellow bikini and her boyfriend. She was almost unrecognizable—hair all stringy, face puffy, limp as a rag doll, eyes like buttons. The boy was the same way. A few times they glanced at each other without recognition.

At four in the morning they finally let us go to sleep. This was Tuesday. I'd gotten up at eight on Sunday, which meant that I hadn't slept in forty-four hours. Not exactly a record, but when you're forty-one years old, no picnic either.

I slept on a floor, on a thin blanket, wearing my clothes, with about sixty other guys (males and females were strictly segregated at bedtime), shoulder to shoulder, head-to-foot, wall-to-wall. It stank, it was hot, it was uncomfortable. And I slept like I was dead. But even then they didn't let up with the programming. Tape recorders played all night long, spewing out Scripture.

When I woke up in the morning, after about three hours sleep, it occurred to me that I'd better start making a plan for splitting. In spite of all my precautions, I was getting worn down. Believe it or not the propaganda was getting to me too. There *were* things wrong with America, I'd find myself sleepily agreeing with a leader or a MO-letter. And yes, my parents hadn't always been wise in their decisions about raising me. And the Bible *did* urge you to forsake all if you wanted to be saved.

Then I'd give myself a mental slapping and wake up and snap out of it, feeling scared. The problem was, it wasn't going to be easy to escape. You were under constant surveillance. And it was pretty clear by now that these Children of God weren't above employing ungodly rough stuff to keep you there.

For example, that morning a nicely dressed woman around my age, white, obviously well-off, drove up to the gate and got out of her car. She was the mother of a female member who had been given the Biblical name of Rachel (you had to forsake your name too; my new name was Solomon). She said she knew her daughter was there and she wasn't going to leave until she spoke to her.

Some of the Elders tried giving her a hard time at first, denying that the girl was there, but the woman was angry and stubborn and at last they allowed her to see "Rachel." But they wouldn't let her talk to her daughter alone. Rachel was accompanied by five Elders. "Rachel doesn't want to talk to you alone," they told her. "We are a family here. We do everything together." When the mother insisted, she was told, "Your daughter is of legal age. She has a legal right to do what she wants. She's here of her own free will." They argued back and forth, Rachel at first not saying anything, then interrupting to tell her mother, "I don't know you. This is my only family. You want to kill me. If I leave here I'll die. I'm doing the work of the Lord, and you want me to serve Satan. You have the Devil inside of you, you are possessed by demons!"

The mother, not surprisingly, proceeded to become hysterical. She grabbed for her daughter, trying to drag her out of the house. But the Elders jumped her. One of them struck her in the mouth, two others pinned her arms behind her back, and they all fell to the floor. The woman was screaming and crying, the Children of God were roughing her up, and her daughter just stood there staring, without any expression at all on her face.

They finally got hold of the woman's arms and legs and carried her to the car and told her to get the hell out.

Back in the house there was a celebration. "Praise Jesus for Rachel!" they were hollering. "Rachel has withstood the test. Praise God! This is how Satan tempts you, in the guise of the flesh of your earth parents who are vessels filled with the stink and filth of Satan." And then they began making plans to move Rachel immediately to a commune in Colorado so her mother couldn't locate her again, which is a favorite tactic of all the cults.

So I figured they meant business. And I figured that if I didn't get out of there in the next twenty-four hours, I might never get out; they'd have my mind too.

Trying to figure out an angle for escaping is probably what kept me together the rest of that day, which was the exact duplicate of the previous day, the same mind-numbing tapes, the same idiocy, the same warping and distorting of the Bible and of the minds of hundreds of victims, this incredible mass kidnapping which as far as I could tell enjoyed the protection of the law. Until then I'd been a model subject, pretending to go along with everything, without doubt, without question. That was in my favor, I thought—the element of surprise. Another card I could play—in fact, the only card—was the lure of earthly possessions. I'd told them on Sunday night about my car, stereo, and musical instruments. Now I also told them I had a couple of thousand dollars in a savings account and an uncashed pay check at my home.

I expected much more trouble with the leadership than I got. And in the process I learned a lesson that would prove immensely valuable to me in the years ahead. Most of the leadership of the cults in America are themselves robots, zombies, incapable of rapid thought, decisive action, or instantaneous improvisation. With the exception of David Berg and a few of his close associates, the people doing the brainwashing in Children of God are themselves true believers. So they are very easy to catch off guard.

"I want to serve the Lord one hundred per cent," I told an Elder that night. "I want to forsake all. I want to do the Lord's work." And I explained about the money. "Every minute that money belongs to me, I can feel Satan tugging at me. I want to get rid of it, I want the Lord to have it, I want to give it to you."

He really couldn't put up any argument. The money is what they've been programmed to go after.

The precautions established for my trip home the next morning were more or less automatic. They always travel in groups, less to prevent anyone from escaping—because after a couple of days they are so brainwashed they actually *like* what they are doing and can no longer distinguish between life in the commune and life in the real world—than to discourage any accidental meeting with a relative or friend who might try to physically abduct them, as Rachel's mother had done.

Knowing that I would be leaving in the morning allowed me to endure the rest of that long evening and night in a better frame of mind. I also began to formulate the outline of the report I intended to send to Sacramento, and I entertained myself with imagining the reaction it would provoke up there. It felt good to know that the information I'd obtained in Santee could be instrumental in seriously interrupting and perhaps even mortally damaging what struck me as the filthiest quasi-underworld operation I'd ever seen. That night when we were finally allowed to go to sleep again, I dreamed about Moses—David Berg. No doubt hundreds of my fellow sufferers did too, but I'm sure my dream was a little different from theirs. I dreamed of seeing him behind bars.

In the morning I climbed into a Ford van with two Elders and two kids, whose new names, as I recall, were Jobab and Aggabus. Jobab drove, with an Elder beside him, and I sat in the back with Aggabus and the other Elder. When they'd come to Santee on Sunday, the two boys—both about eighteen—had hair down to their shoulders. Now, Wednesday, they were shorn, like lambs. Berg is always talking about his "lambs" in the MO-letters, and that's what they were like as we drove toward San Diego, shorn lambs, and as mindless and docile and conformist as sheep.

I tried to make conversation, just to test them, asked them what they had done before joining. They could only answer in Scripture, or with quotes from Berg, or parrot back the nonsense from the tapes. It was spooky and depressing. The idea did cross my mind at one point that I ought to see if I could take them along with me and send them back to their parents. But there would be no way of finding out who their parents were without a tremendous hassle. And then they'd probably only escape and go back to Santee at the first opportunity.

When we arrived in San Diego, I told them I'd better make a phone call to insure that no one was at home. They didn't argue. We parked in front of the Greyhound bus station.

"Be right back," I said.

And I walked into the station and kept walking out the back door where I caught a taxi and went home.

The first thing I did when I reached my house was to take a bath. I lay in the tub for two hours, my head spinning, soaking all the filth I'd been subjected to out of my soul and body. Then I cooked a huge steak. Then I went to bed, but as so often happens in circumstances like that I was too fatigued to sleep.

I could still hear the tape recordings, the loudspeakers blaring, the voice of Moses Berg, as if it were happening again, all over, right there in my bedroom.

I dozed off for a few minutes. Then Ruth Ann was beside me saying, "Where in the heck have *you* been?"

I sat up, grinned, gave her a kiss and said, "I've been in hell, darling."

"What do you mean you been in hell?"

"You're looking at Lazarus," I told her. "I just come back from the Kingdom of the Dead."

CHAPTER TWO

The architect who drew the blueprints for the Children of God was a TV huckster by the name of Fred Jordan, who operated out of California. Jordan was the head of a highly successful religious enterprise that produced "The Church in the Home," a series of weekly telecasts characterized by a sort of primitive fundamentalism combined with a used-car salesman's pitch for cash. It was a lucrative formula, and in 1971, seeking to expand the scope of his operation, he joined forces with David Berg, a one-time Baptist minister whose church had expelled him for unbecoming conduct.

Berg was the author of the MO-letters that were read to Ted Patrick at Santee, and they, plus the description of the recruiting tactics that prevailed at the commune in Santee, provide a fair measure of the man's character, psychology and personality. More insight into the nature of this person—who, to the present day, is worshiped by thousands of young people as though he were the Lord Almighty—comes from the testimony of Berg's former daughter-in-law Sarah, which is contained in a report delivered in September of 1974 to Louis J. Lefkowitz, the Attorney General of the state of New York, by the Charity Frauds Bureau, a bureau of the State Attorney General's office. The report, originating in Lefkowitz's office, was the result of a public outcry against the *modus operandi* of the cult, which by 1974 was recruiting vigorously up and down New York State and reaping increasingly unfavorable publicity.

On page 52, the report says of Sarah Berg:

When she was about 15 years old, her mother, a missionary, permitted her to travel on several trips with the Berg group. Paul Berg [David Berg's son] suddenly demanded that she marry him. When she refused, she was subjected to the following "prophecies" by both Paul and David Berg:

"My daughter, this is my will for you. I have chosen this match that is made in heaven. I have ordained it. Don't be afraid to slip into my plan, my will. Why are you questioning God, are you trying to bring God's wrath on you? Don't you believe these prophecies? If you don't cooperate or do what God told you to, He is going to strike you dead. Obey God, He has ways of making you."

Frightened, she was forced to have intercourse with Paul in the presence of David Berg. Similar incidents occurred thereafter until her spirit was broken. She then was compelled to obtain her mother's permission to marry Paul because she was terrified and believed mistakenly that she was pregnant.

A year later, after the birth of her first child . . . David Berg wanted to have intercourse with her stating: "I see you with Paul's son. Why can't you have my son?"

On a later occasion, when she declined to perform sexually with her father-in-law in front of a group of the Children of God, she was severely beaten, even though she was pregnant once more. She subsequently ran away.

When Jordan met Berg he was looking for a group of youngsters he could feature on his Sunday morning television show, presenting them as drug addicts, pimps, whores, and drunkards who had been saved by the Lord. Berg already had the nucleus of such a group—a small band of youngsters called Teens for Christ—and he had been casting about for schemes to make money with them. Jordan offered him a headquarters in the skid row section of downtown Los Angeles, and—according to Patrick—paid him one thousand dollars a month to enlist in his religious group young people who could then be used on Jordan's television show. Berg sensed the potential of the arrangement, and promptly accepted. With a bankroll behind him, and a staging area in L.A., he began to recruit under the banner of the Children of God.

For a while the venture flourished. Fred Jordan had his witnesses for Christ, claiming he had saved them, and Berg gathered the dividends of the free publicity that his organization, the Children of God, received each Sunday. His followers allowed themselves to be misrepresented on Jordan's show, believing—as most cult members do—that it is no sin to deceive an unbeliever. As the membership grew—nourished as it was by that strange climate of religious hysteria that seems endemic to California—Berg saw the possibilities of an empire, and set about organizing it after the pattern Patrick discovered when he infiltrated the cult in Santee.

In a few short months there were communes or colonies in California and Texas, and plans for expansion into several other states. Fred Jordan had donated a 40-acre ranch in Mingus, Texas, about seventy miles west of Ft. Worth, which was soon operating along the lines of the Santee commune.

Patrick's infiltration and its consequences proved to be the undoing of them all. He initiated a major investigation of the sect, and skillfully utilized the media to publicize his activities. He founded an organization of parents who had lost children to the sect and called it FreeCOG (Free the Children of God) which became an effective propaganda and lobbying arm for exposing and attacking the Jordan-Berg axis.

Responding to the pressure Patrick was applying, Jordan called him and invited him to inspect the cult's headquarters in Los Angeles. Patrick went and was appalled by what he saw. When it became clear to Jordan that Patrick was not going to desist in his campaign to expose the Children of God, he sent a telegram to Ronald Reagan, Governor of California, seeking to get Patrick fired. But Patrick had the support and the confidence of the Governor's staff, and once Jordan realized that Reagan's people would not dump his antagonist, he had second thoughts, and decided that David Berg was a liability. Accordingly, he apologized publicly to Patrick, saying that Berg had deceived him, and forthwith severed his relationship with the Children of God, and expelled them from his properties.

When the dispossessed cult announced its intention to set up a base in Dallas, Patrick and some concerned parents rushed down and picketed the Federal Court Building with signs demanding that Attorney General John Mitchell investigate the cult. Television and newspaper coverage of this event was enormous, which is what Patrick had hoped for. He needed a forum, and the media provided it.

The same thing happened a few weeks later in Seattle where another anti-COG picket line established by a host of angry parents ignited a public controversy which the media obligingly kept fueled for days. COG was seriously damaged. The cult was like a fungus growing in the dark and damp. Exposure, sunlight, scrutiny, the Children of God could not abide.

With the publicity attendant on these confrontations, more and more distraught parents contacted Patrick seeking his help in locating their lost children. Which in turn led to the evolution of the technique (some have called it crime) that inside of a few months made Patrick a figure of national interest and debate: deprogramming is the term, and it may be said to involve kidnapping at the very least, quite often assault and battery, almost invariably conspiracy to commit a crime, and illegal restraint. Patrick disputes the charge that saving children from a cult entails illegal behavior; in any event, he contends that no alternative exists.

TED PATRICK: I tried everything to impress on the authorities the dangers of the setup at Santee. But no one was interested. FreeCOG wrote letters to congressmen, senators, the Justice Department, even the President, and received form letters in reply. We got a lot of helpful publicity, but no one would take official action. Freedom of religion is an issue that few politicians are willing to tackle. If guts were dynamite, most politicians wouldn't have enough to blow their noses. No one seemed to understand that with the Children of God religion was not an issue. Psychological kidnapping was the issue—brainwashing, white slavery, prostitution, fraud, false advertising, alienation of affection.

But the laws, and the politicians who administer and interpret them, were protecting David Berg, and the parents' hands were tied. It seemed wrong to me. I thought something had to be done. And, everything considered, nobody seemed better prepared to do it than me.

I admit my getting into the fight was partly an emotional decision. I was sickened by what I'd seen at Santee, and infuriated by the callousness of the government in the face of the grief and torment of the by now hundreds of parents I'd interviewed who had children in the cults and were looking to me as their last hope.

There really weren't many alternatives for me, given the sort of man I am. I hate to lose; I refuse to quit. And it seemed to me that if I gave up in the face of bureaucratic indifference and legislative cowardice and abandoned the parents and let Berg continue to infect the country with his poisons, I could never live with myself, could never face my children or teach them anything about pride and honesty and having the courage of your convictions.

I knew what the price might be. Possible threats to my family, maybe real violence. I could lose my job, be arrested, be imprisoned. I could imagine law suits, endless litigation, my private life and my motives being ruthlessly attacked and maligned in the media. I might even be killed. Nevertheless, I decided I would have to pay whatever the price might be. And I hoped and assumed that after a reasonable amount of time, I would have plenty of allies.

Addressing a meeting of FreeCOG at my house in August, 1971, I told the assembled parents, "We have to be willing to do whatever is necessary to rescue your children. The cult operates illegally under legal sanctions. We have to do the same thing. There's no other way to fight them. Hopefully, in the long run, as a result of what we're doing, the laws will be changed. Until then, we do what we have to do."

What I'd concluded we had to do was bodily abduct the children from the communes and colonies they were living in. I did not feel that I would be disregarding the free choice of those young people who had become members of the cults. Once they had been programmed, like the kids I watched at Santee, there was no longer any question of their exercising anything that could reasonably be called free will. They stayed with the cults because they had been programmed to stay, brainwashed into believing that it was Satan who was tempting them to go. True, the kids at Mission Beach had willingly boarded the bus for Santee. But my question was this: If the Children of God, looking so harmless in their suits and ties, had clearly explained exactly what would happen at the commune that weekend—the harangues, the loudspeakers, the lack of food and sleep, the abuse of the kids' parents, and the end, in effect, of their normal way of life—how many would then have set foot aboard that blue and white bus? When the cults start recruiting like that, I'll stop rescuing and deprogramming. ming.

From my research into the subject I was reasonably well assured that a parent would not be prosecuted for kidnapping his own child, especially if the child was a minor. With that in mind, I began to formulate the basis of my approach to seizing the children and deprogramming them. The first rule was always to have at least one of the parents present when we went to snatch somebody. The parents would have to make the first physical contact; then, no matter who assisted them afterwards, it would be the parents who were responsible. And if a parent was not committing a crime by seizing his or her child, no one else could be considered an accessory to a crime. I also counted on the fact that only the abducted child could bring suit against anyone. I was confident of being able to "deprogram" the child —counteract the brainwashing he'd undergone—so that once he had come out of it he would have no desire to press charges. In any case, we have to have proof if we were to win over the authorities. That meant getting hold of a cult victim.

The Sunday after the meeting with the parents, I got a call from a woman who had a daughter in Children of God and had heard of me from the parent of another COG victim. The girl had dropped out of the University of Southern California and gone to live at the COG commune in Phoenix. The woman begged me to save her daughter.

I decided to grasp the opportunity. I explained to her what would be involved—taking the girl out bodily—and she said she would consult her husband and call me back. I had just returned from church when the phone rang. "My husband," she said, "says he doesn't care how we do it, just do it." I told her I'd assemble some helpers and we'd all leave for Phoenix that afternoon. At seven in the evening we were on the street outside the comune.

I had made an attempt on that same Phoenix commune three weeks before, as it happened. Mrs. Jackson's son had been there, and we'd tried to rescue him using private detectives she had hired. But the detectives refused to set foot on the commune's property, and the attempt was a disaster. This time, I resolved, things would be different. I had a plan—involving nine trusted helpers and two cars.

The first car rolled up to the house. In the front was the boy from USC and the girl's mother. In back, hiding, were two helpers. Five hundred yards behind that car, down the block, was a back-up car, driven by me. On the sidewalk was a helper pretending to be strolling by.

The mother and the USC classmate went up to the house and knocked on the door. Their instructions were to coax the girl out of the house and, if they could not do that, to enter and scream bloody murder the minute they saw her—whereupon all the rest of us would burst in and take her away.

When the door opened, the mother and the classmate had an awful surprise: a commune meeting was going on, with 125 youngsters sitting on the floor in every direction. But the girl saw her mother and came to the door. The classmate grabbed her from behind and started pulling her out. The man on the sidewalk ran up and helped. As the angry commune members began pouring out of the house after them, they jammed the girl into the first car and off it went. I rushed up my car and picked up the rest of our people, and we zoomed off too. The whole thing had taken less than three minutes.

We drove straight to San Diego and checked in at the Royal Inn Motel. I picked the fourth floor so the girl couldn't escape out the window. If the girl escaped, I was in trouble. I'd lose my job with the governor for sure. But I resolved to pay whatever price I had to get the goods on the cults.

From my own experiences in the COG center at Santee, I knew the girl had been programmed to the Bible she'd be carrying—that it was a device for self-hypnosis—so immediately I took it away from her. She was enraged and slapped her mother, who stood next to her. Then she started quoting Bible verses at me. But she was misconstruing them badly, and so I began reading out the whole chapters in which the quotes appeared, showing her that the meanings were different from what the cult had programmed her to believe.

She began to call us all "Satan," and she said God would strike us dead. I replied that God was a God of love, not wrath and hate. I said God had delivered her from the pits of Hell and she should be grateful to God that she'd been rescued by her parents.

Then we went back to our Biblical debate. Gradually she began to listen and respond. She'd challenge and I'd explain— until I saw that she was actually beginning to use her mind again. It was exciting to watch.

After two days of talking, with three of us taking turns, she suddenly gave in. She snapped, just as if someone had turned on a light inside her. The change in her appearance, her expression, her eyes—it was startling. I was amazed. It was like seeing someone return from the grave. It was the most beautiful thing I'd ever seen.

"I told you earlier that your daughter was programmed," I

said to her mother. "Now she's been 'deprogrammed.' " It was the first time I'd ever used the word.

Almost immediately, news of this success got out, and I began to get dozens of calls. I went up and down the West Coast deprogramming. The more I did, the more stringent security precautions the COG communes adopted, and the harder it got. It was about this time that they gave me the nickname Black Lightning because of the way I'd strike out of nowhere. The more difficult it got and the greater the danger and risk on my part, the greater became the need for very strict and elaborate counter-security and detailed planning.

The case of the girl I'll call Pamela Collins is a good example of the sort of thing I had to cope with in those early days of what some people have called my crusade.

Ralph Collins was a Denver realtor. His daughter Pam, a sophomore at the University of Colorado, was engaged to be married to a boy who was also attending Colorado. The wedding plans were far advanced—the invitations had been mailed, the church reserved, the hall for the reception booked, the wedding cake ordered—when suddenly their daughter vanished without a word.

What had happened was that Pam's financé—the son of a prominent physician—had entered the Children of God colony in Woodland Park, about 100 miles from Denver, and when Pam went out there to try to talk him out of it, they got her too.

Collins had contacted the boy's father to determine whether he wanted to cooperate in trying to free their children. But the boy's father wasn't interested. He argued that his son was of legal age, that he seemed to have found a religious focus to his life which was meaningful and rewarding, and that he did not feel it was his place to interfere. Nevertheless, Ralph Collins was determined to get his daughter out, and asked me to make the attempt.

The security precautions at Woodland Park were the toughest I'd seen. The colony was way up in the mountains, some twenty-four miles back on a dirt road five miles off the main highway. There was nothing else on the road except the colony, which consisted of three buildings—old farm buildings—surrounded by a seven-foot-high fence with a locked gate. There were 350 kids living there. The grounds were patrolled by three vicious German shepherds. And one of the buildings was topped by a watchtower so that no one could come up that road without being detected at least five minutes before he reached the gate. I had to feel vaguely complimented when I heard these details; the security arrangements were a direct result of the heat I'd been putting on them.

Evidently Ralph Collins did not know that I was a black man, because when I got off the plane in Denver he was visibly shocked and disappointed. I'd brought along a friend I'll call Roger Holmes, who had been an ally from the beginning of the fight against the cults, and I guess neither of us were physically impressive on first sight. Holmes is tall and thin, and I'm kind of short, and you could tell right off that Collins was wondering just what the hell he was getting into.

The drive to his apartment was very uncomfortable. No one could think of much to say. I tried to question Collins about his daughter, but he looked preoccupied and would only reply in monosyllables.

The apartment building they lived in was very handsome—a new high-rise in a fashionable neighborhood, with swimming pool, security people at the entrance, spectacular views from all the apartments. I remember thinking as we rode the elevator up to Collins' apartment that his real estate business must be all right.

Mrs. Collins was a pretty, gracious, but extremely nervous woman who wanted reassurance from me that we would indeed get Pam out. Her husband was appearing more pessimistic every minute. As Mrs. Collins served us coffee, I caught him eyeing me with a thoughtful, dubious expression on his face. We made awkward small talk for a while, and then Collins suddenly asked me if I had any credentials or identification. I realized for the first time that he could not believe I was even the right person. I showed him my driver's license and said, "Yes, I'm really Ted Patrick. And I've snatched and deprogrammed a lot of children just like yours."

"Do you guarantee success?" he asked.

"Can't guarantee anything in this life, Mr. Collins. But I'll guarantee you this—I'll give you my best."

"The police and the FBI told me it would be impossible to get inside and take Pam out. We were up there with them the other day. It's like a concentration camp. The police told me the only way is to catch her when she's outside, on the street."

"I don't have time for that," I told him. I was still working for Governor Reagan, and had to confine my deprogramming to the weekends. "If Pam's in there, then we're gonna go in and get her if it's possible to get her."

The doorbell rang and a young well built boy named Danny came in. He was a friend of the Collinses who had volunteered to assist in the job of getting Pam back. I was glad to have him, especially when I learned that he was expert in karate. I believe firmly that the Lord helps those who help themselves—and a few little things like karate, Mace, and handcuffs can come in handy from time to time.

As soon as we were all introduced, I said, "Okay, let's get down to business. First, I want you to call Woodland Park and ask for your daughter. They'll probably lie to you and say she's not there, but don't be put off. Act friendly, real friendly, and tell them that you're leaving for Florida to do some business and you won't be back for a long time. Say that you have a check for her for eight hundred dollars, the money that was in her bank account." When Collins learned his daughter was in the cult he'd withdrawn that money from Pam's account to make sure she didn't turn it over to the group. "Say that you have a lot of her clothes and things, and that you'd like to bring all of it up to her before you leave. Tell them you also want to leave her the key to the house so she can come up and stay while you're gone. Ask for them to have her call you back and when you hang up tell them 'God bless you.'"

Collins continued to be very gloomy, but he agreed to do as I told him, thinking, I suppose, that he might as well, since there were no alternatives.

In spite of his doubts, Collins carried the thing off nicely; he sounded perfectly convincing, even to his "God bless you" which must have made him want to gag. But the ruse worked, and ten minutes later Pam was on the phone.

"Daddy!" she said. "Daddy, oh, God bless you, Daddy, oh how I love you. I'm so glad you finally understand how I have to do the Lord's work." She proceeded to give him directions how to get up there, and said they would be looking out for him.

"That's fine," I said. "They fell for it. Okay, now here's what we're going to do." And I began to outline my plan. "Danny, you drive the car. I'm going to give you the Mace. And Mrs. Collins, I'm going to give you some of it too. Whatever happens, I want you to hold on to it. Don't let go of it, and use it if you have to."

Mrs. Collins turned very pale at this, but nodded gamely, accepting. Danny said, "I'll use the Mace, but I'm also gonna use my feet. I'll be barefoot, with my feet taped. I'm quicker with my feet than with my hands."

At this Mr. Collins changed color, and looked as if he wanted to object, but I ignored him and went ahead outlining the plan.

An hour later we were on the highway, in two cars, the Collinses' and Danny's. As we drove I rehearsed the plan over and over with the Collinses, and made them recite it back to me.

As we approached the twenty-four mile cut up into the mountain, Danny pulled his car off to the side of the road, parked it, and joined us. Then we drove on up, stopping once at a restaurant for some coffee, and I went over the plan still one more time.

"Remember," I said, "we can't make any mistakes. There are over three hundred people in there. They have guards, a warning system, vicious dogs. This is strictly a one-shot deal. If you mess this up, you'll never see your daughter again, and we're all going to get hurt and maybe even killed. Okay? Okay, let's get rolling."

The back of the car was heaped with Pam's belongings—dresses, coats, slacks, shoes. Holmes and I lay down on the floor beneath a blanket as we entered the five mile stretch of deserted dirt road. Danny was driving, Mrs. Collins with her can of Mace was next to him, and Mr. Collins was by the door.

No one said anything. Holmes and I were all scrunched up together beneath the blanket, jouncing up and down and swearing under our breath as one or the other of us caught an elbow in the throat or poked a finger into an eye.

Long before we reached the gate we could hear the dogs barking.

"I hope they're on chains," Mrs. Collins said worriedly.

"If they're not, you Mace 'em right in the face," Danny said. "That'll take care of 'em."

I was hoping none of that would be necessary. I was counting, as I always do, on the elements of swiftness and surprise.

Danny drove up to the dead end of the road, turned the car around, and brought it back in front of the gate. Mr. Collins and his wife got out, each scooping a bundle of clothes from the back seat.

The guard at the gate, a young boy in khaki pants and a flannel shirt, opened the gate, and welcomed them. "God bless you, welcome, we all love you," he said. The Collinses gave him strained smiles and moved up the path to the house.

Pam, a pretty, slight, graceful girl with light brown hair to her shoulders, ran out onto the porch and embraced her parents. "I'm so glad to see you, God bless you, Mommy and Daddy!"

"We're glad to see you too, Pam," Mr. Collins said.

"My name is Sarah, now, Daddy," the girl corrected him. "We've forsaken our earth names."

Collins swallowed. "Yes, Sarah. We're so glad for you," he forced himself to say. "So glad you've found peace with all these nice friends."

"It's wonderful," the girl said, as other members, including her fiancé, gathered around. The Collinses greeted the boy, were introduced to the others, and then Collins took the check out of his wallet and handed it to his daughter.

"This is for your expenses—if you need anything while we're gone."

"Bless you," she said and kissed him.

"We have some other things of yours in the car, darling," Mrs. Collins said. "Come help us get them out."

No one suspected anything, but as a matter of course Pam was accompanied by a gang—five guys, including her fiancé, and three girls. Mrs. Collins fingered the can of Mace in her coat pocket, mentally reviewing her instructions, picking out possible targets, thinking that the girls would pose no problems, selecting two of the ugliest boys to Mace, thinking that if it came down to it she probably could not bring herself to Mace Pam's boyfriend, whom she had once been very fond of.

Holmes and I could hear them approaching. They were talking and laughing. Danny said, "They're about eight feet away, coming around the back, Pam first." I heard the dogs barking, and prayed we'd pull this off before they turned them loose. I heard Danny opening his door and getting out. It had to be fast; as soon as they saw those bare taped-up feet there was going to be tension. The back door opened. It was now or never. I flung back the blanket and found myself staring into Pam Collins' very amazed face.

There was a frozen instant. Then she gasped, "Kidnap!" and started to back away. But her mother was behind her and pushed her hard, and I got my arms around her shoulders and sucked her in on top of us like a vacuum cleaner—whoosh!— and she vanished inside. Immediately her boyfriend piled in on top of her, or tried to, and I remember thinking even in the middle of all the action what a pity it was that his father had not been interested in rescuing him because I could have had him too. As it was, I had to get rid of him, so I kicked him in the stomach and he went reeling back and Mrs. Collins tripped him and sent him sprawling.

In the meantime, Danny was mixing it up with three of the other large dudes, clipping one in the jaw with his feet, and Macing two of the others. Fortunately the three girls did not get themselves together in time to do anything. They just stood back and shrieked.

Collins fought his way around to the driver's seat, and shouted to Danny to get in. Mrs. Collins had already made it back

inside. Holmes and I were wrestling with Pam who was screaming her head off. I was sitting up by this time and saw people
running from the house, and one of the dogs sprinting
towards us. Danny decked Pam's boyfriend with his fist, and
dove in just as the first of the German shepherds arrived and
lunged at the door, banging against it as Danny swung it shut,
and we went rolling off down the hill, leaving a scene of great
confusion and disruption behind.

The entire operation had taken less than three minutes.

"You did just fine and we're in good shape," I told them.
"They've probably got our license plate number and they'll be
calling the police, but there's nothing to worry about. It will
take the police half an hour to get up there, and another hour
or so to take the complaint and get the story from all the eye-
witnesses. We'll be a long way from here by then, believe me."

In fact, the police were quicker than I thought; we met them
coming up the mountain about fifteen minutes later. When we
reached the highway, we stopped the car, let Danny out,
thanked him, and said goodbye. Then we changed positions,
the Collinses getting in back with Pam, and Holmes and I in
the front with me driving. I headed for San Diego and we never
stopped except for gas. I drove all the way.

Pam behaved the way almost all of them do. She put up a
terrific struggle for the first few minutes. Then, realizing she
was trapped, she calmed down. Some try to use silence as a
weapon. Pam was a talker. She wouldn't keep quiet. Things
like, "You're not my father and mother—you're demons, sent
by Satan. You're possessed. My real family is back there at
Woodland Park. Look at him, that black devil driving. Don't
you see the evil in him? You're all going to be punished for this.
I have my rights. You can't kidnap me. I'll bring charges
against all of you. Don't call me Pam! My name is not Pam!
My name is Sarah, and you're not my parents. My family is
back there."

One of the occupational hazards in this business—aside from
German shepherds—is the monotony of listening to this fairly
limited repertoire that the kids have at their command. They

parrot the same old Bible verses at you, spew out the same monotonous programmed rubbish. It's mindless and it's boring, the more so because it's so utterly predictable.

The trip was without major incident. When we stopped for gas we would all accompany Pam to the bathroom, me in front, Holmes in the rear, and her parents on either side of her. It must have looked pretty strange to the filling station attendants, but no one ever said anything. We arrived in San Diego about o'clock the following afternoon and I checked into the Royal Inn Motel. And then we got right down to the business of deprogramming Pam.

Deprogramming, I think, is widely misunderstood—I mean, what I do, what goes on. To read some of the accounts that have been written by reporters who have never witnessed a deprogramming, you would think it was a cross between the Spanish Inquisition and an orgy sponsored by the Marquis de Sade. It's nothing of the kind. Essentially it's just talk. I talk to the victim, for as long as I have to. I don't deny that that's the catch for many people—"for as long as I have to." Yes, in some cases that means restraint. Yes, it also means the victim may not be free to leave when he wants to. When a victim is exceptionally vigorous, it may even mean a measure of physical restraint.

But let me say this. The techniques I employ do not in any way approximate or parallel the psychological kidnapping and mind control that the cults employ. The cults strike at random; they will approach anyone anywhere, without regard to the person's age, background, sex, or occupation. When they go out into the streets to witness—which is their dressed-up term for proselytizing (which is only another dressed-up word, in this instance, for psychological kidnapping)—they attempt to snare people indiscriminately. The Children of God, for example, have attempted to recruit children as young as nine years old. Once they get a victim, they consciously and deliberately set about to destroy every normal pattern of living the victim has known; he is separated from his friends, he is turned against his family, he is led to renounce his education, his career, his responsibilities. He is literally robbed of whatever financial assets he may possess, and his parents are as a matter of course blackmailed into contributing large sums of money to the cult merely in order to be occasionally permitted to see their child. He is physically abused and often expected to work as much as twenty hours a day fund-raising for the group. He is frequently undernourished and psychologically manipulated to the degree that he cannot distinguish between reality and the grotesque fantasies and illusions the cult fosters. He is programmatically turned against his country, taught that patriotism is sinful, the system Satanic. He is urged to become a revolutionary, to destroy the institutions of society in the name of David Berg or some other phony god. Discord, division, hatred, grief—those are what the cults bestow.

Against that, the deprogramming method is first of all very selective. I don't go into a commune and indiscriminately grab the first person I see, as, in effect, the cults do when they are witnessing on the street. The parents of a young person will contact me—usually after months of deliberation, fear and uncertainty. When we take the person into custody he is, admittedly, held against his will. But it's arguable whether at that stage of his indoctrination he can be said to *have* a will, any will, let alone free will in the sense that we normally use that term. Regardless, the child is rarely held in custody by the parents and me for longer than three days. Usually it takes me less than one day to deprogram a person. I've managed to do it on occasion in an hour.

The important things to remember here are how the cults treated the individual, what their motives were, and how we treat him, what our motives are. The child is with his family throughout the process. He is well-fed. While I admit that limiting his sleep is a basic element in deprogramming, he sleeps at least as much as he did in the cult, almost all of which use fatigue as a strategic weapon. I do not brainwash. I ask questions, basically, and I try to show the victim how he has been deceived. Whereas, in the cult indoctrination, everything possible is done to prevent the person from thinking, in deprogramming I do everything I know how to start him thinking.

All deprogramming is is talk—a lot of talk. It only lasts two or three days. Not thirty or forty days as when a person joins a cult. Not three or four years of constant indoctrination and slave labor. I'm criticized for holding these children against their will. But once you go into the Children of God, or the Unification Church, or the Hare Krishna movement, you are not, practically speaking, free to leave either. Now, that seems to suggest I'm fighting fire with fire—or that, at best, I'm no better in my methods than the cults.

But let's look at motives. I do not make money off the deprogrammed person. His parents pay for my travel and living expenses, and whatever other expenses are incurred during the snatch and deprogramming. He certainly does not become a follower of mine, selling plastic flowers in the streets to support me in a life of great luxury. I do not seek to implant in him any dogma, any preconceived or manufactured view or philosophy of life. Once he is deprogrammed he is absolutely free to do whatever he wants to do. Go to school, go to work, lie on a beach and look at the clouds. Whatever. That's none of my business. All I want and all I do is to return to them their ability to think for themselves, to exercise their free will, which the cults have put into cold storage. I thaw them out, and once they're free of the cult, with very few exceptions they begin again to lead productive lives—and not necessarily conformist lives. Deprogrammed people are as various and individualistic as any group in the society. Motives *are* important. The cults' motives are destructive—this can be demonstrated. My motives, I hope I have demonstrated here, have nothing in common with those of the spiritual gangsters who populate outfits like the Children of God.

With Pamela Collins, the deprogramming took about two days. We arrived in San Diego in the early afternoon, following a twenty-hour journey from Colorado. I was pretty tired so I left Pam with her parents, Betty Spahn, and her daughter Linda, who was a former COG member, and went home to take a nap and catch up on some business.

I returned to the motel early in the evening and stayed until about one in the morning. I was back at the Royal Inn early the next morning and stayed until late that night when Pam came out of it.

The arrangements there more or less typified what had become and would continue to be our standard operating procedure. I rented a room in which there is no bathroom window. We removed the lock from the bathroom door and the mouthpiece from the phone. Somebody was with Pam at all times. Legally, of course, it's vital that the parents be present throughout, and it's helpful psychologically too. The victim has a constant pressure on him from the parents, reacts subconsciously to their constant expressions of love, their unhappiness over his condition, their tears. It's helpful to have the parents soften up their child with questions and arguments. The same goes for the others there, former cult members who know in advance all of the victim's arguments, responses, and psychological tricks, and can counter them effectively.

The sleeping arrangements were also typical. Mrs. Collins slept with her daughter in one bed. Mr. Collins slept in the other bed, which was pulled over so that it was blocking the door. The others who were helping slept on the floor.

My approach to deprogramming Pam was also more or less standard. Since a cult's basic point of attachment to a person's psychology is the convert's relationship with his parents, I concentrate on that. I stressed to Pam how unnatural it was for her to renounce her parents. "That's nowhere in the Bible," I told her. "The Bible says you should honor your father and mother, that the days may be long upon the land which thy God gives thee." She argued that the Bible meant to honor your *spiritual* father and mother. "Then why doesn't the Bible say that?" I replied. "Show me where it says that." I kept hitting her on her inconsistencies in that area, on her ignorance of the Bible in general. I pointed out how the cult had taken certain selected verses out of context and distorted their meaning. I forced her to read the whole chapter from which the verse was taken, forced her to think about the real context of those words.

She was sporadically violent, slapping her mother in the

face at one point. "What kind of God do you worship?" I asked her. "What kind of God tells you to slap your mother, to hate her, to renounce her? That's no God telling you to do that, that's Satan. You are a Devil worshiper."

Gradually, Pam began to soften, began to think about some of the things I was telling her, gradually began to perceive the truth about how she had been deceived. Suddenly, late that night, she broke. The moment when that happens is always unmistakable. It's like an emotional dam bursting. Pam began to weep, and she embraced her parents and kissed them. I went out of the room and left them alone for a while. When I came back, Pam turned to me and said, "Ted, I feel so terrible about all the things I said to you, all the names I called you."

"You called me some pretty good ones," I said with a grin. "Some I never heard before. I mean to write them down so I can remember them. Might come in handy some day."

"Really, I didn't know . . ."

"I know. You don't have to explain."

"I'm so grateful to you, you've saved my life. I really feel like I've just woke up from some incredible nightmare. Do you forgive me?"

"Of course I do. Don't worry about it. You were a different person saying those things."

"I'll never forget what you've done for me," she said, and came up to me and kissed me.

It's a very beautiful thing to see when a kid comes out of his bondage. It makes the whole business worthwhile to me, it's what keeps me going.

As a side effect, let me add that after one of these experiences the family is greatly strengthened. They have all gone through an emotional and psychological and philosophical experience very rare and very meaningful. They have literally gone through hell, and the victim has been brought back from the dead.

When I prepared to report to my office that Monday morning, I assessed the weekend and came to a couple of conclusions. One, if I was going to continue to deprogram kids I would obviously have to leave my job with the state government. I had about fifty requests to rescue children piled up on my desk, and more were coming in every day. I either had to do it full-time, or not at all. It seemed to me worthwhile doing it full-time. However, and this was number two, there was going to be a survival factor involved if I resigned my position. How was I going to support my family? I couldn't bring myself to charge distraught parents anything more than my expenses for a de-programming. My wife is a teacher, but could not possibly make enough money to support a family of seven, and I could en-vision ending up losing everything in my fight against the cults (that, unfortunately, proved to be all too accurate a prognosti-cation). But finally money did not seem to be a major considera-tion. I would do what I had to do, and provide for my family however I could. Three, I now had the confidence that I could get a kid out of anywhere. I wasn't likely to run into security precautions any more ironclad than those that I'd dealt with at Woodland Park. The FBI and the local police had informed Mr. Collins that there was no way to get Pam out of the com-mune. I'd gotten her out. After that weekend I felt confident that with enough careful planning, the right sort of helpers, with guts and daring and resolution, I could snatch a kid from Alcatraz if I had to.

The next morning, after conferring with my superiors in Sacramento, I sat down and drafted my letter of resignation. From now on, it was all-out war against the cults.

CHAPTER THREE

The Children of God are in Europe now, most of them, in-cluding David Berg. They began fleeing the United States in the early winter of 1973, arguing that the comet Kohoutek was a herald of the destruction of the U.S. In reality, they were fleeing the impact not of a comet but of the Charity Frauds Bureau report to New York State's Attorney General Lefkowitz, which they well knew was going to discredit their operations once and for all. The report confirmed their fears;

it was explosive. It was also a direct consequence of Patrick's crusade, his all-out war.

Under the heading "Mind-Manipulation (Brainwashing or Thought Control)" the Charity Frauds Bureau report states:

> The COG engages in a particularly reprehensible course of conduct by tampering with the personalities of converts. They proceed in a calculated, systematic manner, albeit without even the informal consent of the victims, to change established behavior patterns.
>
> By manipulation and constant monitoring of thought processes, by making younger members uncomfortable and exposed to psychological cruelties such as bodily deprivation of all sorts and forced memorization of biblical passages, a total assault on the psyche is accomplished. Brainwashing techniques are deliberately employed under the rationalization that it is in the service of a good cause.

The report is a detailed, sober, objective, and remorseless indictment of every aspect of the cult's activities. The headings and subheadings of various sections in the report tell their own story. "Physical Coercion and Solitary Confinement." "Mental Coercion." "Fatigue and Tension." "Uncertainty or Fear." "Fear-Inducing Vicious Language."

And the list of six "common experiences of former COGs and their parents as disclosed in our inquiry:"

1. A sudden (unexplained) decision by a new "convert" to drop out of school.
2. An initial refusal to leave the COG commune by a recent "convert" based on fear.
3. A complete personality change resulted in a bitter hatred for parents.
4. An unexplainable and uncontrollable compulsion of a "convert" to return to COG commune despite vicious brutalization while there.
5. An uncharacteristic and self-destructive compulsion to transfer all personal assets and those of parents to be contributed to COG.

6. The failure of "converts" to receive monies requested from and forwarded from their parents.

The cult's hasty and disorderly retreat across the Atlantic in the face of these indictments was tantamount to a plea of *nolo contendere*. Nevertheless, the public-at-large was slow to take Patrick at his word. The attitude of the average American continued to reflect the sentiments expressed by *Time* magazine in an article about Patrick's methods in the spring of 1973. "Parental abduction," *Time* wrote, "is, to be sure, not novel in the annals of religion. St. Clare's family tried to retrieve her bodily after she ran away from home to join St. Francis of Assisi and his band of pious mendicants. Legend has it that St. Thomas Aquinas' family locked him in a room with a whore to dissuade him from joining the Dominican order. But the deprogramming practiced by today's soul-snatchers seems suspiciously like a religious version of the Ludovico technique— that brain-blowing treatment administered to Alex, the anti-hero in Anthony Burgess' *A Clockwork Orange*. It was designed to make him acceptable to society by ridding him of his sado-sexual violence. In the process, Alex also lost his free will."

One of the battles Patrick has had to fight is trying to convince people that a fundamental difference exists between the Children of God and the Dominicans; between David Berg and St. Francis of Assisi; between benumbed, bewildered, automatized kids and St. Clare or Thomas Aquinas. The public was reluctant to heed his admonitions about the dangers of the Children of God, and once he was vindicated people were grudging in their recognition of the role he had played in exposing the cults. More frustrating for Patrick was the refusal of nearly everyone to concede that the Children of God were not an isolated phenomenon—that the cult movement had as many heads as Hydra.

TED PATRICK: I had never heard of Hannah Lowe or the New Testament Missionary Fellowship until January, 1973, when a man named Joseph Lockwood came down to San Diego to talk to me about his son, Wes, who had become ensnared by the cult. He told me that Hannah Lowe was an old woman who claimed to have visions and possess the gift of prophecy; she had organized a sect operating out of New York City which preyed upon exceptionally intelligent Ivy League college students. I'd been deprogramming for over a year, and the story Mr. Lockwood told me was a familiar one.

Wes, an only son (the Lockwoods also had a twelve-year-old daughter), was handsome, cultivated, outgoing, and popular, with no obvious personal or psychological problems. Raised as a Roman Catholic, Wes had discovered Pentecostalism as a high school student, and had become what fundamentalists call "a born-again Christian." That means that Wes experienced a sudden reinforcement of his faith, of his belief that Christ was his Savior. This took place the summer before he went to Yale for his freshman year. Lockwood was disturbed, but decided it was just a phase his son was going through and that he would eventually grow out of it.

But during that summer, Wes—along with all the other incoming freshmen—received a copy in the mail of a newspaper called *The Yale Standard*. It was a highly professional-looking product put out by Hannah Lowe, professing to tell the religious history of Yale and suggesting to recipients that as Christians away from home they might consider the New Testament Missionary Fellowship as a fraternal haven among friends whose spiritual personalities had something in common with theirs.

When he got to Yale he was introduced to the Fellowship and got interested in their program. The whole process of entrapment was much slower, more subtle, more sophisticated than in any of the other cults I've dealt with. Wes was gradually isolated from the rest of the university as a result of frequent Bible study sessions and prayer meetings. Then step-by-step he was turned against his family and that made him feel guilty, and served to make him even more dependent on the group. As that first semester wore on the emotional level of the prayer meetings grew more intense. The members would engage in singing, dancing, speaking in tongues—so-called ecstatic devotions—that went on nonstop for up to four or five hours a session, and which left the converts exhausted and confused, emotionally wiped out. Then the leaders would indoctrinate them, when their resistance was broken, and would hammer at them with denunciations of the university, the political system, their families, the institutions of government, all of which they were told were of Satan.

By Christmas, Wes had been taken over by them completely. It was at Christmas that he called his parents to inform them he was not coming home for the holidays as he had planned. He had previously written and spoken on the phone with a lot of enthusiasm about the prospects of reunions with his high school friends. Then, suddenly, a few days before he was due to arrive in Los Angeles, he called to tell his astonished parents, "I've met these people who have a whole new concept about serving the Lord. There's a man here named McCandlish Phillips who gave a lecture last night. He's a writer for the N.Y. *Times* and he's really good. He said we had to come to a decision about God. He said now is the time to put God first in our lives. He said the Lord has more for us to do than go home for the holidays. He convinced me. I'm going to stay here and do the Lord's work."

His parents were upset by what he said and even more bothered by his odd tone of voice, and Lockwood began making inquiries about the group. He discovered that all four freshmen members of the New Testament Missionary Fellowship had cancelled their holiday trips after hearing Phillips' lecture. He also discovered that the Fellowship consisted of forty young people from different schools in the East who met weekly at Hannah Lowe's apartment in New York; that Hannah Lowe owned an estate in Yonkers, and a farm in Colombia, South America, to which members of the group were sent from time to time; that all of the members worked at part-time jobs and gave all their money to the group.

Alarmed by all he'd learned, a few days after his son's phone call Mr. Lockwood flew to New Haven to try to talk Wes into coming home. When he saw his son he was shocked. A tremendous personality change had occurred in him. He was withdrawn, uncommunicative, and hostile. Furthermore, he had lost so much weight he was nothing more than skin and bones.

There was an angry confrontation between them, Wes insisting that his father had no right to interfere with his life. The following morning when Lockwood went to see Wes at his dorm, to resume the discussion, he discovered that his son was gone, having fled during the night to Hannah Lowe's place in New York.

Mr. Lockwood followed him to the city and had a long and bitter meeting with Hannah Lowe, who told him in effect that Wes belonged to the Fellowship now, body and soul, and there was nothing he, Lockwood, could do about it.

For the next two years it appeared that she was right. Finally, after reading about me and viewing a television program on my work, Lockwood decided to get in touch to see what I could do.

Mr. Lockwood, a stockbroker, is a very thorough man, one who is accustomed to getting results from his efforts. In the two years his son belonged to the cult, he hired private investigators to get the real story on Hannah Lowe and her operation, and what he found was intimidating. They were very tight, very secretive. He made it sound as though getting Wes out would entail the sort of daredevil expertise you saw on "Mission Impossible."

When he was through with his story, I said, "Look, Mr. Lockwood, I'm pushed for time and I don't want to waste your time. How far are you prepared to go to rescue your son?"

He frowned and said, "What do you mean how far am I prepared to go?"

"Just what I said. Would you be willing to do *anything* to get your son out of that cult?"

"Anything?" he said. "Anything at all?"

"Anything at all. And that means everything."

There was a long pause. He looked at his wife and fidgeted in his chair. Then he said, "Well, we've suffered through this thing for two and a half years now. Suffered! He's my only son. We've discussed this a long time now, and we've decided that this is *it*. We want him out. We wouldn't have come down here otherwise." Then he hesitated a moment, and asked, "But exactly what do you mean by doing anything or everything?"

"You have to understand," I told him, "that you're not dealing with your son anymore. You're dealing with a robot. A zombie. You can't reason with him. He's beyond reasoning. The only way you can get him is to take him out bodily. And I won't kid you. That means a lot of risk. You could go to jail. You could be physically injured. You can wind up paying enormous legal and medical bills. There's a possibility that you'll never see your son again for the rest of your life. The question is: are you or are you not willing to take those risks? How far will you go?"

He looked very thoughtful. He was stalling for time, still not certain in his mind of the answers to my questions.

"If we did it, when could you start?" he asked me.

"Tomorrow," I said. He was shaken; he clearly didn't want to be pressed, and was fishing around for some loophole.

"What's your average of success on other jobs you've done?"

"My batting average is one thousand, Mr. Lockwood. I have never yet failed to get a kid out of a cult. We've lost two or three once we got them out, when the parents let their guard down and the kids went out the window before they were deprogrammed. But so far every time I've gone after a kid, I've gotten him. And out of some pretty tight places too." And I told him about the Collins case.

He was still squirming, looking for some objection to peg a refusal on. He struck on money. "How much will this cost me? What do you make on it?"

"All I charge is expenses. Plane fare, hotel accommodations, food. If you're satisfied with the job afterwards, you can make a donation. If you don't want to, that's okay too. A lot of people don't."

He couldn't think of anything else, but he still wasn't ready to commit himself, so I said, "Why don't you and Mrs. Lockwood talk this over for a couple of days and let me know what you decide. If and when you're ready, I'll drop everything and go."

That was a Saturday. They returned to Los Angeles and I had a chance to be with my family for the weekend; what with all the traveling around the country I'd been doing for the past twelve months, I hadn't seen my wife and children very much and I wanted the luxury of a weekend alone with them.

Monday morning, Lockwood called and asked me if I'd come to L.A. for dinner on Wednesday. "We've decided to go through with it," he said. "To hell with the risks. Life without my son isn't worth living anyway."

So on Wednesday I flew to L.A. and the three of us went out to dinner. Mr. Lockwood turned over to me all the information he had gathered on the cult, as well as schedules of Wes's activities, and maps of the school. He also gave me a check for five hundred dollars. I wanted to spend a lot of time at Yale looking the situation over, so we agreed that I would depart Friday night and spend Saturday, Sunday, and Monday in New Haven. Lockwood would join me there on Tuesday when we would make the snatch. It was Lockwood's opinion that we should take his son from his dorm at 10:30 P.M., which I tentatively accepted.

Then, because I could tell that he was still very nervous about the whole business, I said to him, "Please try to understand this: I haven't found a psychiatrist, or an attorney, or a doctor or anyone else who knows anything about this cult brainwashing and mind control. That's part of my job, and in a way the toughest part—educating the ignorant public. The law wasn't designed to handle this situation of the cults. Now if you call your attorney for advice, if you're going to do that, then I might as well give you back your money right now. Your attorney will give you all the legal aspects of the case, and the legal aspects are all negative. Plain and simple, what we are going to do in New Haven is against the law. That's why I asked you last week if you were willing to do anything to get Wes out."

"We are, we are," he protested quickly.

"Don't worry about him," Mrs. Lockwood said with determination. "He's not going to call any lawyer. We're in this thing to stay."

All the same, the next day while I was talking to some parents in L.A. about snatching their daughter from a cult in Seattle, Lockwood telephoned his attorney. What he heard almost produced a coronary. The attorney had him hanged, electrocuted, in jail for life, flogged, put in the stocks, gassed, fined a hundred thousand dollars—the works. He was scared so badly, he went home and told his wife he was pulling out. They had a heated argument.

"You can't pull out," she said. "It's our only chance to rescue Wes."

"This could ruin me. Bill said I was out of my mind if I went through with it."

"Patrick hasn't failed yet. He's been doing this for two years. Nobody's gone to jail."

"How can we be sure? How can we believe him?"

"Joe, if you back out, then I'm going East and do it myself. And I mean it. I'm getting Wes back and that's all there is to it."

Lockwood didn't sleep that night. He paced the floor, drank coffee, drank liquor. He later told me that he picked up the phone a hundred times to call me and cancel the deal. But his wife never let up the pressure on him, and in the end he caved in. "Jail or no jail," he said. "To hell with it. I'll go."

I arrived in New Haven on Saturday morning and checked into the Park Plaza Hotel. Wes Lockwood worked at the Yale Faculty Club on Elm Street washing dishes twice a day, and from my room I could look down onto Elm Street, and study the flow of traffic and the vicinity of the Faculty Club. I guess even then I'd subconsciously rejected the idea of snatching Wes from his dorm and was hoping that it might be feasible to hit him somewhere else.

I had a bite to eat in my room, and then went down onto the street and reconnoitered the Faculty Club and the immediate vicinity, making mental notes. Next to the Faculty Club was another building, and then an alley, and then a kind of university laundry used by a lot of people. There was a great deal of movement in and out of the laundry, cars pulling up and parking in front and departing every fifteen minutes or so. The traffic was heavy on Elm, which was a one-way street, and four lanes wide. Across from the Faculty Club was a park.

Then I proceeded to Wes's dorm to check that out. As soon as I saw the building I began to get bad vibrations. One of my unbreakable rules is that when I'm taking someone out of a building I have three minutes, no more, to get him out, into the car, and rolling. If you take more than three minutes, you lose the elements of surprise and confusion; the person is struggling and hollering, and bystanders are likely to intervene and interfere. Which is why I always prefer to hit them on the street, where my time limit is thirty seconds.

This dormitory was not well-situated for my purposes. Parking the car would be a problem. Then there was a quadrangle we'd have to drag him across. "Take three minutes just to get him across the quadrangle," I thought.

I went inside and strolled around, looking. I checked the exits and entrances, trying to find an angle, some way in and out that might possibly fit within the three-minute rule. It continued to look bad. It looked worse the longer I cased the place. "Another element you have to think about," I told myself, "is the problem with the other students here." A college campus is not like a city street—students don't give a damn about the dangers of getting involved. On college campuses you don't find any Kitty Genovese cases where thirty-five people watch somebody get murdered and don't lift a finger to help. The kids would jump right in if Wes started hollering. I shook my head. A Yale dorm was not the Children of God commune, with a seven-foot fence and vicious dogs, but it presented its own set of problems. "No way under the sun I can get him out of here," I thought. "No way in hell!"

Leaving the dorm I wandered around the campus, button-holing students here and there, asking them if they knew anything about the New Testament Missionary Fellowship. Generally I drew blanks. A few of the kids had heard vaguely of the organization. Only one student's face really lit up with recognition. "Oh yeah, you mean the God Squad," he said. "Yeah, they're pretty strange. Impossible to have a rational discussion with them. Fanatics. Not that I have anything against fanatics."

"Well, brother, I have," I thought. I took a lot of notes and made diagrams of the street patterns around the dorms, trying to get the feel of the area and get familiar with my surroundings.

Back in my room I went over the file Mr. Lockwood had provided me with, studying pictures of Wes, reading his letters, jotting down more notes, thinking. I would stand at the window and gaze down at the Faculty Club for ten and fifteen minutes at a stretch. The traffic on Elm Street never seemed to let up. "Rough," I kept muttering. "Really rough. This is gonna be a bitch all right."

That evening I sat in the park across from the Faculty Club for an hour, studying not only the flow of the vehicular traffic but the pedestrian traffic too. Bad. And the club itself seemed to be mobbed. I hoped Saturday night in New Haven was not typical of the way things went during the week.

Later, in my room again, I sketched the street, the location of the Faculty Club and the laundry, traced the probable route Wes must take each day from the dorm to the club, and tried to figure out a workable plan. When I went to bed I still had not come up with anything satisfactory.

Sunday was more of the same. Back to the dorm to case it once more, to see if I'd missed any openings that might be exploited. But no. It was hopeless. Then retracing my steps to the park, where I sat for another hour and a half staring at the Faculty Club. The same thing: heavy traffic on the street and the sidewalk. On a hunch, I got up and crossed the street and entered the laundry. Not bad to hang out in. Plenty of movement, lots of people up and down the stairs. You wouldn't be noticed loitering near the door. Good view of the street for several yards in both directions. Parking meters in front of the building. Wes would have to pass here on his way to and from work. Just a few feet away. Open the door, spring out, grab him, into the car and hit the highway . . .

A possibility anyway, I thought. Beats hell out of trying to hit him in that dorm.

I knew Wes would be returning from his weekend meeting at Hannah Lowe's in New York in time for classes Monday morning so I was up early the next day and went over to his dorm. They were still having breakfast in the dining room when I got there. I walked up to the second floor and knocked on Wes's door. He opened it and I asked him if he knew where Jim Smith lived. As he answered I looked him over quickly, estimating what kind of fight he'd put up, and glanced behind him into the room trying to see how it was laid out. He was very thin, but tall—taller than his father, who would have to handle him initially. But not very alert. He was polite, but distant, aloof, cold. No, he said, he'd never heard of Jim Smith. Was I sure I was in the right place?

I thanked him, and went downstairs to wait for him till he left for class. I planned to shadow him all day in hopes of finding something in his pattern, in his schedule, that might suggest a way to hit him the next day.

He came out of the building about fifteen minutes later and I fell in behind him. He walked a couple of blocks to a classroom; I waited in the hall, reading the bulletin boards, chatting with students. Class was over in about an hour, and he went back into the street, and made a telephone call from a public phone booth. I stood in front of a men's clothing store and pretended to be window shopping. When he emerged from the phone booth he headed back towards his dorm, with me twenty yards or so behind, shadowing him. He never noticed me. He was in his dorm for nearly an hour. I walked up and down the street waiting. He reappeared at fifteen minutes before noon and headed for the Faculty Club, going in at exactly twelve.

I took up a station on a bench in the park and waited for him. It was a very cold January afternoon and I wasn't even wearing a hat. I was nearly numb when, at 2:03, Wes came through the door of the club and went off up the street, past the laundry, and returned to the dorm. The traffic, I noted, was as heavy as ever on Elm Street. But I had pretty much made up my mind by that time that the snatch would be in front of the Faculty Club.

I stayed close to Wes the rest of the day. He went to a class at three, returned to the dorm at four-thirty, and at five-forty-five came out to go to the club for his evening dishwashing stint. He seemed very punctual, very mechanical. I figured it was a fair bet that he could be counted on to behave the same way every day.

I was hoping that the traffic at night on the street might not be so active, but I was disappointed. It didn't change. I sat in the park, on a bench, shivering in the dark, staring at the club until eight-fifteen when Wes reappeared. At that point I'd had it for the day. I'd been on the go for twelve hours, most of the time outdoors in the cold. I hadn't eaten, I was tired, and I'd seen enough. It was far from an ideal situation, but we were going to hit him tomorrow night as he came out of the club. At eight-fifteen, on the street—come hell or high water or interfering Yalies or traffic jams or whatever.

I telephoned Mr. Lockwood that evening and told him what I planned. "The dorm is out," I said. "No way to get him there. We've got to take him in front of the Faculty Club."

"Well, he called me today," said Lockwood. "He needs money. He says his tuition is due. And he wants to move off-campus into an apartment."

A few things clicked in my head at that point. "What did you tell him?"

"I said I'd send the tuition and we'd have to think about the apartment. He said it was urgent. He said he would call me tomorrow afternoon, after he was finished washing dishes."

That did it. Suddenly all the elements of the plan came together in my mind.

"Okay, Mr. Lockwood. We're going to get him at two o'clock tomorrow afternoon. Can you be here by then?"

He said there was a night flight out of L.A. to Hartford. He and his brother-in-law would be in New Haven by nine in the morning. I warned him to be sure he rented a two-door car and told him I would see him at the hotel in the morning. I hung up and went to dinner, feeling excited. I don't like uncertainty. I like to move ahead. The detail Lockwood had supplied—that Wes was going to work on Tuesday at noon—was all I needed. He might not work every night; he might not be there tomorrow night; but now we knew that he would be at the Faculty Club for lunch on Tuesday. And the idea of snatching him in broad daylight—for all its dangers—appealed to me. I went to bed in a very optimistic frame of mind.

By the time Lockwood and his brother-in-law, a man named Alan, knocked on my door the next morning, I had packed my bags and drawn up a careful plan of attack. Without any preliminaries, I sat both men down and began to explain what we were going to do. Alan, who was a man of about fifty, had obviously never really grasped the dimensions of the project. I'm not sure what Lockwood had told him, but he clearly wasn't counting on this.

When I finished explaining the job, we went down to the lobby and I checked out. We placed my bags in the trunk of the car, and then drove to the Faculty Club. I pointed out where their stations would be in the park, showed them the laundry, indicated Wes's route. Then we drove out to the highway, returned, went over everything a second time, and drove out to the highway once more. "You understand?" I kept asking. "You got everything straight? We can't afford any mistakes. This is a one-shot deal."

At ten-thirty we pulled into a parking space about twenty yards down the street from the laundry, and sat there waiting. "As soon as a car leaves the space in front of the laundry we move in. And we stay there till two o'clock. It doesn't matter if they give us a parking ticket. We stay there."

In a short while one of the laundry customers drove away,

opening up the space I wanted, and we slid into it. As it turned out the meter was broken—it would accept coins but the time wouldn't register. As Mr. Lockwood was fiddling with it, a kindly old New Haven police officer came by and stopped to talk. Lockwood explained that the meter was broken, the officer said that was all right. Lockwood mentioned that he was in town on business from California, which led to a discussion of the weather and God knows all what else. The officer wouldn't leave. He gossiped and joked with Lockwood for about half an hour before he moved on.

It was then around eleven. We crossed over to the park and I told Alan and Mr. Lockwood to sit down and wait there. I went off to Wes's dorm. Punctually, at ten minutes before noon, Wes appeared, hands in his pockets, head down, heading for the Faculty Club. I walked along a few feet behind him. He entered the club at the stroke of noon.

Crossing over to the park, I said to the two men, "Okay, he's in there. He won't come out for two hours. We might as well have some lunch. No telling when we'll have another chance to eat for a while."

In a nearby five-and-ten we sat at the counter and had sandwiches and coffee. I went over the plan yet another time.

"You really think we can pull it off?" Alan asked.

"We're *going* to pull it off," I said as emphatically as I knew how. "Can't afford not to pull it off. We *have* to pull it off. This is our one and only chance."

We were in the park again at quarter past one. It was a bright but cold day—very cold. The other two men were all bundled up with hats and scarves, but as usual I was hatless and gloveless, and my nose was running. There wasn't much to say. We just sat there staring at the door of the Faculty Club and waiting.

At quarter of two, I said, "Okay. Here we go. Alan and I will take our positions in the laundry. You go to the car and sit inside. Make sure you put your briefcase on the back seat where Wes can see it."

Lockwood took up his position and we took ours. The minutes dragged by. "When he has him, get around the other side of the car *fast,*" I told Alan. "Thirty seconds is all we have. First Wes goes in, then you on the other side, and I'll get behind the wheel and off we go. It's gotta be quick and decisive, otherwise we're in lots of trouble." Alan nodded and didn't say anything. He was sweating and breathing fast.

Then, at two o'clock, the whole thing almost came unraveled. Lo and behold, as we're waiting for Wes to appear, who should stroll up to the car but that same friendly and talkative New Haven police officer! I couldn't believe it. Wes was due momentarily. The officer was laughing and chatting, leaning on the door, talking to Lockwood through the open window. Lockwood was rolling his eyes at us. Alan had gone a bit pale. I didn't feel too good either. "Do something," I was thinking. "Get rid of him, make up an excuse, get out of the car, *get rid of him!*"

At last the officer gave a friendly wave and strolled off. Wes appeared on the steps of the Faculty Club. Lockwood signaled to me, "What shall we do?", pointing to the officer who was only a few yards down the street. All I could do was give the thumbs up sign. "Stay cool," I said to Alan. "I don't care if the cop is sitting on top of the damn car. This is it! We're going to go!"

"But what about the cop?" Alan wailed. Wes came into view walking with his head down.

"To hell with the cop. He's on foot, we're driving. There he is, man. This is it."

Lockwood took a deep breath, opened the door, left it open and stepped in front of Wes.

"Hi, Wes, how you doing?" he said, extending his hand.

Wes jumped. "Dad! What are you doing here?"

Lockwood played his role to perfection. "Oh, I had to come to New York all of a sudden on business and I thought I'd drive up and say hello to you. How are you?"

"I'm fine," Wes said, showing absolutely no pleasure at this unexpected meeting with his father.

"I brought the money you asked for, for your tuition. I've

got the check in my briefcase." He gestured at the briefcase on the back seat of the car. "Why don't we get in and I'll give it to you, and then we can talk about that apartment you want to take. Your mother and I have decided it's okay for you to move off-campus. Come on, get in, it's freezing out here."

But Wes was wary, and he balked at getting in the car. "No," he said, "we can talk right here."

Suddenly Lockwood grabbed the boy without warning and hurled him headfirst into the front seat. It was perfect. "Come on," I yelled to Alan and we went charging out.

Wes was grappling with his father, and beginning to yell. Alan went running around to the passenger's side and opened the door. I was right behind him. Then what I was worried about happened. Alan, who was shocked to see the awful change in his nephew's appearance, momentarily froze. He just stood there with the door open and Wes came bolting out into the street next to the car, shrieking and waving his arms, yelling at the top of his voice, "Help! Help! They're kidnapping me. Call the police! Help me!"

Alan quickly recovered his wits and began wrestling with Wes, but Wes was now impossible to handle. Lockwood started the car. Traffic was piling up, coming to a halt, people gawking. A crowd was collecting on the sidewalk. A woman was screeching.

Wes had taken up a position facing the car, with his hands on the roof and his legs spread-eagled. There was no way to get him inside while he was braced like that. I had to make a quick decision. I reached down between Wes's legs, grabbed him by the crotch and squeezed—hard. He let out a howl, and doubled up, grabbing for his groin with both hands. Then I hit, shoving him headfirst into the back seat of the car and piling in on top of him.

"Let's go!" I yelled. Alan dove in, slammed the door, and Lockwood pulled away from the curb as the friendly old cop came running up. We were in traffic and moving. It had all taken less than thirty seconds.

Both Lockwood and his brother-in-law were excited and

terrified. I tried to calm them down, which wasn't easy with
Wes going crazy beneath me. "Don't run any red lights. Just
take your time and drive normally. The police will take half an
hour to arrive. So they got our license plate number. So what?
By the time the police get there and take a report from all the
witnesses we'll be out of the state. Nothing to worry about."

In a few minutes we were on the Connecticut Turnpike heading for New York.

"Pennsylvania Turnpike. I've got some friends in Pennsylvania. We'll deprogram him there. You got quarters? Use the
exact change lanes at the toll gates. Wes is going to be raising
hell." And then I said to Wes, "Look, boy—you might as well
knock off the screaming and the yelling and the fighting, 'cause
you ain't going anyplace except with us. You and me are going
to be married, you know that? I'm going to live with you night
and day for the next four months. You might as well get used
to the idea. Either you're going to prove me wrong or I'm going
to prove to you that you're wrong. One or the other."

But he wouldn't calm down. He kept beating on the windows,
waving at passing cars, screaming to people to call the police,
that he was being kidnapped, that we were going to kill him.
We all smiled and laughed and pretended it was a joke, and
the other drivers would laugh back and wave at us.

Wes went out of his mind then. He began chanting, and then
speaking in tongues. He quoted Scripture nonstop. He sang "Oh
What a Friend We Have in Jesus." I sang along with him. He
sang "Amazing Grace." So did I. Then he started to pray.

When we approached a toll gate he would go berserk. But
by hitting all the exact change lanes we didn't attract much
attention.

It was dark, around six I guess, and we were somewhere in
New Jersey when we pulled over to the side of the road to
relieve ourselves. We made Wes urinate out the door. Then I
took over the driving. Once, we had to stop for gas and Wes
began to do his number again. He was really tireless—this tremendous frantic kind of energy. Alan quickly got out of the
car and explained to the filling station attendent that Wes was

his nephew, that the other man was his father, that the boy had a mental problem and that we were taking him home for psychiatric care. That was fine with the attendant. One thing I've found in this work is that you can always count on bystanders not being eager to get involved.

After that he finally seemed to calm down a bit. I thought he was asleep as we approached the eastern end of the Pennsylvania Turnpike and I pulled up to the gate to get the ticket. There was a black man on the gate, and when we stopped, and I rolled down the window, Wes erupted. "Call the police. Please. Call the police," he screamed. "They're kidnapping me!"

I snatched the ticket from the man's fingers and got out of there fast. I told Wes, "Look, Wes—that was a brother on the gate. I'm the only black man in the car. You think he's going to call the police on a brother?"

As it turned out, the brother did exactly that. About half an hour up the road I saw two state police cars, facing each other, their headlights making a barrier across the road which every car had to pass through. I knew at once what they were looking for: color of car, license plates, description of passengers.

Sure enough, as soon as I drove by, they peeled off and fell in line behind me. I considered pulling over to the side right away but then I thought, "Well, if they want me, they'll turn on their flashers." So I kept going, being very careful to maintain the speed limit. Wes didn't notice this, and neither did his father or uncle. In fact I think they had all fallen asleep.

We went on maybe another fifteen miles, the two police cars tailing me, and came around a bend onto a scene that looked like a carnival. It was lighted up like the World's Fair: sputtering red flares; about fifteen cop cars, their flashers on, red and blue; cops with spotlights, and big flashlights weaving paths of light and shadow across the road. It was a roadblock, with only a single lane of traffic open. The cops behind me turned their flashers on and I pulled off the road. Police poured out of the parked cars and came running towards us.

"Oh my God!" Alan exclaimed, waking up. "What's this? What's happening?"

"This, friend, is the Law—which has caught up with us," I said.

Wes was alive again and jumping. "See?" he screamed. "See? See what happens when Satan takes over your body? Now you're going to get it, now you're going to suffer! I told you. I'm going to press charges against all of you. You'll all go to jail!"

We were surrounded by troopers armed with rifles, shotguns, pistols, all pointed at us.

"Get out of there—slow, with your hands in the air!" came the command.

We crawled out, very carefully, and spread-eagled ourselves against the car while the troops frisked us for weapons. Mr. Lockwood was thinking about his attorney's warnings—life imprisonment, hanging, the electric chair.

Wes was babbling away, and one of the troopers told him, "Shut up! When we want you to talk we'll ask you."

They then demanded our identification. Fortunately, Lockwood was carrying a letter from the Yale Psychiatric Department concerning Wes, and this had a most dramatic softening effect on the attitude of the troopers. My suitcases were filled with newspaper accounts and magazine stories about my work, and once I'd produced these, and we'd all explained what we were up to, the police became very sympathetic.

"Well," said the lieutenant in charge of the affair, "I guess this is a family matter." He called his headquarters from the car and relayed his reading of the situation to his superiors. Then he went over to Wes and said, "Okay, young man—you're going to get back in the car and go with your father and your uncle. They're not trying to hurt you, they're trying to help you. And you need help."

Wes began to argue. "I don't have to get back in the car. I'm twenty years old. I have my rights."

"I don't care if you're forty years old, you are going to go back in that car," the officer told him sternly.

"I won't do it. These people have kidnapped me. They've violated my civil rights. I want a lawyer. I want to press charges."

"Fine," said the officer. "You can do all those things once you get back to California."

"I won't go!"

"You will too go because we're not staying out here on the highway with you any longer."

At that point I got my arms around Wes and pushed him into the car. One of the officers asked where we were going. He said he would call ahead to the toll gate at our exit and warn them we were coming so there wouldn't be any more interference. We thanked them very warmly and left.

Wes, realizing now how completely isolated he was, put his head in his hands and wept like a baby.

It was a little after midnight when we pulled into a small town at the western end of the state. I'd deprogrammed a boy I'll call Gene from that town who'd been caught up in a California-based cult called the Tony and Susan Alamo Christian Foundation some months earlier, and I thought he would be able to help me find a place to deprogram Wes. Gene's parents lived in the town and he was working there now with his father in the family grocery store. That morning, before Mr. Lockwood and Alan had arrived at my hotel, I'd phoned him and asked him to get me a hotel room somewhere nearby. Gene said he would and told me to call him as soon as I arrived.

Well, the main street was not designed to make me feel awfully confident about the reception a black man abducting a white boy might receive if there were trouble. The only thing I could think of as we drove in was Dodge City. It looked like a set from an old Western cowboy movie. Dark, deserted, just a couple of blocks long, a small, mean-looking town.

I cruised up and down with an eye out for a phone booth. There were none. I also had my eye out for a black person I could approach, but there weren't any of those either. There were two bars open and I figured I'd have to go inside to call Gene. I didn't relish that; if Wes began making a fuss, I could see myself being lynched in the town square by a bunch of redneck steelworkers.

I sat in the car at the curb outside the bar for a few minutes looking in. There were six or seven big guys at the bar drinking beer. I could hear a juke box playing. Didn't like the set-up at all, but there was nothing to do but go ahead.

The minute I walked in, everything stopped, including—so help me—the juke box. Dead silence. All eyes right, fastened on me. In my friendliest voice I asked the bartender, who was a burly guy too, if they had a telephone I could use. He pointed to a room in the rear. The tension was really thick, and as I walked back to the phone I could feel their eyes boring into my spine. "What the hell," I thought. "You can walk into a bar in Alabama and it's not this heavy."

What I had no way of knowing at the moment was that six black convicts from the state prison had escaped that night, and there were bulletins and alerts out on radio and TV. Naturally they thought I might be one of the cons. The bartender took a pistol out of a drawer while I was gone and kept it handy.

I dialed Gene's number and he told me he'd reserved a room for us in a hotel about twenty miles away. He gave me directions and said he'd see us in the morning. He was very interested in helping deprogram Wes.

I returned to the bar and decided, hostility or no hostility, lynch mentality or no lynch mentality, I needed a drink after this long and difficult day and I was going to have one.

I sat down at the bar and, in as friendly a voice as I could manage, asked the bartender if he had any Cutty Sark. He said he did.

"Give me a double," I said. "On the rocks."

Pouring the drink, he set the glass down in front of me.

"How much?" I asked.

"A dollar-twenty," he said.

"Then that's two-forty for the double?"

"No. Sixty cents a shot."

"Sixty cents a shot! Hell, I've paid two-forty for a single where I come from. At prices like that, buy everybody a drink. Let's liven up the place."

Everybody seemed to relax a bit at that, and somebody put

some coins in the juke box. Obviously if I was an escaped con I wasn't going to be buying the bar in a place like this.

"Where you from?" the bartender asked me.

"California. I'm here visiting a friend. Maybe you know him. He's supposed to have a store in town." I mentioned Gene's father.

His eyes got big. "California," he said. Then he looked at me real hard and suddenly snapped his fingers and said, "Are you Ted Patrick?"

"That's who I am."

"Damn!" he shouted, smacking the bar with his fist. "You're Ted Patrick? Look, you put your money away. You can't spend your money in this town. After what you did for Gene, your money is counterfeit in this town. I'm Gene's uncle. His dad is my brother. Hey, you guys. This is Ted Patrick, the man who got Gene out of that damned cult!"

All of a sudden I was a celebrity. "We can't tell you how grateful everybody in this town is for what you did for Gene, Mr. Patrick. There's no way in hell you can spend a penny in this town. There's no way we can repay you."

I told him that I had another boy out in the car that I had to deprogram. "Gene's got me a reservation in a hotel."

"You ain't going to no hotel. I got a furnished apartment upstairs. The lights are on, you got hot and cold water, we'll give you everything you need. The apartment's yours as long as you want it. Bert, get behind the bar. I'm going up to put sheets on the beds. Bud, call Jimmy and tell him Ted Patrick's in town. And tell Gene to cancel the reservation at the hotel!"

The apartment was perfect. There was an outside entrance, and it was on the second floor, too high for Wes to jump out the window. I put Wes and his father in one room—they slept in the same bed. My room adjoined theirs, and I dragged the bed across the doorway in case Wes tried to get out during the night. Alan slept in the living room, on a couch which we placed across the outside door. Even though I didn't think Wes would go out the window, I asked Gene's uncle to nail the windows closed.

For a big tough guy he was very gentle and sympathetic with Wes. "We know what you're going through," he kept telling the boy. "Believe me, this man is here to help you, not hurt you." Wes didn't say anything.

I had a couple of more drinks and then we turned in; it took me a little while to go to sleep. I kept thinking about how strangely everything worked out in life, how again and again really good and honest people would turn up when you were in a jam, wanting to pitch in and help, giving you their homes, their time—people who cared, who wanted to be involved, who, once they understood the danger, wanted to help as much as I did.

We got up early the next morning, Wednesday, and I went to work on Wes even while we were eating breakfast. I was standing in the doorway with a cup of coffee in my hands, launching into the customary recital of how he had been deceived and was worshiping Satan, when he suddenly shot up from the table and made a rush at me. He hit me like O. J. Simpson. The coffee cup went into the air, the coffee hit the ceiling, the cup and saucer smashed on the floor. Wes grabbed for the door, trying to jerk it open. But I got my arms around him and put him out of commission in a matter of seconds. Then he began screaming, "You've got to kill me, I won't stay here, you can't make me stay here, you're going to have to kill me, to beat me and beat me and beat me, because I won't stay here and listen to you!"

I shoved him to his bedroom and shut the door. He rushed behind the curtains to hide. I tried to talk to him, but he plugged his ears with his fingers. I continued to try to reason with him; he began to sing and chant and speak in tongues. Then he rushed into the center of the room and began to do what in cult circles is called the Sanctified Dance. I laughed at him and danced along with him, making gargling nonsense syllables in my throat, mocking his speaking in tongues. "Talk English," I told him. "A baby can make noise like that. Talk to me in English." He was really wild. I'd never encountered anyone as wild and energetic and determined as he was.

Finally I told him, "Wes, I want you to get something through your head. I can do the 100-yard dash in 10.4. Now unless you can do it in 10.3 there's no point in your running away because I'm going to catch you and bring you back. This whole town is on my side. Nobody's going to help you. So you might as well just calm down." His response was to jump in bed and pull the pillow over his head.

Deprogramming that young man was a battle. It was like Sugar Ray Robinson fighting Joe Maxim for the light-heavyweight title. Robinson kept hitting him and hitting him, but Maxim wouldn't go. You wondered what was keeping the man on his feet. But unlike Sugar Ray I had no intention of wilting from the heat and losing by default.

All the same he gave me a hell of a workout. Generally speaking I think I would prefer to confine myself to arranging the snatches and let someone else do the deprogramming. It gets repetitious after a while, and it's a stationary, locked-up, mental sort of thing. I'm a man of action. I don't like sitting in an airless room day after day talking. I'd rather be out in the open, on the move. But I had to admit that Wes was so strong he was stimulating. I love a good fight and he was putting up a beauty.

Around noon Gene arrived with another uncle, a barrel-chested foundryworker named Mike, and they went at Wes for a while, giving me a break. A little later food began to flow in. It seemed like everybody in town wanted to help and their way was to send food. Cakes, pies, kettles of beef stew, pots of spaghetti-and-meatballs, loaves of homemade bread, baskets of fried chicken. We were practically buried in food. It was enough to feed a cult commune of thirty kids for a week.

We kept after Wes, with breaks for lunch and dinner, until around two in the morning. He was unbudgeable.

"I don't think he's ever going to crack," Gene sighed late that night. "I never saw anyone so strong."

Mr. Lockwood was of the same opinion. "I think we'll have to put him in a mental institution. This just isn't working."

"Don't worry," I said. "We'll get him."

We slept about four hours and were up early Thursday

morning, hammering at him again. We took turns. I'd go for a couple of hours, then Uncle Mike would relieve me. He was so concerned that he stayed home from work that day to help. Gene would relieve Mike, and then I'd come back. We kept the pressure on him, but he was as firm as boiler plate.

In the afternoon Gene informed me that a Catholic priest who taught at a nearby college was interested in having a go at Wes. The priest was writing a thesis on cults and mind control but had never witnessed a deprogramming. I didn't have any confidence that he'd accomplish anything, but I said, sure, why not, let him come.

Wes almost ate that poor man alive. In the first place he knew the Bible better than the priest. Unlike most cult members, he knew it inside out. In the second place he was stronger than the priest. The priest was a very nice young man but a bit innocent, and Wes wouldn't let him get a word in edgewise. Of course the priest had never met a person it was absolutely impossible to reason with. He never imagined that such things happened to kids like Wes. Wes just kept tearing into him, screaming and shouting insults at the priest, calling the Roman Catholic Church the Whore of Babylon and things like that, until the priest was literally reduced to tears and had to leave.

I had to admit that ordinary techniques were not going to work with Wes. He was so rough I thought I'd have to play a little rough too.

That night he and his father got into a violent fight. Wes had been screaming that his mother was evil, was of Satan, all sorts of filthy and outrageous things, and the father lost his patience finally and smacked him. At that Wes leaped on his father and the two were at each other's throats—I mean they were trying to strangle each other. They were overturning furniture and lamps were crashing to the floor. I jumped between them and pried them apart, and dragged Wes into the bedroom. My own patience was a little thin about then, and I threw him down onto the bed and said, "Now you sit there, sit your ass down, and if you so much as move a muscle again I'm going to knock the shit out of you. You understand?"

This is not my normal vocabulary when I'm deprogramming, but I felt I had to shock him, jolt him, and it worked. For the first time since we snatched him, he came to a dead stop. His eyes bugged out and his mouth hung open and he just gaped at me. I think he believed I would do all that (I wouldn't have), and he was scared, which was what I wanted. I had to make him listen to me, and there wasn't going to be any listening on his part as long as he was doing Sanctified Dances and talking in tongues and trying to strangle his father.

Having gained his attention, I was able to begin talking to him, analyzing his beliefs, showing him the contradictions he was hanging on to, pointing out step by step what had happened to him and forcing him to think about who Hannah Lowe really was and what she really represented. I knew once he began to listen to me that it was only a matter of time before he broke. I don't think his beliefs were all that structured or complicated, otherwise he wouldn't have had to throw up that smokescreen of frenzy and craziness and physical energy. I suspect that deep down he knew that if he had to try to rationalize his beliefs they'd come apart like wet tissue paper.

Anyway, around midnight he snapped. We were talking about Hannah Lowe and I was going at her pretty hard, and he'd been trying to defend her, when all of a sudden he began to cry. I called for his father to come into the room, and Wes threw himself at his father again, only this time not to strangle him but to embrace him. He kissed his father and they hugged each other, and he apologized over and over for what he'd done, what he'd said, how awful he'd behaved. Uncle Mike came in too—this big mean-looking foundryworker who'd scare the pants off you if you met him in a dark alley—and he began crying too. We were all crying, as a matter of fact, and shaking hands, and laughing at the same time, and Wes was saying he wanted to call his mother right away to talk to her, and how important it was that we call the parents of his ex-roommate, Dan Voll, and get Dan out of the cult too. It was a fine, satisfying, moment. There was a great sense of celebration, kind of like a welcome-home party for someone who'd been away a long time.

*The Children of God, the first cult Ted Patrick attacked, was origi-
nally a California group and has now spread throughout the country.
Recruits are starved, exhausted, and harangued into a brain-washed
state, then taught to hate their parents and obey the cult leaders
blindly. Above, at the UN in 1973, they proclaim that the comet
Kohoutek foretells the destruction of America.*

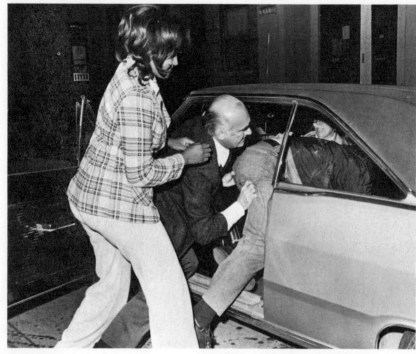

The next four photos show the actual deprogramming of a Children of God victim named Marc Manecke. Above, at midnight outside the Children of God headquarters in Boston, Walter Manecke suddenly grabs his son Marc and shoves him into a car. At left is Patrick's aide. Visible in the front seat is Marc's mother; Patrick is in the back, yanking Marc inside the car.

The next day Marc is rushed to the Maneckes' home in Connecticut. The Children of God had tried to get the Boston police to stop the car at a toll booth the night before, but the police were sympathetic to Patrick and refused. During the start of the deprogramming, Marc escaped out a window, but the local police were sympathetic too and returned him.

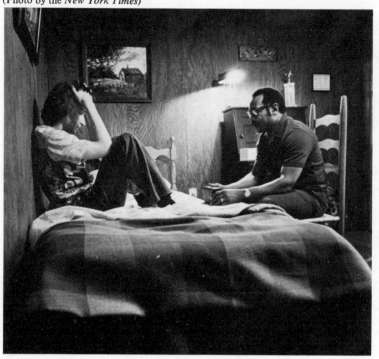

Marc and Ted Patrick square off as the deprogramming gets underway. Marc fights hard, and at one point he cries: "If you don't let me go back, I'm going to kill myself." But Patrick persists, refuting Marc's arguments, helping him see that he has been exploited by the Children of God and duped into behavior he could not be blamed for.

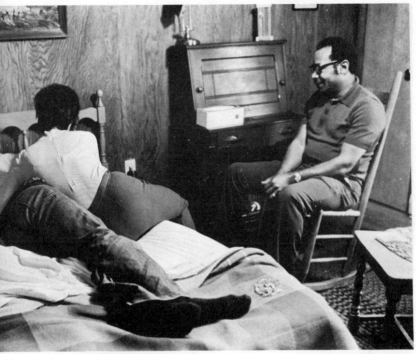

After three and a half days, Marc breaks down and is deprogrammed. Patrick leans back and smiles as Marc's mother embraces the boy. "Welcome home, baby," she says. And Marc replies: "I'm sorry for all the trouble I caused you, Mom. Please forgive me." But it was almost a year before the last traces of the brainwashing disappeared.

(Photo by the *New York Times*)

Sun Myung Moon is a Korean industrialist who has created a cult called the Unification Church, whose membership is large and growing rapidly. Young disciples are sent out into the streets to beg for Moon. They are trained to consider him the Messiah and they give him all their property. Some forge checks and abuse their credit cards for him. With the millions he has wrung from these children, Moon has bought mansions for himself, and political influence.

Taffy Bunt (center) was recruited into Moon's cult in California, when her college roommate joined. Her parents became alarmed when they learned she had been forced to beg the streets eighteen hours a day and when fatigue began to hurt her health. Ted Patrick deprogrammed her in twenty-four hours. "When I realized that Moon wasn't true," says Taffy, here with her parents, Dr. and Mrs. Frederick Bunt of upstate New York, "it was hard to think that somebody could be so evil, doing this to kids."

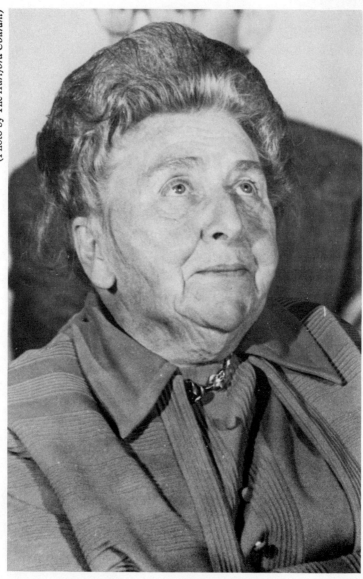

Hannah Lowe is the founder of the New Testament Missionary Fellowship, a cult that preys on Ivy League students. Members believe she is a prophetess. "We were told to break ties with families and friends," says one former member, "because they were demon-possessed, and we were encouraged to lie and even steal if it was for our salvation."

Dan Voll, a member of the Hannah Lowe cult, performs what is called a "sanctified dance" during a prayer meeting at Columbia University. Other members accompany him. Voll was a close friend and Yale roommate of Wes Lockwood, a cult member Patrick had successfully deprogrammed.

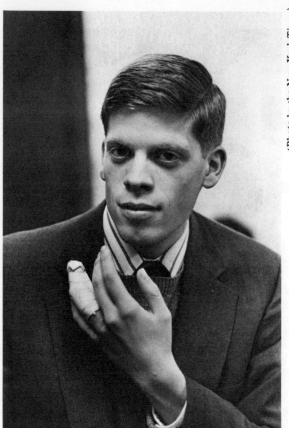

Dan Voll shows photographers the finger he injured during the tussle when, in early 1973, Ted Patrick helped Dan's parents capture him. Before the deprogramming could take place, police intervened and Dan took Patrick to court for kidnapping. The not-guilty verdict reaffirmed Patrick's argument that parents are justified in using physical force to prevent psychological injury to their children.

A few months earlier, however, Patrick had been jailed after an attempt to rescue someone from the Lowe cult. At right, Patrick and his attorney, Pat Wall, leave the New York Criminal Courts Building.

Hare Krishna members and some bystanders. "This is an international movement," says Patrick. "It is rich, powerful, and growing fast. It is militant and inflexible and very harsh. Some adherents believe they have a divine sanction to kill when necessary. I believe that in Hare Krishna you have essentially another Charles Manson movement—only many thousands of members strong."

Randy Sacks of Cleveland was playing Frisbee at school on his fifteenth birthday when he was recruited by Hare Krishna. "My first reaction," he says, "was, 'These people are really weird.' Then they really socked it to me, the heavy hypnosis, and I was in."

Once he joined, Randy kept his big smile—at least for this passport photo—but frequently told his mother he hated her. He eventually dropped out of school and went off to live in the Krishna temple. Mrs. Sacks was grief-stricken, since Randy had been a cheerful, loving son.

119

(Photo by Barney Peterson, San Francisco Chronicle. © Chronicle Publishing Co., 1975)

Mrs. Sondra Sacks, Randy's mother, heard of Ted Patrick and persuaded him to come deprogram her son. When Randy saw Patrick he yelled: "Get this man out of here or you'll never see me again." After he was deprogrammed, his first words were, "Mom, I love you." Says Mrs. Sacks: "I hadn't heard that for two and a half years. I'll never forget that moment."

Today both mother and son devote great amounts of time to helping Patrick save other cult victims. Here is Randy with Carmencita Esteve of Dallas, a girl Patrick saved from the Children of God.

Kathy Crampton, a member of the Love Israel cult in Seattle, Washington, is one of Patrick's few failures. The cult is one of the worst, according to Patrick—"a wild, nasty, filthy bunch." He deprogrammed her, but while she was still "floating"—the period during which backsliding is possible—she escaped. Patrick was again charged with kidnapping and exonerated.

Brother Julius, who says he is Jesus, is a fifty-one-year-old former engineer from Brooklyn whose real name is Julius Schacknow. His headquarters are in New England. He is a master at brainwashing and high school students seem especially attracted to him. Ted Patrick regards him as a particular adversary.

CHAPTER FOUR

Because all of the cults are so secretive, it's extremely difficult for anyone to obtain an objective, balanced picture of what goes on inside. Descriptions given by cult leaders differ so greatly from the accounts of men and women who have left the various cults that they would seem to cancel each other out. Hannah Lowe, who was an Evangelical missionary in South America for forty years before she organized the New Testament Missionary Fellowship in 1964, declares, "We are a small group of Christians who come together for prayer and Bible study. There are no rules or regulations or church. We believe in Jesus Christ, we believe most surely." McCandlish Phillips, formerly a writer for the New York *Times,* is convinced that Hannah is a prophetess. "When a prophet, or a prophetess," he wrote in his book, *The Bible, the Supernatural, and the Jews,* "speaks by the momentary inspiration of the Holy Spirit, the words may come like lightning or like dew, but they are always fresh and arresting and right to the point of immediate need."

Calvin Burrows, who gave up his medical studies at Yale to become a minister in Hannah Lowe's cult, says, "The American family is being broken up by all kinds of things. We are trying to put families back together." A lawyer for the Fellowship, John Lamoult, has been quoted as feeling that his clients are "really fine people."

On the other side, we have the testimony of Calvin Burrows's father, a research professor in nuclear medicine at Boston University: "The Fellowship absolutely insists on a sort of religious blackmail—that children separate from the family unless the family signs up."

The way the Fellowship tries to induce a family to "sign up" would seem at variance with Hannah Lowe's description of their simple purpose and high-minded function. The Hartford *Courant* of April 29, 1973 gives the following account of the Fellowship's attempt to enlist Dr. and Mrs. Burrows:

Dr. Burrows said Cal, Mrs. Lowe, Warren [another son who eventually left the cult and now denounces it energetically] and other Fellowship members have tried twice to bring him and his wife into the sect as "born again" Christians.

During one six-hour session, Mrs. Lowe said she was "rebuking demons in me," said Dr. Burrows. "I was amazed my sons didn't see her as an idiot and when I called her a crazy old lady, Cal said that was blasphemy."

When the conversion attempts failed, Mrs. Burrows was told her husband was "carnal" and when she tried to ask her son for more information on the Fellowship, "Hannah told Cal that I had devils in me," said Mrs. Burrows.

Bob Bakker, a geologist, is another member who eventually quit the sect. In the same *Courant* series, he gives the opinion that Fellowship members "can't evaluate themselves or the group. You automatically reject any argument that is critical of the fellowship's beliefs because you feel guilty and afraid the Devil will take over your brain."

Warren Burrows says, "Hannah is the conscience. There is no sense of self in the group. She was always reminding us that we were inadequate, that we were like children."

Mrs. Marie Voll, the mother of Dan Voll (Wes Lockwood's roommate at Yale), began trying to convince him to leave the cult when he dropped out of school, convinced by a Fellowship leader that the university was "of the Devil." During one of their confrontations, Mrs. Voll lost her temper and made a disparaging remark to Dan about Hannah Lowe, who is a very fat woman. "I compared her to a rather plump teacher Dan once had and disliked a lot, but he said, 'No, Mom, she's not like that at all. Mrs. Lowe is thin.' Now, Hannah Lowe," said Marie Voll, "is many things, but one of them is *not* thin."

In spite of the iron curtain of secrecy Hannah Lowe tried to maintain, glimpses were obtained into what went on inside her New York headquarters. The *Courant* gives this account of a prayer service provided by a former member named Charlotte Shenikin:

They play tambourines, guitars and other instruments, sing hymns and dance. You sing and sing, the instruments get louder and some dance in the center of the singers and players.

Then the rhythm builds up and gets frenzied and you begin talking in tongues and some get revelations. Hannah sits in a chair screaming in tongues and getting visions.

Pretty soon all thirty people are doing something. You can't help yourself—it builds up to a pitch.

A non-member witness was a girl named Kathy Blanchard, who had been a high school friend of Dan Voll. While visiting him in New York, she was introduced to Hannah Lowe:

They wait on her hand and foot, her wish is their command, and all eyes are focused on her every movement . . .

It was not what I expected. The apartment was filled with expensive furniture, Persian rugs, paintings, and afghan dogs—the whole bit . . .

She kept telling us about the wonderful miracles Daniel had been performing. She wouldn't let him talk. We would ask the questions and Mrs. Lowe would answer. I couldn't stand it any longer and I finally caught Dan's eye and blurted out, "How are you?"

He started to answer but Mrs. Lowe interrupted.

It was scary. We left with an uneasy feeling. Dan had a smile on his face the whole time we were there—always the same smile.

Margaret Rogow, a Hamden, Connecticut girl, quit Columbia in her freshman year to join the Fellowship. The San Diego *Union* of December 12, 1974 gives the story:

The two daughters [Margaret Rogow and her sister, Elizabeth] joined the fellowship in late 1972. Elizabeth was working for a New York attorney and Margaret was a freshman at Columbia.

"We were looking for a wholesome Christian group," Margaret said, when a fellow college student took them to a meeting.

Two months later, Margaret left school and Elizabeth quit her job. They refused to meet with their parents and joined the forty-member group, founded twelve years ago by a penniless widow, Hannah Lowe.

They followed a rigorous schedule of work, Bible study, prayer and personal deprivation that outlawed dating, and absolute obedience to the Elders, Margaret said.

"We were told to break ties with families and friends because they were demon-possessed and we were encouraged to lie and even steal if it was for our salvation."

After the kidnap attempt of another sect member, Daniel Voll, and the acquittal of Voll's father, the sect sent the women to a twenty-five-acre farm in South America, fearing another kidnap attempt.

"We worked daily from 5 A.M. to 5 P.M. doing farm work, housecleaning and cooking," Margaret said. "We received no wages for our labor, but had to pay Mrs. Lowe $30 a week for room and board. We quickly used up our savings and were placed in a very difficult situation of bondage."

But Margaret began to suffer from headaches and depression and became doubtful when she broke her arm. Contrary to what the sect leader said, the Lord did not ease the pain.

On the morning of December 17, 1973, she told the group she would skip lunch to fast and meditate. She walked two miles to a bus and took a plane home, using a return ticket she had been originally provided.

Who and what is one to believe in all of this? Patrick cannot conceive of anyone in his or her right mind asking the question.

TED PATRICK: Look, Hannah Lowe makes money off these people. Wes Lockwood gave all the money he made at the Yale Faculty Club to her. Dan Voll, when he lived in New York, held down two jobs, and kept only what he needed to pay for his room and board; he turned the rest over to the cult. Hannah Lowe and her friends have a very good reason for lying. The kids who have been deprogrammed don't have any reason to lie, they don't stand to gain anything by blowing the whistle on Hannah Lowe except maybe to make sure that other people won't join the cult the way they did.

The problem is that any one cult can make what seems to some people a pretty convincing argument to defend what they're doing. You can always get some psychiatrist, or college president, or other prominent member of the community to stick up for a particular cult. The cult invites him over to observe, they do a snow job on him, and he goes away feeling pretty good about them.

It's only when you begin to see one after another of the cults —and there are hundreds of them around the country—all doing and saying the same things, when you begin to see the pattern of the movement, the psychological fear they all employ, the turning of the kids against their families, the rip-offs, the glorification of the cult leader, and so forth, that you can see someone like Hannah Lowe for what she really is.

How the cults differ from each other is interesting. But what they have in common is the point of my argument. For example, the Church of Armageddon.

In the spring of 1973, I successfully deprogrammed a girl named Vickie Sinunu, who had been a member of the Church of Armageddon in Seattle, Washington. All the cults are rotten, but in many ways I think this outfit came close to scraping rock bottom. Worse, they were like something you find when you turn the rock over.

Evidence we gathered from a variety of sources (and evidence that eventually stood up absolutely in court) indicated that in the cult, babies were beaten with sticks from the age of six months when they "disobeyed." Then they were locked in dark closets until they stopped crying. From about the age of two, children were forced to sit cross-legged on the floor for periods up to an hour "meditating." They were punished when they failed to behave.

Two members, both young men, died while sniffing Teluene, an industrial solvent. They were found with plastic bags over their heads by the founder of the sect, a man named Paul Erdman who called himself Love Israel. They had turned blue, but were still alive when he found them. But Erdman delayed summoning help for three hours while he prayed over them and tried to heal them. When the emergency squad finally was called, the boys were pronounced dead on arrival. Erdman told his followers that the boys had died because they had been disobedient.

Then Erdman convinced the authorities that autopsies should not be performed immediately because—to quote an article in the Seattle *Post-Intelligencer*—"The Church of Armaggedon has a belief that the men are not really dead and will revive in three days." This really says something about the power of the cults to intimidate law enforcement agencies.

Another boy fell to his death from a tree. Apparently he had leapt from it in the belief that he could fly. The group again managed to postpone an autopsy for three days as they tried to bring him back from the dead.

One of their pastimes was to connect themselves to an electrical device to see how much electricity they could stand passing through their bodies. They also gathered mushrooms from a nearby cemetery and ate them without making any attempt to determine whether they were poisonous or not. "We believed that all substances are given to us by God. We thought we could take anything into our bodies and it wouldn't hurt us, as long as we took it as a gift from God," said Vickie Sinunu after she was deprogrammed.

If a member's eyes were defective, he was forbidden to seek the care of an ophthalmologist. "The vision we had was the vision God wanted us to have," said Vickie, "and it would be impudent to try to correct it." The same went for dental care. "We really believed that if we prayed hard enough God would fill our cavities." If their teeth fell out it was proof that they were sinful. A number of cult members came down with jaundice and hepatitis, but none ever received any medical assistance because Paul Erdman saw all illnesses as a sign of a lack of faith.

When a cult member became pregnant, she was not allowed to consult a doctor at any time during the pregnancy. Babies were always delivered without medical assistance in one of the cult's houses. Birth certificates, death certificates—they were very loose about these things, as all cults are. You could have a baby and whether it lived or died, no one would know.

The cult also shared with the others the usual characteristics: censorship of mail; persuading members to sign over powers of attorney to the cult, along with bank accounts and other assets; programmed hatred of parents; and intense Bible study—except that the Bibles used by the Church of Armaggedon were altered so that every reference to the Deity was replaced by the name Love Israel. Erdman was anointed "King" and all the donations and contributions that flowed into the cult went directly to him. He lived in comparative luxury, keeping what he wanted and distributing the rest to his disciples as he saw fit. He was considered "Christ's administrator" or Christ's go-between between the members and Heaven. Obedience to leaders was paramount. The group was taught "not to think. Don't use your little mind inside. Use your big mind, the collective family's mind. We're your mind."

These leaders weren't just playing authority games. The consequences of disobedience were real, all right. One of the members disobeyed the injunction against having sexual relations with women outside the cult. He was beaten on his bare buttocks forty times with a sawed-off pool cue, in the presence of the other members. The leaders told them that the time could be foreseen "when someone might have to be killed for disobedience."

It was a wild, nasty, filthy bunch, and when we took Vickie out we had to leave her two-year-old baby inside. I told Vickie's mother, "Don't worry. Once we get Vickie deprogrammed, we'll get a court order making them release the baby."

The child's father was a medical student who did not belong to the cult. When Vickie disappeared, the Church of Armaggedon tried to obtain a birth certificate that said one of their members was the real father. I got a court order in Seattle a few days later when Vickie signed a statement renouncing the cult and demanding her child back. We took the order to the police department and set out for Erdman's headquarters on McGraw Street in the Queen Anne Hill section of Seattle—a storefront five or six blocks from the house Vickie had been living in. While we were at the headquarters, about nine or ten carloads of police surrounded the house to make sure the cult didn't try to smuggle the baby out a back door.

Erdman met us at the headquarters. He is a medium-sized youngish man—about thirty-four then—with long hair and a beard. The police had suggested it would be simpler if we could get him to turn over the baby without serving the papers, so that we wouldn't have to go to court the next morning. But Erdman was arrogant and uncooperative. He said he didn't know anything about the baby, didn't know where it was. The detective with us called his men at the house and told them to move. But Erdman had ordered that the police should not be permitted to enter the house, that they were to be stopped at all costs.

When we got to the house, all the members were lined up on the lawn daring the police to try to enter. It was a crazy scene. I warned the lieutenant in charge that they were programmed fanatics, and there might be bloodshed before the police got inside. He suggested it might be best to go back and get a warrant for Erdman's arrest, which he did.

They never arrested him, though. Instead they arrested the people who were actively opposing their entry into the building. (One of them was the son of comedian and television actor Steve Allen. He went by the name of Logic Israel.) In court they testified that Vickie had been kidnapped and that they were refusing to give up the baby because they feared for its safety. They couldn't really believe that Vickie was deprogrammed, and wanted her produced in court.

That was a mistake for them. The judge did what they wanted. He ordered Mrs. Sinunu to bring Vickie to court the following day. And he told the cult members to bring the baby. Mrs. Sinunu was very worried that if Vickie had to confront the cult face-to-face she might fall under their spell again. But I was certain that she had come out of the deprogramming strong enough to resist them.

The next day Vickie wavered a bit as the cult's lawyer questioned her but she generally stood fast in saying she did not want to return to the Church of Armaggedon and wanted her baby back. The baby's father also testified, and then the judge ruled that he was convinced that Vickie was telling the truth. "Where's the baby?" he asked. "We didn't bring it," they said. "All right," said the judge, "you are all going to jail and you're going to stay there until this woman's child is produced."

The group went to jail and stayed for twenty-four hours before Erdman gave in and turned over the child. One of those imprisoned was Logic Israel. Some time later Steve Allen, who is obviously an intelligent man, issued a statement to the press in which he said, "It's fine with me that my son and grandchildren are living in a religious commune. I decided that if it was reasonable and productive for him, it was fine by me. The one important question about social experiments is the fate of the children . . . the happiness of the children is ultimately one of the society's measuring mechanisms . . . These people are living something twenty-four hours a day, which is a distinction from other religions, which usually practice forty-five minutes on Sundays."

Statements like that make me want to climb walls. It is so difficult to alert the general public to what is going on. What did Steve Allen see up there? What did he want to see? To call what goes on in Love Israel's tribe "a social experiment" is like feeding a baby to a shark, and then calling it a social experiment to see how the baby will react.

Anyway, Vickie got her child back, and she and her boyfriend got married, and they are both free of the nightmare of cultism now and doing fine.

If it hadn't been for the Sinunu case, I probably wouldn't have gotten involved in one of my best-known cases—probably the first and only time in history that a kidnapping was televised nationwide in front of millions of people.

Mr. and Mrs. Curt Crampton of Redondo Beach, California had lost their daughter Kathy to the Love Israel family in January of 1973, about the time I was snatching Wes Lockwood from Yale. By all accounts, Kathy was the last person in the world you would suspect could be sucked into a cult. She was bright and artistic, a very strong-minded Roman Catholic.

Like most parents, the Cramptons didn't know anything about cults, and thought Kathy was living in a commune in Seattle. They also didn't know anything about communes— only that a lot of kids were living that way, and while they were a bit uneasy about it, they trusted her good sense and accepted it. Then one day they got a letter from someone who called himself "Kathy's older brother." (Kathy has two sisters, no brothers.) The letter was signed by a person calling himself "Strength L. Israel." It said, "Kathy is finding her place here in the family and feels better all the time. It seems certain that soon she will be baptized into the family. Through baptism she chooses to die to the past, take the name of Israel, and become a servant to mankind, 'a new creature in Christ.'"

The Cramptons were stunned. Getting better? Had she been ill? Dying to the past? Was there something so wrong with her past she had to "die to it?" Baptized into the family? Something seemed very wrong, and Mrs. Crampton went directly to Seattle to talk to her daughter.

"I knocked on the door of this house on McGraw Street where Kathy was living. A tall thin girl with long dark stringy hair, a vacant look in her eyes, and scabs all over her face came to the door. It took me several seconds to realize it was my daughter. She looked absolutely terrible. She'd lost about thirty-five pounds. 'My God, Kathy—what's happened to you? What's wrong with your face?' [A doctor later diagnosed it as a kind of staph infection.] 'Oh, it's getting better now that I don't doubt,' Kathy said. 'This happened to me because I doubted.'"

Mrs. Crampton was introduced to the other members who all had names like Strength, Serious, Willing, Sun, Light and so on (Kathy's new name was Corinth), and was given a tour of the other houses belonging to the group. It shows how re- moved these people are from reality that they would willingly take her around and expose her to the kind of life they led without suspecting that she would find it terrible. Everyone she met regurgitated the same empty expressions of contentment and peace. "I was told everything from the outside world is of the Devil. Everything written by Man is wrong. Only the Bible is true. All the people there said they loved me. They called me by my first name and said 'isn't this a holy way to live.' It was like a broken record. I was staggered. I certainly saw no indication that any of them were doing anything that would qualify them as 'servants of mankind,' which is what Strength Israel said in that letter."

When she returned home with her upsetting account of what she'd seen and heard, her husband and she set about at once to find some way of getting Kathy out. For a time they considered committing her to a mental institution, but a lawyer told them that it's a very tricky business where religion is involved to prove the difference between religious behavior and insanity.

Mrs. Crampton continued to visit her daughter, and Kathy told her about Vickie Sinunu's abduction and recanting. The Cramptons then contacted the Sinunus who gave them my phone number.

I went to Redondo Beach to talk with the Cramptons, who had made up their minds that my route was the only one available to them. They wanted to go ahead. At the time I had a lot of other deprogrammings on my schedule, but I agreed that as soon as I could I'd contact them and we'd proceed.

Shortly after deprogramming Wes Lockwood, I'd also tried to snatch his friend Dan Voll from the Hannah Lowe cult. For reasons I'll go into elsewhere, the attempt blew up in my face and I was charged with unlawful restraint and assault. It made big news in New York, where the attempt was made, and at my arraignment I met for the first time a news reporter from CBS by the name of Steve Young. Young was interested in doing a television documentary in which he would follow a case from the moment of the snatch through the deprogramming. I was doubtful about the idea and put him off, but every time I came back to

New York to go to court (the case kept being continued through the spring) he would call and pester me about the idea. He was very persistent.

Then one night he and his producer, a man named Bob Syms, came up to my room in the New York Hilton and we had some drinks and they pressed me once more about the project. They did a snow job on me, I must say. They had me convinced of their sympathy with my work, and told me how much they wanted to get my side of the story on the air.

"Well," I told them, "it's hard for me to arrange anything like that. I'm on the go all the time, from one part of the country to another. I can't wait around for you to assemble a camera crew, and I don't know two days in advance where I'll be."

"Okay," Syms said, "but if anything ever comes up where you have some advance notice, here's our phone numbers, home and office. Call any time of the night or day and we'll come running."

We all parted on the friendliest possible terms. In June, following my acquittal in the Dan Voll case, I let the Cramptons know I was ready to snatch their daughter Kathy and we made the necessary arrangements.

Quite by coincidence, the Sunday I was preparing to leave for Seattle, my phone rang, and it was Steve Young wanting to know what was happening. "We're still awfully interested in doing that documentary," he said. "We think it's important for the whole country to be made to realize the dimensions of this thing and the role you're playing in it."

I said, "Well, as a matter of fact I'm going to pull off a snatch on Tuesday up in Seattle. I'm packing my bags to go right now."

"Great!" Young said. "I'll get a crew together and be there."

"Wait a minute! I'm not sure the parents will agree to let you go along. It's their decision, after all. And I can't get in touch with Mrs. Crampton. She's staying with Julie, another daughter, in Eugene, Oregon. I don't want you flying all the way out here and then have the Cramptons say no."

"Don't worry about it," he said. "I'll do it on speculation.

For me, it's worth the gamble. What time you getting into Seattle?"

I told him when I was arriving and where I was staying. He said he'd be in touch and hung up.

I was still of two minds about this documentary, which was supposed to appear on the Walter Cronkite show. I knew that it would be valuable from the point of view of publicizing how dangerous the cults were, and how widespread. The chance to get my side of the story on network television was tempting. But I was also worried about the possible effects a TV crew would have on Kathy as I deprogrammed her. My first responsibility had to be to the girl and her parents.

Then I thought—why get all worked up about the thing? There's no way Young is going to get a crew together and to Seattle on such short notice. He'd have to be half crazy to try.

However, incredibly, when I got off the plane late that afternoon, who was standing there to greet me but Steve Young!

"What'd they do, launch you from Cape Kennedy?" I asked him.

"Have to move fast in my business," he grinned.

"Mine too," I said.

He drove me to my hotel, informing me that he'd gotten together a top-notch film crew from San Francisco, and that they were all ready to roll.

First, though, I had to get the Cramptons' permission. Mr. Crampton wasn't able to come up, and Mrs. Crampton was accompanied by the boyfriend of one of her other daughters. His name was Greg Temple. They'd also brought along a sort of hippie-looking kid named Mark—a very humorous boy who liked to play blues on his harmonica.

I explained in private to Mrs. Crampton what Young wanted, and emphasized that it was her decision to make. She thought about it for a while and then said, "If showing this on television can prevent one child from ending up like Kathy, then I'm all for it."

Once Young knew he had a green light, he telephoned the police department, informed them he was from CBS without giving his name, asked them questions about me and the Love Israel family. The police really didn't understand what he was driving at, though the Vickie Sinunu case was still fresh in their minds and they generally approved of what I'd done with Vickie and disapproved of Love Israel. Young was satisfied with that—for some reason he felt he'd covered himself and the network from any possible legal tangles.

The plan that evolved over the next twenty-four hours was this: On Monday Mrs. Crampton was going to spend the night with Kathy at the house, as she had occasionally done in the past. (In order to have access to her daughter, Mrs. Crampton had pretended to approve of her daughter's involvement.) In the morning she would suggest to Kathy that they go into town to do some shopping. They were supposed to walk down from the house to a bus stop where we would be waiting and grab her. We set the time for nine in the morning.

On the corner near the bus stop, there was a house set back from the street on a kind of hill. The lawn rose about six feet above the sidewalk and there was a stone wall running along beneath the lawn. At eight the next morning, we stationed Mark up on the lawn, pretending he was waiting for the bus. He was wearing a baseball cap, and when he saw Kathy and her mother coming down the street, he was supposed to turn his cap around as a signal to me and Greg who were parked around the corner in separate cars. We would then signal the television crew, parked in two big Lincolns on a side street and they would go into action. As soon as I had Kathy in the car, we would all head for the freeway and San Diego, with the CBS people following. Mark would pick up the other car and return it.

That was the plan and it was a good one. Trouble was, it didn't work. What we didn't know was that on the way down from the house a bus from another line came and Kathy flagged it down. Not wanting to arouse her daughter's suspicions by objecting to any particular bus, Mrs. Crampton was forced to board it and the two of them went downtown shopping.

In the meantime we were waiting. Mark was sitting up on

the lawn playing his harmonica. The film crew was in place. Nine o'clock came and they didn't show. The bus arrived and departed. Nine-thirty. Nothing. Ten o'clock. Zero. Young came over to my car and asked what was going on. I said I didn't know, something had happened. At eleven, I went cruising around the neighborhood looking for them. I went up past the house and then drove over to their McGraw Street headquarters. No sign of them. Back to the bus stop where we waited until three.

"Just like I said," I remarked to Young. "You have to move fast in this business."

Around three-thirty Mrs. Crampton appeared. Mark had been playing his harmonica on the lawn since eight-thirty. I think by then he'd moved from blues to Beethoven's nine symphonies.

Mrs. Crampton was crying. She thought we'd failed, and that it was all over. After I'd calmed her down and got her to explain what happened, I took her to the hotel and gave her some Scotch to steady her nerves.

"Don't worry," I kept telling her. "It's okay. Kathy doesn't suspect anything. We'll get her some other way. Now tell me everything that happened while you were in the house."

She talked for a long time, and then—without thinking it was anything significant—she mentioned that she and her daughter had gone jogging that morning.

"There was this little boy, three years old, he's always wetting the bed. He woke up around four in the morning, crying, and Kathy got up to clean him and change his clothes. I helped her. Afterwards we couldn't get back to sleep, so Kathy suggested we go jogging. We did. Through the cemetery."

"You went jogging!" I said.

"Yes," she nodded, wondering why I was so excited.

"Okay," I said. "You're gonna go jogging again tomorrow morning. Come on. Show me the route you took."

We got into the car and retraced their route. They had come down a few blocks from the house, turned right, gone a few more blocks, then entered the cemetery where the cult gathered their mushrooms. They jogged through the cemetery and emerged at the other end, where they had to climb over a wire fence.

"Okay," I said. "This is where we're going to hit her. Right here, as you come over the fence. I'm taking you back to the house. You behave the same way you did yesterday. Friendly. Nice. In the morning, if the baby doesn't wake up, you wake him up. Same as today. Then suggest another jog. When you come through that fence you're going to jog right into my car, the two of you."

The next morning, at five o'clock, we were all out near the cemetery—Mark, Greg Temple, Steve Young and his camera crew, and myself. Pretty soon we saw them coming through the fog, a couple of blocks away. They turned and entered the cemetery. The camera men sprawled on the hoods and fenders of the Lincolns with their equipment. If anyone had come along just then it would have seemed extremely unusual—all those cars parked outside a cemetery at dawn, sound equipment, cameras, guys lying on top of cars. Thank God the street was deserted. About ten minutes went by and then we saw Kathy climbing over the fence. She stopped to hold the wire down for her mother and Greg and Mark and I poured out of the car and snatched her. It went so fast she didn't know what was happening. She didn't even have time to scream. We had her in the car inside of ten seconds. It was so smooth I couldn't believe it. As it turned out, I would have been wise not to have believed it.

A few minutes later we were on the freeway headed for San Diego. Kathy was in the back seat with her mother and Greg, and I was driving. Kathy was very calm, not saying anything, and I was thinking she might be easy to handle. The worst was over and it had gone without a hitch.

An hour or so out of Seattle, I stopped for gas. The two Lincolns pulled in behind us, still taking pictures. We gassed up without incident. No outbursts from Kathy. I felt encouraged. If Young and his crew had got gas at the same time, we might have avoided a lot of grief, but I guess they were so involved with what they were doing they didn't think about it.

An hour later, Young flagged me down, indicating he needed fuel and we all pulled into a little filling station in Kelso, Washington, a sleepy one-horse sort of town.

Off to the side of the station was a small lunch counter. While I was having my tank topped off, and while the CBS people were being serviced, I went for some coffee. Kathy was behaving perfectly; we'd made one stop without any trouble, and I didn't anticipate we'd have any now. But as I was at the lunch counter, and Kathy and her mother were going to the bathroom, all hell seemed to break loose. I heard screams. People were leaping out of the Lincolns, cameras grinding. Young was shouting. Someone else hollered, "Police!"

I left the coffee and went running. Kathy had made a break, catching Greg and her mother by surprise, and jumped the filling station attendant who was also the manager of the place. She had her arms around him when I got there, and was screaming at the top of her voice, "Help, please! They're kidnapping me!"

Mrs. Crampton was frantically trying to explain to the bewildered station manager what it was all about. I shouted at her, "We don't have time to talk! Let's get out of here, let's get a *move* on!" I pried Kathy loose from the man and stuffed her into the car. She was screaming all the time. Then I realized that the attendant had my credit card and my license plate number. I decided to stay and deal with the police, which would give the Cramptons time to get away. The manager was already on the phone. I told Greg, who was behind the wheel, "Go to Julie's in Eugene. I'll meet you there!" Greg threw the car into gear and shot out of there. The Lincolns, with guys falling all over themselves, trying to cram their equipment back into the cars, falling down, doors popping open, went squealing out after them. I remained by myself.

By an unlucky coincidence, the filling station housed not only a restaurant but the office of the Kelso Chief of Police.

It was a small room, with a desk, a couple of chairs, and a two-way radio. The chief arrived in about half an hour, having been awakened, no breakfast, and in a bad mood.

"What the hell is going on here?" he demanded.

"I'll be happy to explain," I said. I had with me copies of the New York *Times* account of my acquittal in the Dan Voll case a few weeks before in New York. That case had made national news, and the chief had heard about it. He'd also heard about the Sinunu case in Seattle. "So you're the guy," he said.

"I'm the guy," I smiled.

"All right, fill me in on the particulars."

I did. When I was through, he was very sympathetic. "Yeah," he said, stirring sugar into his coffee, "these damned cults. I've been reading about them. Kids getting all screwed up. But damn it, Patrick—why did you have to pick this little town to stop for gas? We ain't equipped to handle stuff like this. I have to put out a description of the car on the radio. If anyone sees them I have to bring them back here. Maybe nobody will see them."

A few minutes later, having heard the radio calls, a young deputy sheriff drove up and asked to talk to me. At first he was friendly and seemed sympathetic. After he'd interviewed the service station manager, however, his attitude changed completely. He said, "I have reason to believe that you've been involved in a kidnapping, which is a federal offense." Apparently the manager had fingered me as the one directing the whole operation. "I'm placing you under arrest." He advised me of my rights and presented me with a paper to sign, attesting to the fact that he had advised me of my rights. I signed it. What the hell. I'd been arrested before; it's no big deal.

The deputy then telephoned the prosecuting attorney. "I've got something really hot for you," he said. "A kidnapping. Guy named Ted Patrick."

As it happened, the prosecutor also knew about my acquittal in New York. "They let him off before," he told the deputy.

"Judge ruled a parent can't be found guilty of kidnapping his own child. You better be careful with this one."

I could see the deputy beginning to have second thoughts. Then, a few minutes later, the phone rang and it was the sheriff. He was hot. It was a small room, and the sheriff was raging, so I could overhear quite a lot of what he was saying, and guess most of the rest based on the different colors of green the deputy was turning. The sheriff's words ran something like this: "You moron, you idiot! Who the hell is running this goddamned show—you or me? Who the hell do you think you are? Where the hell do you get off calling the prosecuting attorney? *I* make these decisions here. You got that man under arrest? Well, you better get him *out* of arrest, and fast! Otherwise you're gonna have a lawsuit on your hands and you're gonna be looking for another job!" Oh, the man was on the warpath! He was making the walls shake. I'm not revengeful by nature, but I couldn't help enjoying the deputy's discomfort. He had that phone pressed so hard to his ear so I couldn't hear he was denting his skull—but I could hear anyway.

After he hung up there was a long silence. The deputy blew his nose, and then said to me, sheepishly, "Well, Mr. Patrick, you're free. You're—uh—you're not under arrest after all."

I couldn't resist. "The hell I'm not! I signed that paper, you placed me under arrest in front of the chief here. You can't just arrest me one minute, and then un-arrest me the next!"

"It was a mistake . . . a procedural error," he said, biting his lip. "You know—um—sorry about that."

I would have hassled him a little more, just for fun, but at that moment, over the radio, came a message from the state police that they had the Cramptons and were bringing them in to Kelso.

"Damn!" swore the chief, shaking his head.

The state police had nabbed them on the freeway, parked on the side of the road near an exit ramp. Evidently, in all the confusion, Greg and Mrs. Crampton could not agree on what I'd shouted to them about meeting them at Kathy's sister's in

Eugene. They seemed to think I'd be coming along and were waiting for me, though naturally that would have been impossible since I had no car.

For a glimpse of what went on out there when the state police, curious to see why three cars were stopped at the side of the road, pulled over to investigate, we cut now to the CBS Evening News with Walter Cronkite (Roger Mudd substituting), August 13, 1973:

GREG TEMPLE: A Mr. Ted Patrick [sound of highway traffic] is the man who takes religious people out of love families, so to speak. He has just taken the mother's daughter out of the Love Family in Seattle, and we're on our way down to San Diego for a deprogramming.

D. O. MAHONEY (state trooper): My God, it's . . . [Pause] I feel awful uncomfortable.

YOUNG: Uncertain what to do he radios for assistance, and a state police sergeant responds to the call.

L. E. WALTER (trooper sergeant): Hi, how are you?

KATHY CRAMPTON: I'm fine, [Indistinct: much highway noise throughout this sequence.]

SGT. WALTER: What is your name?

KATHY: Corinth Israel.

SGT. WALTER: Corinth what?

KATHY: Corinth Love Israel.

SGT. WALTER: Corinth Love Israel. How old are you?

KATHY: I'm eighty-five.

SGT. WALKER: Eighty-five years old? I see.

I should interject here that not only does the Love Israel Cult give each other Biblical names, and have their own calendar and their own time scheme (the day begins at six in the morning, which is their first hour), but they also add sixty-six years to their "earth age." Now back to the Cronkite show.

YOUNG: The sheriff's department is next to arrive. A gas

station owner has reported a possible kidnapping, he says. Ted
Patrick has been placed under arrest.

SGT. WALTER: The mother and he and the fiancé of one of
her other daughters went up to get this girl. They took her
from this environment. The girl is so out of her mind and
drugged. I asked her a minute ago, for instance, if this was
her mother, and, of course, she gave me something like, no,
my mother is somebody, the mother of the universe. So she's
all ripped up inside.

DETECTIVE R. COVINGTON (sheriff's office): Rattled. Right.

TROOPER: In the physical life, who is she?

KATHY: She claims to represent my mother.

TROOPER: Is she? In the physical life?

KATHY: No, my mother is the spiritual—is the spiritual vision
of peace.

TROOPER: But in the physical life, is this your real mother?

KATHY: I don't see that this is the question. The question is
that I've been taken against my will. I would prefer to go with
you, sir, to the police station, than to go with these people.

TROOPER: Well, we have to identify you and establish who
you are.

KATHY: I'm Corinth Israel.

TROOPER: You're Corinth Israel. Is that your legal name?

KATHY: Yes it is, as far as I know.

TROOPER: Do you have any legal documents to show who you
are?

KATHY: These people kidnapped me, and I don't have any
papers with me. We were jog . . . we were running, this
woman and I were running, and I didn't carry my papers with
me just to run around the block.

TROOPER: Well, I'll let the deputy sheriff talk to you, okay?

COVINGTON: How old did you say you were?

KATHY: I'm eighty-five.

COVINGTON: You're eighty-five.

YOUNG: At the Cowlitz County Courthouse in Kelso, Washington, the question, what to do? They checked the statutes

and doubt this is a kidnapping. Kathy's mother was present. There was no try for ransom, and the Seattle police confirmed they knew in advance. Legally, Kathy is an adult, but Patrick insists he and the others are acting within their rights.

PATRICK: Well, I'll say the parents got a right to rescue their child, if they feel they are under some type of spell or influence of drug or alcohol, or in trouble period. They have a right to go and give as much help as possible. That's a human right and constitutional right.

YOUNG: Asked if she is a menace to herself or the community, a psychiatrist says no. Charges against Patrick are dropped, and Kathy is released. Her freedom is short-lived.

KATHY: Okay, now. I don't want to go. [Indistinct] I'm gonna . . . you're gonna physically take me . . . I'm going to walk this direction. [Indistinct] I'm free. [Indistinct]

MRS. CRAMPTON: Greg! [Sound of running footsteps.]

KATHY: Let me go. Let me go.

YOUNG: For the third time today, Kathy is forced against her will to go with her mother and Ted Patrick.

What happened at the Cowlitz County Courthouse was, of course, a lot more interesting and a lot more involved than the CBS show indicated. The deputy sheriff who had "un-arrested" me, drove me to the courthouse and I sat down and had a long talk with the sheriff while we waited for the Cramptons to appear. The sheriff was an intelligent and interesting man. He'd heard about what I was doing and had strong opinions about the cults. It's been my experience that almost all the police departments I've dealt with in the past few years share my convictions about how evil the cults really are. I guess the American Civil Liberties Union automatically discounts and disqualifies the police on this score, as if having the police be in favor of something means that it must automatically violate some concept of civil liberties. Which strikes me as an example of amazing tunnel vision.

Anyway, once I'd explained the situation, the sheriff said to me, "Well, Mr. Patrick, the only thing I can do is bring in a psychiatrist. That's the law. He'll examine her, and then release her. I have to let her walk out that door."

That was fine with me. But the psychiatrist couldn't come for a couple of hours, so Mrs. Crampton, Gregg and I went out to have lunch. Kathy, in the custody of a policewoman, had food sent in to her in the jail.

By the time the psychiatrist appeared, the sidewalk was crowded with bystanders, gawking and curious. It was a small town, Kelso, and the word had spread rapidly about what was happening. The psychiatrist talked to Kathy for about ten minutes and declared that she was neither a danger to herself nor to society. Then the sheriff released her, telling her she was free to leave.

She walked out the front door and I was right behind her. She began to run down the street. Her mother was tailing her, trying to reason with her, trying to explain that what we were doing was for her own good. I yelled out, "We don't have time to talk, Mrs. Crampton. Come on. We've gotta get rolling!" I grabbed Kathy around the waist and hustled her into the car. My memory is that one of the Kelso police held the door open for me as I shoved her in. A police car escorted us out to the highway and the cops waved goodbye as we drove off.

Kathy behaved quietly during the rest of the trip. We stopped in Eugene, Oregon where we saw her sister Julie, and then we went on, with the film crew hanging on to every turn of events and photographing everything. We followed Route 5 all the way to San Diego, an absolutely beautiful run through mountain country, glimpses of the Pacific opening up when we hit the California line.

We drove to L.A. where Kathy's father met us at the airport, which was the drop-off point for the rented car. Needless to say, he was very relieved to see us. We returned the car and then went to the Cramptons' house. They had a large van which Mr. Crampton told us we could use to drive on to San Diego, and after we had something to eat, we took off. During all of this, the camera crew, the lights, microphones, cameras, and sound equipment were very much in evidence. Steve Young was excited; you could tell he thought he was in on a major story.

The major story, unfortunately, kept getting in the way of my deprogramming once we were in San Diego. The lights and cameras and mikes were a major distraction. Kathy kept performing for the cameras, which only complicated my task. Then too, she escaped again that first night.

Some good and well-meaning friends of mine—the Spahns, already mentioned—had come over to the motel to help deprogram Kathy. They had a child in a cult, and were interested in helping other children. I left Kathy and her mother and the Spahns at the Royal Inn Motel and went to my home, which is only ten minutes or so away. I was exhausted. The long drive down from Seattle, plus all the dealings in Kelso, had taken a lot out of me. I renewed acquaintances with my family and then hit the sack.

It must have been around one-thirty in the morning when the phone rang. I was reaching for my pants before I had the receiver off the hook. I just knew.

"Ted. She's escaped!" It was Mrs. Spahn.

"How could she escape from the motel?"

"She wasn't at the motel. We brought her home with us for the night. She seemed so nice and calm, we thought it would be okay."

"Jesus Christ!"

I sprinted out of the house, half dressed, and jumped into my car. On a hunch, instead of heading for the Spahn house, I went out toward the freeway, figuring that Kathy would be intent on hitchhiking to Seattle. Sure enough, a few minutes later, I saw her walking along the side of the road. I had already driven past before I noticed her, and I had to turn the car around. As I was making the turn to come back and pick her up, a Ford van stopped and she got in.

I took off after that van like Mario Andretti. I hung on his rear bumper and flashed my lights. He speeded up, I speeded up. He slowed down, I slowed down.

He was a young musician playing in the band at the Royal

Inn. He was scared. Kathy was saying, "That's the Devil back there. That's Satan on our tail." He thought she was nuts and he was afraid of me.

Finally, he pulled into a gas station and I put my car in front of his van where he couldn't go anywhere.

"What's this all about? What the hell's going on?" the driver said as I got into the front seat next to Kathy. She shrank away from me and began to cry, "That's him, that black devil, that's Satan and he's trying to kidnap me."

"My name is Ted Patrick," I said, and launched into my standard explanation of what had happened and what we were doing. "The girl's mother is about ten minutes from here. If you don't believe what I'm telling you, how about driving us over to see her mother? If you're not satisfied after you talk to her, then you can call the police if you want to."

He remained leery, but I was calm and friendly and Kathy was talking all her nonsense, so he took a chance and we drove to the motel. The Chula Vista police were already there; Mrs. Crampton had called them. The police and I were pretty well acquainted by this time. They went through a few formalities and then took off, and so did the musician.

We put Kathy into the motel room again, and I told my well-meaning friends: "Look. I have to get some sleep. This girl doesn't move from this room, you understand?"

"We thought she was cured," Mr. Spahn apologized.

"I'll tell you when she's cured. You watch her. You keep her here. I'll be back in the morning."

The next few days I got nowhere with Kathy. Young and his crew were shooting a story, but it wasn't the real story. I mean, their presence affected the business in such a fashion that they were really running the deprogramming. I suppose that accounts for the fact that after a week of seeing and hearing what went on, Young came away from the episode with absolutely no understanding of what Kathy's problem was or what the cults represent. He didn't learn a thing in all that time.

Eventually I decided to take Kathy to my house. I thought we needed a change of scene, and I thought too that in my own house I could arrange things so that I'd have some privacy and could get the job done. I was really annoyed. It was five days since we snatched her and she wasn't deprogrammed yet. That almost never happened to me, and I informed Young as politely as I knew how that I wanted his crew to lay off until I was finished.

Well, he wanted some shots of my house and family, and a few shots of Kathy in the house which he claimed was important "if we're going to tell the whole story."

"Okay," I said, still trying to be cooperative. "But make it fast will you, please? I have to get to work."

They did not make it fast. I asked the crew to stop. One of them replied that they took their orders from Young. I informed them that they were guests in my home and that in my home I give the orders. Still they continued. By this time I'd had it. I believe I then suggested to Young that I was in a mood to take a hammer to his cameras. Young didn't understand much of what went on that week, but I must say he did understand that. The cameras came down and the lights went out with amazing swiftness and I was left alone to deal with Kathy.

The deprogramming was a snap after that. I guess I worked with her about four hours and she was out of it. Young and his people were camped out on my lawn waiting, and I permitted them to interview her. We'd already invested so much time and energy in the project I felt obliged to let them talk to her to round out the story. But I was still seething over what I considered Young's bad manners. After all, everything else aside, he'd been a guest in my house and I thought he'd abused my hospitality. My own manners were somewhat strained just then and I am afraid I called him a no-good son of a bitch.

Later, I calmed down and invited the whole crew to a party I was throwing out at the Bahia Hotel. It was Fourth of July holiday again and I was laying on my annual bash. Since I was moving my whole family out to the hotel, I gave the Cramptons the keys to my house and told them to make themselves at home.

Now, one thing people have trouble understanding is that

deprogramming involves more than that initial breakthrough.
The kids are filled with psychological fear. They have been
programmed to believe that if they leave the cult terrible things
will befall them. They have been taught to see Satan everywhere.
When they come out of it, they are often confused and uncertain. For months, sometimes years, independent thinking, independent decision-making has been discouraged. The cult does
their thinking for them. So, a period of rehabilitation is crucial.
This lasts an average of a couple of weeks. You can compare a
kid coming out of a cult to someone who's been confined to a
bed or a wheelchair for a prolonged period. His first steps are
going to be shaky. He will totter. He will falter. You have to
bring him along little by little as the muscle tone is restored.

Some require less rehabilitation than Kathy did; Wes Lockwood, for example, came out strong and clear and fighting mad
over how he'd been deceived. Even so he stayed with me at
my house for more than a week. Kathy was what I call "a
floater." She would drift in and out mentally; you can see this
happening with kids: the old vacant look will return, they get
restless, they begin to express doubts. It's important for whomever is with them—preferably their parents—to recognize these
symptoms and make a vigorous effort to bring them back to
reality. Occupy their minds. Talk to them. Get them involved
in some physical activity. And keep an eye on them to make
sure they don't suddenly bolt.

In Kathy's case, this was basically her mother's responsibility. My idea was to have Mrs. Crampton stay with Kathy at
my house for a couple of weeks for her rehabilitation. I assumed that Mrs. Crampton understood what precautions were
necessary. Unhappily, she did not.

The Spahns, who had taken Kathy to their home that first
night, came around to the house the day I was moving my
family to the hotel, and invited Kathy and her mother to go
to church with them. Now, going to church is the last thing a
girl in Kathy's condition needs. This is a critical stage, the
person is psychologically fragile, and anything doing with religion, church picnics even, work on a person like poison. (In

case anyone is thinking that I go around turning zealous fundamentalist Christians into atheists, I don't. After deprogramming —after the rehabilitation—the kids do what they want about religion. Some go to church, some don't; some experience a renewal of faith, some are indifferent. All of which is fine with me.)

Evidently Mrs. Crampton either didn't understand my warnings or didn't believe me. Whatever the reason, she took Kathy off to church, assuming I suppose that my friends were acting in my behalf and could be trusted. Naturally Kathy got confused, and asked her mother to buy her a Bible. Mrs. Crampton granted the request.

I don't mean to be too hard on Mrs. Crampton. For any parents in this situation everything is so foreign to them they have a hard time dealing with the simplest problems. It's like learning a new language or something. The parents are always saying things like, "This has been a nightmare." Or, "I feel like I'm on a different planet." They feel caught up in something deeply bewildering; it's as though they can't believe it even as they see it. I guess that was Young's problem to some extent too. It *is* hard to credit your own senses at times, and some parental confusion is to be expected. In the Crampton case, though, it proved disastrous.

I was entertaining a mob at the hotel. Mrs. Crampton called from my house asking if she could bring Kathy out. I thought that it might be all right for a little while; if she showed signs of being disturbed they could return to my house. Of course I didn't know then about the churchgoing and the Bible purchase and how disturbed she already was.

They came over shortly afterward and took a walk on the beach. Then they came to the party, which was jumping. Loud music, drinking, dancing—all the stuff the cult had been hammering into her head was evil and sinful. She asked her mother to take her back to the house; it was all too much for her, she said.

I think if Kathy's mother had done that, Kathy might be all right today. But for some unexplained reason, Mrs. Crampton chose instead to have Kathy take a nap in the van, which was equipped for living with a bed and chairs and toilet and sink. Kathy slept for about three hours and returned to my party one more time. It was only then that I noticed she was clutching the Bible. I recognized the look on her face too—she was "floating" and she needed help.

My hands were full at the moment so I told my two sons to keep a close eye on her. But a few minutes later, when she wanted to take another walk on the beach, the Spahns' son advised my children that he could take care of Kathy by himself. The sequence of events is not really clear to me because of the huge crowd of people I was dealing with. But Kathy went out toward the beach again with this young man, and as they were walking along, she suddenly opened the door of a car parked at a stop light, got in, and drove away. The young man did nothing whatsoever to try to detain her.

It was a crushing disappointment for everyone concerned and we read the accounts of Kathy's press conference in Seattle a few days later with a very morbid interest. It was the usual collection of lies and half truths and I felt very frustrated; the papers made us all look pretty bad, and they treated the cult with kid gloves. The only consolation, I thought, was that at least we would get a large audience for the TV show. I was still innocent enough to imagine that Steve Young and Bob Syms had been serious about wanting to put my side of the story on the air.

In August, when the show was broadcast, I had a rude awakening. All of us emerged looking like villains, kidnappers, violators of Kathy's civil rights. The cult came off looking pretty good. Love Israel appeared at one point with this incredible statement: "We don't really have any big brainwashing program other than loving each other and living a regular life, and our book's the Bible, and that's the one we read, and, as far as cleaning up your mind, you know, I think we're all cleaning up our minds. If that's called brainwashing, I don't know. I just think that we all need it, real well. I think we could all use a lot of it."

This Erdman, with his collection of drugged-up, spaced-out, wired-up mental zombies, sniffing Teluene, beating on each other with sawed-off pool cues, abusing children, jumping out of trees—and there he was talking about loving each other and leading a regular life. It made me sick.

In a statement to the press, Mrs. Crampton summed up our objections to the telecasts:

"Steven Young said we removed Kathy from the cult because we disagreed with her religious views. This is a lie! We took drastic action only because of the psychotic condition of her mind. We explored every means possible for months and found there is no law against destroying a person's mind, i.e., Charles Manson was tried only for murder, not for destroying the minds of his followers.

"The program stated the police did nothing. Wrong again! The Kelso police held Ted Patrick and me and released us only after a psychiatrist they called had examined Kathy. He said she was irrational and psychotic but not violent to the point of being a danger to herself or anyone else. He recommended Kathy be released to me.

"Twice an ACLU lawyer was shown saying the parents interfered with Kathy's civil rights. They did not point out the fact that the cult leader had already removed her rights to medical aid, mail, free speech, and privacy (no one can visit her alone). Her property, money and right to make decisions have been taken from her. We had hoped to restore her ability to think and reclaim these rights.

"The program called the cult a 'fundamentalist Christian' group. The members are taught to believe Love Israel is greater than Christ. The Love Family Charter supersedes the Bible and the laws of our land. Only Bible quotations reinforcing Love's mental domination are included in the Charter. God is Love, Love is God. Can such a group be called fundamental Christians?

"We, her parents, had been interviewed by Steve Young. Not one scene or one line from the interview was included, but the ACLU lawyer was given two different spots to present his opinions."

In spite of all this, the program helped a lot of people. Hundreds of parents who had lost children to the cults learned who I was and realized that I offered some hope to them of retrieving their children. So, inadvertently CBS dealt a further blow to the cult movement, and I thank them.

As for Steve Young, well, after all he'd seen, this is what he concluded about me and my activities: "I feel very strongly about what Patrick is doing. I think he makes broad-brush, unfounded charges against whole religious groups. Some of what he says may very well be true, but my own feeling is that he is a flimflam man, that he is manipulative and that he preys upon desperate parents."

What are you going to do?

At least Roger Mudd seemed to want to balance the account a little. As he signed off after the final segment of the documentary, he read with a straight face the following news item:

"Last week in Detroit, the fifteen-year-old religious leader, Guru Maharaj Ji, was hit in the face by a pie by a young man who said the Guru was nothing but a slick businessman. Today the man who said he tossed the pie, twenty-one-year-old Pat Haley, was operated on in a Detroit hospital for a skull fracture. His condition is reported good. Police are quoted as saying that Haley said he was beaten up by two followers of the Guru."

CHAPTER FIVE

Snatching two, three, sometimes four people a week and deprogramming them, Patrick avoided serious legal problems for the better part of fourteen months. The kind of benign, almost avuncular tolerance of various police departments around the country illustrated by the behavior of the Kelso, Washington police in the Kathy Crampton episode, was certainly a contributing factor to his apparent immunity from criminal charges. Another was his high degree of success—the virtually complete absence of recidivism in the young people he rescued. In those few instances when, for one reason or another, young men and women did return to cults, the cults were reluctant to press charges. None of the cults are eager to appear in a court of law to be cross-examined about their methods, their ideologies, and especially about their bookkeeping. Finally, however, it was meticulous attention to detail that kept Patrick free from legal entanglements for so long—the kind of obsessive strategic planning, as in the Wes Lockwood snatch—that constituted his best insurance against prosecution.

Inevitably, circumstances combined to trip him up. In the winter of 1973, carelessness, illness, impatience, lapses of judgment resulted in a snatch being bungled and Patrick being arrested and charged with assault and unlawful imprisonment. Happily for him, he was assigned a judge in New York City whose intellect and passions, wit and spirit were not embalmed in a pickle jar of briny legalisms.

TED PATRICK: It was a small, neat courtroom. The atmosphere was relaxed, civilized. Judge Bruce Wright didn't exactly run a tight ship but he ran a comfortable ship. Unlike other courtrooms it's been my misfortune to appear in since then, Judge Wright's amounted to an arena for testing ideas and securing the truth. It was a little like going to college, that trial, with a fine gentleman as your professor; the trial turned into a course study in philosophy and law. I enjoyed it very much. So did everyone else connected with it except, I guess, Dan Voll and his leader, Hannah Lowe. They didn't enjoy it at all.

It was a hot July day in New York. The air-conditioning system in the courtroom hummed and wheezed throughout the proceedings. The weather was quite a contrast with what it had been that night in January when I'd committed the act that had me sitting here listening to Judge Wright deliver his charges to the jury of five men and a woman. That night it had been cold, and the New York City streets were covered with snow and sleet. I was sick, I thought I was coming down with pneumonia, as Dan Voll's father and I stood on the corner of 119th Street and Amsterdam Avenue waiting to snatch the former roommate of Wes Lockwood.

Who was Dan Voll? And why exactly were we all in this courtroom in Manhattan engaging in what the Washington *Post* called "the nation's first judicial test of the rights of parents and their agents to remove their college-age children by force from religious groups of which they disapprove"?

Judge Wright explained it better than I ever could in his statement dismissing the assault charge against me.

"Complainant," he wrote, "the product of a pious Lutheran home, was close to that faith's rituals and devotions until shortly before he entered college. A high school valedictorian whose subject was, ironically, 'Reconciliation,' he was originally pointed towards the Lutheran ministry and that branch of homiletics. Instead, however, he elected Yale's Saybrook College.

"At Yale, he was introduced to the New Testament Missionary Fellowship, a charismatic, Pentecostal, and evangelical expression of the Christian emotion. Whereas some Catholics believe in the Real Presence and dramatize the rite of communion as a literal tasting of the flesh and blood of Christ, the Fellowship was in constant combat with the Devil as a palpable existence. This moralistic crusade demanded almost ceaseless prayer, understood the sacred therapeutics of 'laying on of hands,' reacted to the Holy Spirit by oral hieroglyphics spoken through the 'gift of tongues,' and sometimes did an involuntary dance of ineffable joy. Sometimes a tambourine might help summon the movement and rhythm. On others, the inspiration was *a cappella*.

"His childhood religious experiences had been a bit more Gothic and austere. Lutherans, originally rebellious schismatics, torn from the Roman faith, were reformers. Martin Luther's ninety-five Theses, advertised in 1517, were condemned as ecclesiastical heresy and a defiant rejection of papal orthodoxy. His 'Primary Works,' included such titles as 'On the Babylonian

Captivity of The Church of God,' and, by 1520, he had been
excommunicated and his writings publicly burned in Rome.
He translated into German the New Testament, delivered passionate sermons against the fanaticism of the puritanical image-
breakers and he also wrote hymns. Preceding Father Berrigan
by some 448 years, he shed his monk's cowl and, in 1525,
married a quondam nun who had divorced herself from Christ
by renouncing her vows.

"To suit the convenience of his fervor, he authored a new
church service and published catechisms. His life was given
over wholly (and holy) to theological controversy. Believers
and doubters alike still find warm mystery in the lyrics and
melodies of his *A Mighty Fortress Is Our God.*

"The Lutheran creed espoused a basic and rigid belief in
individual responsibility to God, urged strict allegiance to the
truth as expressed in the Bible and an unshakable belief in the
offer of salvation by the grace of God alone.

"It was within this context of rebellious church history and
systematic theology that Daniel Voll was spiritually nourished.
When it ceased to command his undeviating loyalty, questions
arose in his mind and he eventually cast the lot of his soul's
redemption with the New Testament Missionary Fellowship.
Astonished, sorely vexed and dismayed, his parents became
acutely worried about his welfare. So bitter were they over
what they regarded as the seduction of their son by an alien
propagation, that Daniel was reluctant to discuss it with them.
They believed him to be 'demon-possessed,' and indeed, ob-
sessed. Firm in their despair that his promising career at Yale
had been cruelly aborted and that he had been stolen from the
bosom of their home by devices smacking of hypnosis and
trance, they devised a desperate plan to return him to his
family and his Lutheran senses.

"They sought help from the defendant. Ted Patrick had won
a national reputation as one who could 'de-program' young
captives of fanatical and visionary fundamentalists washed in
the rhetoric of Fellowship evangelism, the so-called 'Jesus
Freaks' and 'The Children of God.' His methods, once alone

with those he sought to redeem, apparently involved ceaseless sermons of reconciliation and annulment of Fellowship fanaticism. Retained by Daniel's parents, who were fearful for his welfare and his sanity under domination by Fellowship zealots, he accompanied them to West 119th Street, where Daniel then lived last January. While defendant waited in a car with Daniel's mother, the father went into the street to intercept his son. It was when he saw Daniel and his father grappling and fall to the treacherously iced sidewalk that he left the car and sought to help them up. It was then that a struggle began which has earlier been described. Somewhere between Daniel's physical reluctance to accompany his father, his noisy portage to the car, and the point on Amsterdam Avenue where the police intervened, Daniel's left ring finger was injured."

I watched Dan sitting across from me, his eyes on the judge, his chin in his hand, that recognizable, empty, false smile on what normally would have been a handsome face, and I only felt regret for our having failed to get away with him that night so that we could have restored him to the sort of health his old buddy Wes Lockwood now enjoyed. As important to me as winning the trial was the fact that Dan Voll was lost to that damned Hannah Lowe cult indefinitely.

Dan Voll was described by friends and associates as being, prior to his involvement with the cult, practically another Jack Armstrong. "One of the nicest kids you could imagine," was the opinion of Kathy Blanchard, a high school friend. "He went to all the social things—dances and games—but he didn't do a lot of wild things other kids did, like drinking with guys and racing in cars." His high school track coach said, "He had to be the hardest worker I've ever seen. He wasn't a natural runner. But he made himself one through determination and the desire to be a winner. My relationship with Danny was that of a friend. I loved that kid. I used to hope that my kid would be the same type of boy Danny Voll was." This is Dan's mother on Dan when he was only two years old: "When his sister was only one, she would try to run into the street. I told Danny to watch her. I used to hear her screaming and run out to find

Danny pulling on her with all his might to keep her from running off. Even at that age he accepted responsibility." A model boy from a model family. One of the neighbors in Farmington, Connecticut, where Eugene Voll is the principal of a school: "This kid came from the best background there ever was. They're a terrific family. I've never heard that woman yelling at her children. She never loses her temper. The kids play outside all the time and I've not once heard them scream at each other. They seem very devoted to their children and spend most of their time at home."

Except for the air-conditioning it was very quiet in the room, which was packed with law students, relatives of the prosecutor (who was trying his first big case), relatives of my attorney, Judge Wright's wife, the media. Judge Wright moved his glasses up and down on his nose and read on. "Both Daniel Voll and his father agree, although here on opposite sides of the legal process, that on the early evening of January 29th, 1973, it was the father who approached Daniel first, who grabbed his arms and said to him, 'You're coming with us' or words to that effect . . ."

Jumped the gun, Mr. Voll did. We would have had him otherwise. And wouldn't have been here at the moment with me facing a jail term and already about fifteen thousand dollars out-of-pocket. But the whole case was a matter of jumping the gun. Nothing went right from the beginning.

It all started back in San Diego at my house, where I'd taken Wes Lockwood for a week or two for rehabilitation. Not that he needed much; he was one of those who came out of a cult determined to strike a blow against the people who had conned him.

For starters he was eager to rescue his old friend Dan Voll, and at his insistence his parents called the Volls in Connecticut. Wes was out of the cult, they told the surprised Volls, good as gold, his old self, happy and loving, and he wanted to urge them to retain me to deprogram their son. The Volls were impressed, especially after they'd talked a while with Wes, and amazed that he was free—they'd given up hope of ever seeing

their own son return to normal. Whatever skepticism they felt
about my motives was laid to rest by Mr. Lockwood. "This man
has knocked himself out for us, worked like a dog for a week,
took risks, ignored danger, everything, and he's never asked for
a cent beyond his expenses."

The Volls were convinced in short order, but money was a
problem with them, as it is often for clients of mine. This might
be the place to say a few words about this money issue, because I've been accused of—well, to quote Steve Young again,
"preying" on the parents. *Time* magazine claimed I made as
much as twenty-five thousand dollars on a single case. The fact
that I dress well when I appear in court seems proof to some reporters that I'm making a fortune. One reporter who interviewed
me in my house noted snidely that I had been eating a steak
sandwich, which he called "a luxury."

For the first year and a half or so I lost a lot of money in
this work. All I charged was expenses. But when I was on the
road, my family inevitably suffered financially. I was meeting
my own expenses, but I wasn't earning a salary to help pay
any of their expenses. Since my wife works, we had to spend
a fortune on baby-sitters and nursery schools. On more than
one occasion a client never paid even my expenses. And when
the legal bills began to mount I was plunged quickly and
heavily into debt. I'm still in debt. Today, for an average job
I'm forced to charge fifteen hundred dollars. Out of that comes
a lot of expenses. If I have helpers, I have to pay them their
room and board, and air fare. There's my own plane fare, room
and board. My telephone bills are astronomical. I have one full-
time secretary who earns a modest salary. I have to pay something to the people whose houses I use for the deprogramming
(I almost never deprogram a kid in his own home). It's very,
very expensive. But maybe I shouldn't be sensitive about this
issue. I really don't believe that the people who hate me for
what I do would hate me any the less if I did the work for
absolutely nothing. Then I'd be a Communist, I suppose.

Anyway, the Volls were apparently in a money bind. I'd
quoted a minimum expense figure of five hundred dollars to

return to the East and get their son. They claimed to be able
to lay their hands on only $490. I agreed that that would be all
right, and made plans to meet them in New York where Dan
was living near Hannah Lowe's. I left two days later.

I really should have waited. As a result of spending so much
time staking out Wes in that park across from the Yale Faculty
Club, I'd come down with a very heavy cold. When you feel
that lousy, you aren't going to be thinking too straight, and
your efficiency is going to suffer. But I guess I was moved by
the enthusiasm of the Lockwoods, as well as by my loathing
of the Hannah Lowe operation and my desire to disrupt that
outfit as soon and as much as I could. So instead of climbing
into bed and staying there until I was fit again, I jumped on a
plane and took off for New York.

Wes had provided me with a minute-by-minute schedule of
Dan's activities. Almost step-by-step. They all followed a routine
that never varied, he said. This was an advantage I did not
possess in New Haven, and I hoped it would compensate for
my having less time than I would have liked to study the place
and draw up my plans. But the Volls wouldn't let me operate in
my usual fashion. They had strong opinions about everything,
although they didn't understand anything about the intricacies
of such a maneuver, and thought that their $490 entitled them
to call all the shots.

They simply did not seem to believe that the things I told
them were as crucial as I made them out to be. Within about
five minutes of their picking me up at the airport I knew we
had problems. I had stressed the need for a remote site for the
deprogramming; one reason you cannot take a kid home is
that's the first place the police are going to search. I prefer
removing the subject as far from home as possible. The Volls,
however, weren't perfectly sure where we would take Dan. That
made me uneasy right off the bat.

Then, they had ignored my advice about bringing along a
third party to help in the snatch. "We don't need anybody else.
The three of us can get him," Mr. Voll said. But mothers are

never dependable during a snatch. You cannot trust them to do what they're supposed to do. They invariably freeze at the most critical point, panic, go into hysterics; in general I don't like them around except as observers.

"Look," I told them, "I can go into the street and hire some-one for fifty dollars to help out." I'd done that many times in the past; you'd be surprised how many guys there are on the street willing to make a fast fifty like that. Not one of them hired under those circumstances has ever failed me either. They've been great under pressure.

But the Volls were reluctant to spend the money.

"I had a woman freeze up on me just a couple weeks ago," I argued. "We can end up blowing the whole thing."

"No," Mr. Voll replied, "Marie will be fine. The three of us are enough. Marie is very trustworthy, as you'll see."

Well, I would have preferred placing my trust in some seven-foot black dude off the street who would crush rock with his bare hands for fifty dollars, but I finally gave in.

"We think the best time to get Dan is tomorrow morning when he leaves his apartment," Voll then said.

"Tomorrow morning! No, now wait a minute. No way we're going to do it in the morning. I've never even seen the neighbor-hood. I've never been on 119th Street. I don't know what the neighborhood is like, how many pedestrians, what's the best route to the highway." I went on and on. But they were un-moved. They seemed to think there wouldn't be any problems.

"We can describe the neighborhood for you," said Mrs. Voll. "It's very ordinary."

I was so run-down physically that it was a great effort to try to explain how vital it is for me to observe these small details personally. A large proportion of pulling off a successful snatch is intuitive with me. I have to have a feel for the situation, and the only way to get the feel is to hang around and watch for a couple of days, the way I did in New Haven. I hate to launch an operation with inadequate mental preparation.

But the Volls were impatient. Maybe they feared I would

just be consuming more expense money if we delayed. I finally made them agree to let me spend the day staking out the place and then snatch Dan that evening.

As a final frustration that Sunday night, they had ignored my basic rule about providing a two-door car. Their car had four doors. With only three of us to deal with Dan, four doors was out of the question. We would have to rent a car, which meant transfering Dan from one car to the other, dropping off the rental car, or trying to drive two cars back to Connecticut with a possibly wild (if Wes Lockwood was any example), frantic, fighting, strong young man trying to burst out of one of them. Jesus, talk about bad vibrations.

And the weather was horrible. A big winter storm was moving across the city, it was snowing and sleeting. We would have to be at Dan's place at six in the morning. I should have been under a doctor's care and instead I'd be prowling around in all that mess trying to figure out a way to patch up this operation with a bottle of glue and a few clothes hangers. I went to sleep feeling very pessimistic. I slept badly and in the morning felt like people had been beating on me with black-jacks. I couldn't breathe and my joints ached. But I met the Volls downstairs as per schedule and off we went into the storm.

I have never spent a more miserable hour in my life than that hour standing in the freezing sleet and snow, hatless, glove-less, without overshoes, running a temperature, waiting for Dan to come out of his apartment. I tried to make my brain record the relevant details of the scene, the neighborhood, that might prove decisive in a crisis, but I knew I wasn't thinking clearly or well. The Volls sat in the car, warm and dry with the heater running. I could have done that too, but they were driving me nuts and I had to be alone.

Eventually I went over to the car and said, "I don't think he's in there. He must have spent the night somewhere else. Let's go over to Hannah Lowe's."

Mrs. Voll drove the seven blocks to Hannah's brownstone and as we turned the corner there was Dan going up the steps.

I knew from Wes's account of their routine in the house that the entire cult gathered every morning before work for a prayer meeting. It was one of Dan's duties to walk Hannah's dog afterwards. I wanted to follow him, to try to develop some grasp of his behavior, how he reacted to the people around him, get some sense of the quality of the fight he might make. The Volls could not see the usefulness of this, and were debating why we shouldn't just grab him then when he came out after the prayer meeting. I walked away from them and went into a coffee shop nearby where I had a cup of hot tea and a doughnut. The place was a quick turnover business, with a lot of Columbia University students coming in for breakfast, so I couldn't loiter in there for very long, and I couldn't bring myself to return to the car and have to argue with the Volls, so I had no choice but to hang around outside and freeze.

At eight-thirty Dan emerged, walking Hannah's dog. I followed him. We went around the Columbia campus for about half an hour uneventfully. Then I followed him back to the apartment, waited while he went in, then followed him to the subway which he took to work. It was all mechanical on my part—I was getting no feelings whatever. I just knew this whole trip was shaping up as a bummer.

Nevertheless, I continued going through the motions. We covered the various routes to the highway, and I selected the best one, and we rehearsed our escape route several times. The Volls were determined to grab Dan when he came home from work, as he was on his way to the evening prayer meeting at Hannah's. I didn't want to try to grab him at all. The whole thing was such a mess, so poorly prepared, so hasty. But I'd come all that way across the continent, spent their money, and if they wanted to call the shots, I thought, "Well, it's their responsibility. I'll do the best I can."

Back in the hotel as I thawed out, coughing and blowing my nose, I explained what I thought we'd have to do. We'd check out of the hotel and leave the Volls' car in the parking lot. Then we'd rent a car and Mrs. Voll would drive to Dan's.

We'd hit him as he was coming out of the house. How we were going to retrieve the Volls' car I really didn't know. Worry about that later, I thought.

"Now listen," I said to Mrs. Voll. "I don't care what happens, what you see. If your husband is on the ground being killed, you don't get out from behind the wheel. You drive right up, keep the motor running, and when we're inside, whatever happens, with or without Dan or your husband, when I say take off, you take off, no questions asked." And Mr. Voll, I reminded: "This has to take thirty seconds, no longer. If it takes longer than thirty seconds, forget about it. It's a one-shot deal."

At five-thirty we were outside Dan's apartment. It was already dark, and the weather was still miserable. The street and sidewalks were all icy. Naturally, there was no place to park, so we had to double-park. Mrs. Voll was very nervous. I was feeling a little numb, like a wide receiver on a cold day who can't get his hands warm enough to feel confident about catching a pass. Then Dan was coming down the street and Mr. Voll said, "There he is, there he is!"

And he jumped the gun. I tried to stop him. "Wait! Let him go in. We'll get him when he comes out." That was the plan, that's what I was ready for. But Mr. Voll was already out of the car running toward Dan. Dan was startled. He jumped and threw up his arms defensively. "What are you doing here?" he cried.

"We've come to take you home," said Mr. Voll, grabbing at his son. Dan jerked away and started to run. Mr. Voll got his arms around his waist and sort of tackled him. They both hit the icy sidewalk pretty hard.

Judge Wright, in the courtroom six months later, a hot sun beating out on that same street now, told the jury what happened next.

"Both sides agree that Daniel resisted fiercely this detainer of his person and began a struggle remarkable and intense for a young man of Daniel's size. In the course of the struggle, the father slid down from Daniel's waist level to his legs, in a tackling position. Both father and son then fell to the icy surface of the street. The father then says that he realized that he would be unable to get Daniel to the car then parked in West 119th Street, without some assistance and he called to the defendant, who had remained behind in the car. It was then that the defendant came over. He lifted Daniel's torso, while his father held the son's legs and they succeeded in placing Daniel partially in the automobile's rear seat of a car driven by Daniel's mother . . ."

I was reliving it all. So was Dan, I guess, and his parents. I don't know what was going through their heads in detail, though I imagine their details were different from mine and different from what the judge was saying. Not that what the judge was saying wasn't true. It's just that when you're a defendant in a trial you begin to get new ideas on what truth is.

As soon as Dan and Mr. Voll hit the deck I was out of the car and running, bouncing off bumpers and fenders, trying to keep my balance on the ice, intent on putting Dan out of commission fast and slamming him into the car. He was kicking and screaming and a crowd was beginning to gather. I pounced on top of him and got my arms locked around his shoulders. Mr. Voll got his legs and we tried to lift him. But we kept slipping, and then some guy was climbing all over my back yelling, "Let that boy go, let him go, damn it!" I gave him a hell of a kick in the shin, heard him shriek and felt him fall away off of me. In the meantime Mrs. Voll had—as I'd feared all along—lost her head. Instead of bringing the car up to where we were wrestling with Dan to make things easier for us, she slid out from behind the steering wheel and began to shout to the bystanders that she was the boy's mother, and we were trying to give him psychiatric help and the whole useless bit. By that time I had a woman hacking at me with an umbrella, and someone else was beating on Mr. Voll. Dan was fighting and wriggling like a wildcat and people were pouring out of the apartment buildings.

In spite of all that, in spite of having to carry him through between the first row of parked cars along the curb, and then down several yards to our car where Mrs. Voll was still trying to give the family history to half of New York City, in spite of people beating on us and pulling and tugging and shoving—we still finally got him to the car. Around then Mr. Voll more or less collasped. "I can't move!" he gasped. We were all in a tangle, half in and half out of the car, but there was enough of us inside so that we could get moving. "Let's go, damn it!" I yelled at Mrs. Voll who was at last back where she belonged— behind the wheel. "Move on out!"

"But the door's still open," she squealed.

"Damn the door, lady, get this car rolling!" Well, she went creeping off about two miles an hour with people streaming along in our wake as I succeeded in hauling the rest of Dan into the back seat.

One block later—bam!—it was Wes Lockwood and the Pennsylvania Turnpike scene all over again. Cop cars everywhere. Sirens. Red lights. Guns pointed at our heads. Spread-eagling against the car, being frisked for weapons. A friend later asked me how the police had arrived so quickly. Hell, the snatch had taken so long they'd had time to come from Boston!

The judge sat back in his chair and shuffled his papers. I studied the jurors, looking for a clue to their thinking. We had a couple of blacks and one fellow who was a writer. I didn't see how they could convict me, but you can never be sure in these matters. Once during the trial I noticed the writer dozing off during important testimony. Maybe he'd already made up his mind? Little things you look for, and place significance on. A friendly glance from one of the women. A smile. The raising of an eyebrow. It's a little like handicapping a horse race, studying the jury during a trial.

I'd been lucky to get the attorney I had. Patrick Wall. A young, good-looking, very quick, terrifically hardworking, brilliant man. I'd retained him in the spring, after having been interviewed at Yale by a law professor there named Steven Duke. He was fascinated by my story, and said that if he had a license to practice in New York he'd take the case for free. Which was what I needed: a lawyer who would work for nothing since I had no money. Professor Duke telephoned Wall and arranged for an appointment with him.

I remember walking in to Wall's office and saying, "Mr. Wall, I'm probably the worst client who ever walked through your door. I'm in trouble, and I don't have any money."

When I was finished with my story, he shook his head and remarked, "Well, I'll say this, Mr. Patrick—you're certainly one of the most interesting people who ever walked through that door."

"This case might well be rather simple and straightforward," Judge Wright continued his lengthy instructions to the jury, all of whom, I was relieved to note, were alert and interested. "Except that the defendant has urged, through his witness, Eugene Voll, the father of the complainant, that whatever was done was done under his parental leadership; that the defendant acted only as an agent of the parents of Daniel; that they, as parents, were justified in what they did; and that if they, as principals, committed no crime, then their agent committed none.

"The theory of justification for conduct which would otherwise be criminal, is found in Number 35.05 of the Penal Law. So far as relevant here, it says as follows:

> Unless inconsistent with the ensuing provisions of this article defining justifiable use of physical force, or with some other provision of law, conduct which would otherwise constitute a defense is justifiable and not criminal when:
>
> Such conduct is necessary as an emergency measure to avoid an imminent private injury which is about to occur by reason of a situation occasioned or developed through no fault of the actor and which is of such gravity that, according to ordinary standards of intelligence and morality, the desirability and urgency of avoiding such injury clearly outweigh the desirability of avoiding the injury sought to be prevented by the statute defining the offense in issue.

"In other words, if you find that the defendant believed Daniel Voll was threatened by his membership and indoctrination in the dogmatics of the New Testament Missionary Fellowship, and if you find that his parents and the defendant were justified in their belief that such indoctrination and domination by the Fellowship elders was of a greater injury to Daniel than the conduct of the defendant and Daniel's parents, in taking Daniel from the public streets and attempting to have him deprogrammed by the defendant, then you may excuse the conduct of the defendant as it has been described to you."

I was thinking throughout this, that even if I won, I'd suffered a financial beating that would take a long time to recover from. Legal fees aside, I'd spent a fortune commuting back and forth between California and New York during all the postponements and continuances of the trial in the spring and summer. The trial itself had kept me in New York for more than three weeks, living in hotels. Obviously at that time I wasn't doing any deprogramming. My family was hurting, we couldn't keep up the payments on the house, Ruth hardly had any money to buy food and clothing. My savior in this crunch was Wes Lockwood's father, who called me one night to ask how I was doing keeping my family together, and when I told him, he promptly wrote a check and sent it to my wife. That was the only thing that pulled us through. We wouldn't have made it otherwise, and I'll never forget Mr. Lockwood's generosity.

Anyway, I consoled myself with the thought that if I'd taken a beating, Hannah Lowe and her gang had taken a worse beating, as the judge was making pretty clear. Whatever the verdict of the jury, we'd succeeded in ripping the cover off the Fellowship and exposing their activities.

"You may consider," the judge was saying, "the state of mind induced in the parents of Daniel when they learned that he had dropped psychology because its teachings were, as he said, contrary to the Scriptures, or, as Gordan Wallace said, because the subject involved teachings of the Devil.

"You must consider, also, the effect, as the evidence reveals it, on the parents when they learned that Daniel had decided to drop out of Yale, after such a promising beginning.

"You may also consider the effect upon the minds of the

Volls when they learned that their son was cleaning the apartment of McCandlish Phillips.

"Consider, as well, that Sloan Coffin, Yale Chaplain, had told them that Hannah Lowe was a dangerous woman and that he, Dr. Coffin, was very concerned about what was happening to Fellowship Members at Yale."

Pat Wall had burned them. One damaging revelation after another came out through his cross-examinations. Dan Voll, for example, admitting that he had taped phone conversations with his parents without their knowledge or consent. Bringing out that when he worked in a bookstore, Dan had hidden books that he thought were injurious to the customers' morals (an action he was forced to admit on the stand did not show great wisdom), and getting fired as a result. His destroying his record collection so that it wouldn't contaminate his younger brothers and sisters. His writing letters to one of his sisters trying to turn her against their parents. Forcing him into a ridiculous and embarrassing attempt to define "speaking in tongues."

It was so bad that although the prosecution had announced at the beginning of the trial that McCandlish Phillips and Calvin Burrows would both testify, in the end neither one went through with it. Wall would have turned them every way but loose. As for Hannah Lowe, she'd made herself real scarce; she took off for Bogotá and hasn't been seen since. She is still living in Colombia, on an estate she purchased for two-hundred-fifty thousand dollars.

What Pat Wall managed to do, as the prosecution complained at one point, was to put the cult on trial instead of me. Hannah Lowe's name must have been mentioned a hundred times for every time mine was.

The prosecution gave it all they had, but the young D.A.— a fellow named Ortiz, trying his first big case—knew what he was up against from the start. He was quoted in the papers as saying that everyone in his office was teasing him about drawing "a loser" the first time out. I liked him, though; he was a fighter and he worked hard. But when your clients are snakes, cross-examination is going to make them spit. And it's hard to develop credible character witnesses.

One witness Ortiz had called was the President of Columbia University, Dr. William J. McGill. The jury had heard him testify, and the judge was saying now, "that he [McGill] had had about twelve conversations with Daniel Voll and knew something about Columbia students involved with the Fellowship. He expressed the view that the members were a fine group of young people. He had never attended any services of the Fellowship. He said, however, that as a matter of religious liberty, he would not use force to remove his own child from a group such as the Fellowship, assuming that one of his children joined such a group."

I'm sure McGill was honest and sincere. I think he was also extremely naive. I don't know of very many college presidents who spend a great deal of their time immersing themselves in the activities of radical groups on their campuses. They are fund-raisers, mostly—figureheads at the top of large and complicated bureaucracies. If you'd never been to snake-worshiping services, I imagine that casual conversations on the street might convince you that certain snake worshipers were "fine" people. Unfortunately, my experience is that more than a few college presidents across the land would, as a matter of religious liberty, refuse to employ force to remove their own children from a group of snake worshipers practicing on their campuses. Or at least that's what they would testify in a well-publicized trial.

Ortiz also produced the Reverend Dean Kelley who is the religious-liberty director of the National Council of Churches. He came on as an expert in what he called "high demand" religions. In his charge, Judge Wright reviewed Kelley's testimony, in which he said that he was aware "of the peculiar, bizarre, and dangerous activities which are said to be practiced by persons expressing their high-demand religious zeal.

"Conceding that he had made but one visit to a New Testament Missionary Fellowship service, he spoke of high-demand practices in terms of their deviation from what has come to be known as the orthodox religious rituals of established churches.

"Reverend Kelley told us that he believes that it is a blunt offense against religious liberty to use force in seeking to remove a young person from a group such as the Fellowship, even if done by parents of one of its young members.

"He concluded by declining to answer the hypothetical question of whether he would forcefully intervene to rescue his own daughter from membership in a religious cult which believed in handling deadly poisonous snakes, by way of demonstrating faith."

It seems so clear to me. I don't understand how there can be an argument. Here was a man prominent in the National Council of Churches saying that though he was aware of bizarre and dangerous practices in "high demand" religious groups, he would not interfere with them. Dangerous means dangerous. I wonder if all the orthodox church groups feel so insecure themselves that they can't afford the risk of cracking down on the maniacs and child molesters. Or are we to continue to tolerate a law that gives equal protection to dangerous as well as to nondangerous groups? Is "dangerous" really that difficult to define?

Quite often, I've discovered over the years, legal sense and common sense are far apart. The nice thing about our jury system is that most of the time a jury will vote for common sense and reject complicated and incomprehensible legalisms. I was hoping that would happen that day. Judge Wright is nothing if not the spirit of common sense. The witnesses we had produced had to appeal to any fair-minded man or woman's common sense. The revelations about Hannah Lowe's cult were deep insults to common sense. To call what went on inside that group "religion" was pure nonsense. If it wasn't, I think everyone understood, the principals would not have been so leery of taking the stand.

"Throughout the testimony here," Judge Wright went on, reading from the pages laid out on the desk in front of him, glancing up frequently to look at the jury or direct his gaze out at the spectators, "you have heard Hannah Lowe, Calvin Burrows, McCandlish Phillips, and Frank Boushold characterized as Elders or leaders of the New Testament Missionary Fellowship.

"None of these persons was called as a witness for either side.

"While no presumption arises from the failure to call a witness under the control of a party, and while you cannot presume that the testimony of that witness would be unfavorable to the party failing to call him, nevertheless the failure to call a witness under the control of a party, whose testimony might reasonably be expected to shed light on the transaction may be taken into consideration, in evaluating the weight to be given to the testimony already in the case; that is to say, the failure to call a witness may justify giving greater weight to the testimony already in the case."

Readers of a book have greater leeway in making judgments than jurors in a trial. And I'd like to ask the reader to consider why Hannah Lowe and the others did not testify. All they had to do was convince the jury that Dan Voll was not being harmed and that his parents had no reason to believe he might be harmed. If nothing harmful was going on in that group, why didn't they come forward and bring out the facts favorable to their side? There's one perfect explanation: They couldn't. They knew Wall would murder them if they took the stand, and Ortiz knew it too.

The judge spent some time defining whether or not Dan could be considered a minor and concluded that he could, and then ended his charge to the jury with the words:

"I further charge you that the People's testimony, taken together with that of Daniel Voll's father, if believed by you, spells out an unlawful restraint of Daniel Voll's person and was an unlawful imprisonment of Daniel Voll, and you are entitled to convict the defendant for his role in that unlawful imprisonment, unless, as has been stated, you believe that the conduct of the defendant, taken together with that of Mr. and Mrs. Eugene Voll, and the age of Daniel Voll at the time, was justified and thus excuses the conduct.

"Your verdict must be unanimous, as noted, and it must be either Guilty, or Not Guilty."

With that everybody got up and left. I remained in the courtroom, telling myself to be confident, to be optimistic, assuring myself over and over that there was no way they could convict me. On the other hand, people do strange things under pressure, and juries often develop a logic all their own. I'd been in jail once, and I didn't relish the idea of going back a second time.

I thought about that night I'd spent in the Tombs, in New York City, last winter, also in connection with this damned Hannah Lowe.

There was a whole family that got caught up in the New Testament Missionary Fellowship—a mother and her two daughters and the husband of one of the daughters. The husband's name was Robert DiQuatro. Robert had joined only after his wife's mother had sucked her daughter into the bunch. He somehow managed to keep his sanity through it all and remain what you might call a fellow traveler. Even at that his head was messed up pretty good, and after more than a year he left. Although he and his wife Esther were married while they were together in the cult, Hannah Lowe, he said, forbade them to have sex with each other, calling it filthy and disgusting and of the Devil. According to Robert, in spite of the fact that he had never really bought their program, it was months before he could think straight again.

The younger sister, Charlotte, also came out—of her own accord—after five years (this sometimes happens), but not having anyone to formally deprogram her, it was almost a year before she'd recovered from her psychological fear. During that time she lived with her two brothers and they said that they couldn't leave her alone for a minute, night or day. She was terrified of demons and "Divine wrath," had nightmares, a nervous breakdown, and contemplated suicide several times.

Anyway, in May, two months before my trial for the Dan Voll episode, Robert DiQuatro persuaded me to help get back his wife Esther. I was dead set against it, mainly because I had this legal mess pending, I was overworked, exhausted, and hadn't seen my family in weeks. In fact I was at LaGuardia airport, standing in line to have my bags checked, with my ticket in my hand for a flight to San Diego, when I heard my name being paged.

It was DiQuatro on the telephone, begging me to help get his wife. We'd talked about it several times since I had first met him at my arraignment in April, and he knew what I required.

"I've got two cars, I've got five people to help. We have to do it tomorrow, Ted. Please."

"Robert, look," I said. "I've already told my wife I'm on my way home. I'm beat. We'll do it when I come back, in a couple of weeks."

Then he began to cry. Well, hell it's not easy for me to say no to someone in any case, but when a thirty-year-old man begins to cry I'm sunk.

"Okay, Robert, okay," I sighed. "Come pick me up at the airport. I'll help you."

We grabbed Esther the next morning. It was a replay of the Dan Voll situation—she lived in the same house as Dan—only this time the weather was lovely and the operation went off without a hitch. We had her into the car in fifteen seconds and were gone. Hardly caused a ripple on the surface of the pond. As a matter of fact we came close to snatching Dan Voll again that morning. I mean, we could have had him along with Margaret and Elizabeth Rogow, whose father was helping us snatch Esther. I would have loved to do it, would have loved to see the D.A.'s face as Dan told him he was dropping all charges and calling a press conference to denounce Hannah Lowe. The things dreams are made of! Before we nabbed Esther, they were standing on a street corner like clay pigeons. But just as we were about to pounce, a police car pulled up next to us and we had to drop the idea.

Anyway, we drove to Bristol, Pennsylvania, to the home of DiQuatro's parents where we stopped for something to eat. I'm always nervous about going to the family home because it's the first place the police check out. Sure enough, inside of a few hours we got a tip that the police would soon be arriving and to get the hell out of there.

Well, before we could get out of the DiQuatro house and go somewhere else, the Bristol police arrived in force and, to make a long story short, Robert, Rogow, myself, Robert's brother, and Esther's sister ended up in the local cooler for the night. That wasn't pleasant, especially when I thought about the fact that by all rights I should have been home in San Diego by then, but it was a small-town jail and the cops were friendly so it wasn't too bad.

The next morning, though, when the detectives from New York came on the scene to take us back to the city, the nightmare began. First we were taken to the courthouse where we signed an extradition waiver. Then we drove back to New York and got to the Twenty-fourth Precinct station house around three in the afternoon. Because of my involvement with the Voll case, and because the New York *Times* had been working with me on a long story about deprogramming I was doing in Connecticut, my arrest was big news, and there were about twenty-five or thirty reporters and photographers and TV cameramen waiting for us when we arrived.

The police took us upstairs where we were booked, fingerprinted, had mug shots taken. Then I had to fill out a million papers and questionnaires. They made an inventory of all the things in my bags, which took a long time. Then we went downstairs and the police apologetically slipped the handcuffs on us so the press could photograph us as we were formally booked. The handcuffs were on for about five minutes all told; the detectives who picked us up in Bristol didn't bother with them. "This ain't no criminal case anyway," one of them said. "Whole thing ought to be in a family court."

The police there in the Twenty-fourth were exceptionally helpful and friendly. Their feeling was that we wouldn't have to spend even one night in jail—that the judge would let us all go once we'd appeared. But there was such a ton of paper work to be done that a lot of red-tape-cutting was needed to process us through. Those guys worked overtime to try to speed things along.

Even so, we didn't get to the courtroom downtown until round eleven that night. Pat Wall was there to meet me, and we talked briefly. He was not too happy about the complications in the Voll trial this caper might create. At least Dan Voll had been a minor; Esther DiQuatro was thirty-one.

More processing and interviews and paper work had to be finished before we went to see the judge. It should have been pure formality, but the D.A. dropped a bombshell. Mr. Rogow and the DiQuatros lived in New York, he said, and they'd never been in any trouble, so he recommended freeing them on their own recognizance. However, he said, since I had the Voll trial pending and lived in California, he was asking for a twenty-five-thousand-dollar cash bail.

The judge was a reasonable man. He didn't really believe the state had a case against me, and told the D.A. to take the matter to a Grand Jury to see if they would indict. Nevertheless, he did set bail for me at five thousand dollars. Since I could as soon spin gold out of cotton as lay my hands on that kind of money, I was taken to the Tombs down on Centre Street while Rogow and the DiQuatros went home to their beds.

At moments like that I don't get awfully discouraged and I rarely have second thoughts about what I'm doing, but I certainly do give in to great waves of disgust. It was yet another example of my trying to help someone out against my better judgment and winding up holding the bag.

The Tombs was without question the nastiest, filthiest place I'd ever seen in my life. It made that pig sty of the Children of God in Santee look like the Hotel Americana by comparison. David Berg could have learned something from it about refining his techniques for breaking a person's spirits down in short order.

They put me into a cell with four or five drunks. One was a drug addict. Another was in there for rape. One guy was urinating in his pants, lying on the floor, his head against the wall, in a puddle. Another guy was vomiting. People were screaming and howling up and down the corridor. The stink and the noise was unbelievable. There was constant traffic up and down as they brought people in, the social workers looking about as dirty and disreputable as the inmates.

After a while I had to stand in a line to be interviewed by a social worker, and afterwards we were instructed to turn in all our personal property. Then I was taken to another room with about twenty other guys for a medical examination, then stripped naked, and made to take a cold shower. The floor was dripping wet and there was no place to lay our clothes except in the puddles.

After the shower, us still naked, with police, lawyers, and women social workers strolling around, the doctor came and made us lie down on a table. He examined my rectum, administered a blood test, and listened to my heart.

Then another line, more doctors. "Have you ever been in a hospital? Do you suffer from incurable disease? Have you ever had V.D.? Do you have V.D. now?"

Another line, where they finally issued us clothes. Mine were four or five sizes too large. I had to roll up the cuffs several times to be able to walk. And yet another line where they issued us a sheet and a blanket and a toothbrush and a tube of toothpaste.

All of this happening amidst the worst filth and stink and confusion imaginable. It was like some slaughterhouse in Kansas City, or a stockyard. The smell was about the same, and the noise. The Tombs was certainly an inspired name for that place. You feel entombed, and you tend to get panicky, wondering even if someone signs an order for your release how are they ever going to find you?

At six o'clock in the morning they took me to a cell on the ninth floor. A narrow bed with a mattress about half an inch thick you could feel the springs through. A toilet by the head of the bed, wash basin directly above the toilet, everything out in the open. I was on the third tier of cages (that's all they are, iron cattle pens) surrounded on all sides, above and below, by every description of broken-down, screaming, bawling derelict.

Then, to add insult to injury, they assigned me to the wrong floor. For some unknown reason, I was in the drug addicts' section, and didn't know it. I saw male nurses in dirty white uniforms bringing pills to guys, and one of them asked me if I wanted some methadone. I said no. All I wanted was some sleep. I'd had about four hours sleep in the last three days. But sleep was out of the question. Men were constantly being let in and out of their cells for examinations, to talk to their lawyers, to stand in long lines to make phone calls, and the crashing and clanking of the cell doors as they slid open and closed was enough to shake the fillings loose in your teeth.

From time to time a guard would yell something out, and all the cells in our block would slide open like elevator doors. They were letting us out for exercise, but I didn't realize that, and the doors would slam closed again before I could figure out what was going on. I missed breakfast that way; once the doors opened you had to jump or get caught in your cell.

After lunch, I succumbed to something like despair. There was no way in hell I could raise the bail. God knew how long I'd have to stay there. As I sat on my cot cursing Hannah Lowe, another nurse came in and offered me methadone again.

"What the hell is this about methadone?" I said. "I don't even take aspirin."

"You mean you're not an addict?"

"Addict? Hell no, I'm in for kidnapping."

"Kidnapping! Then what you doing on this floor?"

"You tell me, brother."

"You ain't supposed to be here. No kidnappers on this floor."

"Well then take me to the floor where they keep the kidnappers," I said.

"Been a mistake," he mumbled.

"You're telling me."

"I'll see what I can do."

When my neighbors heard I was a kidnapper they wanted to know all about it.

"Shit, man," one of them said. "You don't look like no kidnapper. You look like a damn preacher!"

"Maybe he's a plant," someone else suggested. "A cop."

"You a cop we gonna bust your ass, nigger."

I tried to explain. I wasn't very successful. How do you explain about brainwashing and mind control to a gang of wild men like that having drug fits and banging their heads against the walls?

Fortunately, in a few minutes, a guard came along and said, "Okay, Patrick, come along."

I assumed they were transferring me to another floor. But the guard said, "Your bail has been paid. You're free to go."

I was dumbfounded. "Who paid it?"

"Don't know. But it's paid."

Maybe another mistake, I thought. But if it was a mistake I wasn't going to hang around jiving about it while somebody corrected it. I didn't ask any more questions. I moved. It took them sixteen hours to get me into those Tombs, and less than an hour to get me out. (Several days passed before I learned that John Moody, an old friend and a supporter of mine from the beginning of the fight back in California, had been responsible for springing me—another kind of debt I can never repay.) When I stepped into the sunshine, in my own clothes, a free man, I felt like I was reborn. I just stood there sucking in the traffic fumes like it was the purest sweetest perfume.

Sitting now, two months later, in Judge Wright's courtroom waiting for the jury to decide my fate, I realized that there was a possibility, however small, that I would be going back to jail. If I were rich, of course, I probably wouldn't be here at all, I thought, let alone facing the chance of a jail sentence. But if I had stood trial and was rich, with all the appeals processes, there was still virtually no chance I'd see the inside of a jail. But Pat Wall, wonderful as he was, obviously was not going to spend the rest of his life representing me for nothing. Appeals cost money. And I didn't have any.

Then the jury returned. They'd been out about an hour and a half. A good sign, I'd been led to believe. And as they took their places, the writer sort of glanced at me in a very friendly way that made my heart leap.

Judge Wright arranged himself at his bench and asked for the verdict. I held my breath.

"Not guilty!"

I had a speech impediment as a child and still have trouble with words, so maybe I appreciate the way language is used more than other people. I admire people who can write books and poetry. The English language is a beautiful thing to me. But I can honestly say, I don't believe I ever heard anything prettier than those two words in my life—*not guilty!*

It was over. I'd won. Pat Wall was shaking my hands, and I was laughing and shaking hands with the jurors as they left. Dan Voll still had that same strange, sad smile painted on his face. His mother was crying. "Now maybe people will understand," she was telling reporters.

Outside, the writer on the jury, whose name was Tuttle, said that the jury agreed everyone had freedom of religion but that they also believed the parents were justified in what they did. Which came close to meaning, as far as I could see, that they'd decided Hannah Lowe's operation was not religious in nature. "Spiritual fascists," Tuttle called them.

I felt awfully good. I thought we finally had a legal precedent to support our work. And I also thought we'd delivered a rabbit punch to the cult movement in general. They all had to sit up and take notice—they weren't immune to legal attacks anymore.

"I haven't been on trial," I told the reporters outside. "The whole movement has been on trial. This is a victory for the whole world!"

CHAPTER SIX

Patrick's reputation—or notoriety—began to assume national proportions. The Lockwood case received extensive media coverage in January of 1973, and then so did the fiasco on 119th Street shortly after. The New York *Times* did a long piece on him in March. There was the Crampton affair, then the DiQuatro abduction. The Voll trial was a topic of conversation around the country, and the CBS documentary followed in August.

Although it hardly seemed possible, Patrick's tempo increased that summer. The dialogue he had been seeking for so long was at last taking shape. The Children of God were under investigation in New York. Hannah Lowe had removed herself to Bogotá, Colombia. David Berg had fled to Europe. The dimensions of the cult movement were encroaching on the public's consciousness. Controversy attended Patrick everywhere. The ACLU issued streams of denunciations. *New York* magazine ran a major piece by Marc Kaufman entitled "Saving Your Children from Salvation." The weekly news magazines kept sniping at him. And requests from parents seeking his help were intensified.

Patrick crisscrossed the country, deprogramming, making snatches, appearing on TV, granting interviews, catching planes, and deprogramming some more. In Detroit for a television appearance, he was at the studio at ten in the evening, taping at eleven, out of the studio at twelve-thirty, and at 1:00 A.M. negotiating in a dingy bar with four black thugs, offering them fifty dollars each to help snatch a girl off the streets at seven in the morning. At two, the deal concluded, he was back in his hotel, on the phone to San Diego, on the phone to Tampa, on the phone to Toronto. At four he was asleep, and awake at six, packing his bags, checking his plans and at seven, along with his mercenaries hired the night before, swooping down on a girl belonging to a little-known cult called The Body of Christ, throwing her into a car, speeding off to a hideaway, flinging himself into the deprogramming.

Two nights in Detroit and an early morning flight to Philadelphia to deprogram a girl from the Divine Light Mission of Guru Maharaj Ji. Six hours later, the girl successfully deprogrammed, he was in a car racing to Pittsburgh to deprogram a boy from the Children of God. One day there, and then down to Tampa. Thirty-six hours in Tampa and then on another plane to Toronto, where, taking a break from a Krishna case,

he did a radio talk-show, then resumed and finished the deprogramming of a young devotee of Krishna, caught three hours
sleep, and headed for Washington to deprogram a follower of
Sun Myung Moon.

What kind of people get caught up in all these cults? Who
is it that Patrick is rescuing? They are white, almost exclusively,
and a large majority are Roman Catholics and Jews. Middle
to upper-middle class. Some of them have family problems,
others don't. Some are psychotic; most are not. A number of
them were intensely religious before joining a particular cult;
an equal number had no interest in religion whatever.

How then are they ensnared? To many people Patrick's
theory of on-the-spot hypnosis is not convincing. The counter-
theory that is, perhaps, the most plausible argues that what
renders all these young people susceptible to the cults' influ-
ences is their relative degree of innocence, naivete, and ignorance. The children Patrick deals with are the products, in
their affluent suburbs, of a world in which there is, in effect,
no crime, no poverty, no hunger, no disease, in which they do
not fear anything, do not want for anything, and do not truly
have to work to obtain anything. Consequently, they are easy
prey for religious shysters who seek to exploit them.

None are exploited more than the devotees of Krishna
Consciousness. In the course of the last several years millions
of Americans have paused on the street corners of big cities
to view the antics of Hare Krishna delegations—beating drums,
shaking rattles, and tambourines, chanting "Hare, Hare, Hare,"
dressed in saffron colored robes, their heads peeled, beads
around their necks, looking vaguely Mongoloid with their un-
focused grins and outlandish dancing—instinctively recoiling
from the sight, offended, perhaps even a little frightened at the
same time they were amused and contemptuous, as one is when
one awakens from a grotesque dream.

Most people tend to dismiss the Hare Krishnas finally as
harmless eccentrics. Recent evidence suggests that may be a
serious mistake.

His Divine Grace A.C. Bhaktivedanta Swami Prabhupada, the founder and leader of the International Society for Krishna Consciousness, is an eighty-year-old religious entrepreneur from Bengal who came to the United States from India in 1965, attached a handful of young drug addicts and various other specimens of society's flotsam and jetsam to his sacred person and quickly established himself at the center of an international cult of personality whose dimensions are astonishing.

The Krishnas preach a life of severe asceticism. They practice a rigorous program of self-denial, abstaining from meat, drugs, alcohol and sex (those married couples in the cult are permitted to have intercourse only once a month, when the woman is ovulating). They take cold showers several times a day "to ward off lust." They meditate for hours at a time, chanting and fingering prayer beads.

And they fund-raise. Their list of books on matters pertaining to Krishna Consciousness constitutes one of the world's most lucrative publishing enterprises. They own the largest and most remunerative incense factory in the country. His Divine Grace is a multimillionaire.

More imposing even than their financial assets is their school in Dallas, Texas, to which adherents from all over the world send their children. It is called the Gurukula, and all the students are small children, under the age of ten. None of these children is protected by state law. The Gurukula is a private school, therefore none of the teachers has to be (or is) qualified by Texas educational standards.

At the Gurukula, the children rise at four in the morning—having slept on the floor—and chant Krishna mantras for two hours. Then they have breakfast and go to classes. According to Mike Wright, an ex-marine who runs the place and who goes now by the name of Dayanada das Adhikari, "We do not teach any science and very little history or geography—they are unnecessary complications in a child's life. They are allowed to read only our religious books—no fairy tales or nursery stories are permitted, and no television. The youngsters see their parents only once a year. This separation is how we show them that they can still love someone deeply even without physical touch—the parents and children are drawn together spiritually."

The children remain in Dallas until they are ten, when they are moved to the Hare Krishna commune in West Virginia to complete their "education." At fifteen, they go out into the streets proselytizing and fund-raising.

Krishna Consciousness is an international movement, but the basic operations of the various local chapters are the same. The focus is always on fund-raising. In September 1974, *Atlas World Press Review* ran an adaptation of an article from the German magazine *Stern* in which a reporter, Conrad Zanders, a Swiss, told about his experiences when he infiltrated a temple in Frankfurt. The average earnings of the devotees in that temple, he claims, total $228 a day per man, except in the summer when, working the beaches, the average goes up, at least in Hamburg, to $380. That's per day, per man. In Zanders' temple, there were twenty men. Forty-five hundred dollars a day.

"These begging achievements," he says, "are the fruit of hard preparation. Each Sunday the devotees of all the German temples gather at Castle Rettershof for a two-and-a-half hour training seminar. The themes: selling strategy, market research, and ritual. There are long practice sessions in how to get the uninitiated (*karmis*) to part with their money."

When Zanders asks one of his partners about the ethics of lying to people on the street about where the money is going, he is told, "It is written in the holy scripture that we can deceive the uninitiated when we do it for Krishna. He who has the transcendental conviction stands beyond good and evil."

When his Divine Grace arrived by jet for a visit in Frankfurt, says Zanders, "I was one of more than seventy German '*prabhus*' who took part in the welcoming. Lying flat on our bellies in the dust, we washed his lotus feet with rosewater, fanned him with a peacock whisk, and offered him superb marzipan. When a pandemonium of drums, cymbals, and horns broke loose, we danced and cried *Hare Krishna!* His Holiness smiled benevolently. 'Such a beautiful army.' "

Zanders began to worry about his own sanity and shortly escaped. A boy from Munich also fled. He concluded the article by saying that, "The chances of his [the Munich boy's] returning to a normal life are minimal after a few weeks of Krishna indoctrination. I asked *Prabhu* August, a former Capuchin devotee, 'Did anyone ever get away from here?'

" 'Not more than half a dozen.'

" 'And what happened to them?'

" 'After a few week of trying to make it on the outside they all wound up in the loony bin.' "

As Ted Patrick's fame spread, he began to receive requests from parents who had children in the Krishna cult. The testimony of the young men and women he eventually deprogrammed was a carbon copy of Wes Lockwood's, of Pam Collins', of Vickie Sinunu's, and that of dozens and dozens of people from dozens of other cults.

"It was a complete mental breakdown," a girl named Betty Stevens from Chicago confirmed. "The hypnosis was so strong that if I was told my parents were in the way of my religion I might have killed them. We ate almost nothing, and getting only four hours of sleep a night, we were kept constantly weak and fatigued. We were never allowed to think for ourselves. My purpose was to sell books and get donations for Krishna. I'd sell books for eight hours and at times fell asleep on the street. The minimum per day I collected was one hundred dollars. Altogether, I probably collected between thirty and fifty thousand dollars."

A Cincinnati boy, Jim Dew, said he wouldn't want to go through his Hare Krishna experiences again. "At first it seemed blissful, but I couldn't use my mind. I couldn't make a decision. In this program they take away your will to think. To advance yourself, you were supposed to chant the Hare Krishna mantra. You kept hypnotizing yourself by chanting. Ted made me think. Eventually I could see it was just for the money. And then the effects of it began to wear off. It's like coming out of a trance."

Patrick contends that the Krishnas are among the easiest of

the cult members to deprogram. "If you cut off their ponytails and take away their beads, they'll deprogram themselves in a couple of days." In about one hour he deprogrammed the son of the woman who is now his secretary. The boy had been in the cult for two and a half years.

One who gave him a lot of trouble, however, was Ed Shapiro, a twenty-year-old Brandeis University dropout from Boston.

TED PATRICK: Ed Shapiro was a diabetic, and the cult let him go to his father's house once a week for a treatment. Dr. Eli Shapiro is a prominent physician in Newton, Massachusetts, not far from the Boston temple. Lee Alan Roth, a friend of Shapiro's and also a member of the cult, was being taken out by his father, a New York dentist, for medical treatment. The two doctors wanted me to deprogram their sons at Shapiro's house.

As the result of some legal difficulties I encountered in Denver after the Dan Voll trial, I no longer was participating physically in snatching the victims, and I insisted that both boys would have to be in custody before I arrived in Newton or I wouldn't come. The two gentlemen promised that they would have their boys at Shapiro's house when I got there. They sounded like sober, responsible men and so I trusted them.

I was supposed to be in Newton late in the afternoon of August 5, 1974, but I was delayed for some hours by an unforeseen accident. I'd been in Delaware, deprogramming a boy from the Guru Maharaj Ji's Divine Light Mission—a kid named Rick. He proved easy to deprogram and he asked if he could come with me to Newton to assist in deprogramming Shapiro and Roth. He had an old van and said we could drive to Newton in about eight hours. We left early in the morning of the fifth but along the way we had a breakdown, and were delayed for several hours while the van was being repaired. We didn't arrive in Newton until rather late that night.

In the meantime, a team I'd put together had flown into Boston the previous night and were waiting at Shapiro's house.

I had deprogrammed a girl named Marcia Carroll a few weeks before in Ohio from the Divine Light Mission also, and, like Rick, she had asked to assist me for a while in my work. So I took her with me to Toronto where I had to deprogram another member of the Divine Light Mission, Maria McEvenue. I deprogrammed her in a couple of hours and then left Marcia and a big burly football player type, Ed Painter (who had got interested in what I was doing because his sister was in a cult) to supervise Maria's rehabilitation at the McEvenue's cottage on a lake outside of Toronto. Afterwards Maria also wanted to participate in deprogrammings, so when the Shapiro deal came up, I called them and told all three to meet me in Newton.

The Shapiros lived in a mansion—three floors—and when the Roth boy was brought in he was taken upstairs. He was very very sick, and with his shaven head and large staring eyes and his emaciated body he looked like he had just come out of a Nazi concentration camp. He was so sick he didn't put up any resistance. Just sat there passively staring, saying nothing. Marcia and Maria stayed with him and talked to him, holding the fort until I could get there.

Ed Shapiro was something else. Once he realized that he was being held (they put him downstairs—he never knew that Roth was in the house), he got violent. He practically ransacked the place, smashing lamps, overturning furniture, chanting, screaming, running amuck.

In addition to my team, about eighteen other people were present, relatives and friends of Eddie's. But no one could do a thing with him. His parents were on the verge of panic, wondering where I was, afraid that Ed would get away, that they would be unable to restrain him.

By the time we pulled into the driveway, six hours late, Ed had turned the house into a shambles and brought his parents to the verge of collapse.

"Thank God, thank God you're here!" Mrs. Shapiro gasped, hugging and kissing me. "He's acting like a wild man."

"Where is he?" I asked.

"Downstairs. Please, do something with him."

We hurried downstairs to the examining room where Dr. Shapiro conducted his practice, and there was Ed, a tall thin boy, his head shaven, still wearing his robes and his beads, chanting and screaming.

"Get me a pair of scissors," I said.

"Scissors? What for?"

"First thing we're going to do is cut that knot of hair off his head."

Ed came to attention. "What? Who are you? What right do you have to go cutting my hair? I have a right to wear this. It's part of my religion. I'm a legal adult. I'm twenty years old."

"Shut up and sit down," I told him. "Just shut your mouth and listen."

"I won't listen. I don't have to listen. I want to leave!"

"Well, you're not going to leave. Where's those scissors?"

Four of his relatives held him down and I cut off the tuft of hair they all wear on the back of their heads and I removed the beads from around his neck. As soon as we let him up, he started chanting again at the top of his voice, "Hare Krishna, Hare Krishna, Hare Hare, Hare . . ." Then he saw my tape recorder on a table, seized it, and smashed it to bits on the floor. Then he made a dash for the door, but was intercepted by the others in the adjoining game room.

In the game room Dr. Shapiro had a lot of lovely and expensive art objects and souvenirs he'd collected over the years and Ed began smashing them, one by one, just ripping the place apart, chanting all the while. I hadn't seen such violent energy since Wes Lockwood. I figured the treatment ought to be the same as it was for Wes, so I took him by the arms and flung him into a corner up against the wall, and I said, "All right, you hatchet-head son of a bitch, you move out of there and I'll knock your goddamned head off."

But he wriggled out of my grasp and ran across the room, screaming, "Get the hell out of this house! Don't touch me!"

At this, Ed Painter got furious and cocked his arm as if to lay Ed out cold. I managed to push him out of the way just in time. "Easy, Ed. Never mind. Just cool it."

Then I picked Ed up by the front of his robes and marched him backwards across the room, slamming him bodily against the wall. "You listen to me! You so much as wiggle your toes again, I'm gonna put my fist down your throat!" His eyes got bigger and bigger with fear. He sat down abruptly. I had a picture of Prabhupada and I tore it up in front of him and said, "There's the no good son of a bitch you worship. And you call him God!" The usual line of approach.

Inside of an hour, he was out of it. The Krishnas are easy. I think the reason they're easy is that they don't really study anything like some of the other sects do. They're simply into self-hypnosis. They are programmed to chanting and their beads and once you prevent them from doing that, it's a snap to make them see how they've been deceived.

With Ed, it was like he was waking up. His personality changed in an instant, and suddenly he was laughing and joking with his parents, relaxed, sensible, and friendly. He went upstairs and changed into a shirt and slacks, laughing at his transcendental underwear. This is a kind of loincloth that goes around the waist and then is looped under the genitals and pulled very tight. It's supposed to discourage sexual desire, and I could see how it would. "That was the one thing I could never really overcome," Ed confessed to me, grinning. "It was one of my biggest problems. I was thinking about sex all the time. Every time I'd begin to think about it, I'd chant until the desire went away. But it was hell."

Leaving Ed with his parents, who were preparing a meal for everyone, I went upstairs to talk to Lee Roth. I never saw a more pitiful sight than that boy. If he'd stayed in the cult another month I think he would have died. Because he was so weak and run down, he was no trouble. In fact the two girls had pretty much brought him out of it before I saw him.

We ate and then went to bed. That was around two in the morning. I'm not sure what happened next. The temple later claimed that Eddie had telephoned them and asked for help. Maybe so. He might have "floated" during the night and got to a phone. I'm inclined to believe that the Krishnas were lying, that they found out he was there some other way. They knew he was going to see his father, and when he failed to return, it would have been logical for them to figure that he was still in Newton.

In any event I was just crawling into bed when Ed Painter came bursting into my room.

"The house is surrounded by Krishnas!" he exclaimed. "They're all over the place!"

I leaped out of bed and pulled on my pants. "Where's Eddie?"

"He's flipping out, but Marcia and the others have hold of him."

"How many Krishnas?"

"About twenty, thirty."

As we ran down the stairs I could hear this weird halloo-ing from outside, in some Indian language, and I could hear Eddie halloo-ing back to them. "Hare Boh!" they would call. "Hare Boh!" It sent shivers up your spine. When we got to the living room, Eddie was chanting again, and struggling to get away. I heard knocking at the front door. I heard banging at the back door and downstairs. They were at the windows, tapping and chanting, trying to get in. They seemed to be everywhere.

Marcia and Maria were terrified. You'd be terrified too if everywhere you turned there were gleaming bald heads pressed against the windows leering at you, knocking, clattering at the glass, chanting. It was like some damned nightmare. "They're crazy!" Marcia was crying. "They're like the Mansons. They'll kill us!"

"If there's going to be any killing," I muttered, "we're the ones gonna be doing it."

I ran up to my room and got my straight razor. I could hear glass shattering in the basement. In the living room we found a couple of big thick sticks, somewhat bigger than pool cues.

"Come on, Ed," I called to Painter. "You and I can wipe out the whole bunch of them. Come on. We're going out there and break some skulls."

The women were hysterical, though, and tried to stop us from going out. By the time we struggled loose from them and jerked the front door open, the police were pulling up and jumping out of their cars. I ducked back inside, dropped the stick and got rid of the razor.

There were about fifteen cops, inside and outside. They ordered the Krishnas to leave the property and then tried to find out what was going on. The house, of course, was in an uproar, and the Shapiros were having a hard time explaining.

I was sitting in the kitchen when this black cop came in, took one look at me, and yelled. "Hey, I know this dude! We helped him a couple of months ago!"

A while back I'd snatched a girl from the Boston Children of God commune and this cop had been a party to it, turning his back, letting us get away. Now, he went to his lieutenant, took him aside, and told him who I was and what we were up to. About ten minutes later, the lieutenant sat down with me and said, "I don't understand this, Mr. Patrick. Is this kid mentally ill or what?"

"No, he's a victim of mind control," I replied. "He's been brainwashed by this cult and I'm here to deprogram him. I had him deprogrammed, but when all these lunatics got here he flipped back in. Let me have him till the morning and he'll be fine. There's another boy up on the third floor with his father." Throughout this turmoil, Lee Roth had no idea what was going on. I knew he was still okay. "Why don't you go up and talk to him and his father and see for yourself?"

The lieutenant sent another officer upstairs with me and he talked to Lee for a few minutes.

"You okay?" he asked.

"I'm fine," Lee said.

"You being held against your will?"

"Absolutely not."

"You want to go back to the temple?"

"No, I want to go home with my father. I'm glad to be out of the temple."

Downstairs, when the lieutenant heard this, he said to Eddie Shapiro, "All right, young man, why don't you stay here overnight? Tomorrow everything will be fine."

"You don't seem to understand," Eddie said, "that I'm being held here against my will."

The lieutenant raised his eyebrows, looked around with innocent surprise. "Held against your will? Really? Isn't this your house? Aren't these your parents? There's no way I can see that you can be held against your will in your own house by your own parents. Doesn't make any sense."

"Oh no? Then you tell me—do I have a choice to leave here if I want to?"

"Why don't you just stay overnight like a good boy."

"Do I have a choice or don't I?" Eddie pressed him.

The lieutenant paused, thought, stroked his chin, then said, "Well, as a matter of fact, no—you don't have a choice."

It's rare when you can't count on the police at a moment like that.

Once they were gone, and the house had settled down again, I told Dr. Shapiro that we had to get out of there. From past experience I knew that in the morning the Krishnas would obtain a writ of habeas corpus in an attempt to free the boys.

It was then three-thirty or so. I thought we could catch a few hours' sleep, and leave before seven. So we all went to bed, with Eddie under heavy guard.

At six-thirty, as we were packing, everybody pretty groggy and having trouble waking up, still somewhat shaken by the incidents of the night, two men came up the drive and knocked on the front door.

"They must have the warrant! said Mrs. Shapiro.

"Can't have," I said. "It's too early. Don't answer the door."

The men hung around for a few minutes and then left. I later learned they were ACLU lawyers. We finished packing in a hurry and drove to a hotel a few miles away, where we took four rooms.

Lee was still calm, but Eddie was in a rage. We worked on him for a couple of hours without much success, largely because there were too many people in the room with him. As I say, I like to work alone. It's a matter of bringing them step-by-step to a certain frame of mind, developing certain patterns of thought in them. If someone interrupts with a question or a comment, the victim's concentration is distracted and he goes backwards several steps and I have to start all over.

Aside from that, Eddie was pulling a Wes Lockwood on me again. He would get down between the bed and the wall, plug his ears with his fingers, and chant.

Eventually, I took a break and Maria McEvenue and I went to the dining room for lunch. Marcia Carroll and Ed Painter were staying with Eddie.

I was just finishing my meal when Marcia came running in, flushed and excited. "He's going to get away!" she cried. "He's escaping."

We sprang for the door and in the hallway almost collided with the manager who was also dashing for Eddie's room; one of the maids had called him, saying there was a fight going on.

What had happened was that Eddie had torn a metal towel rack off the wall in the bathroom and battered his way out of the room. He got as far as the exit leading to the parking lot, where coincidentally Rick was just returning from the van. The door there was a combination screen and glass affair and as Eddie flung it open, it smashed into Rick, who threw his arms up in self-defense, shattering the glass. Rick tackled him, and he and Ed Painter wrestled him back down the corridor and into his room.

The manager was upset and indignant, but he quieted down when Dr. Shapiro identified himself and promised to pay for all the damages. I told the man who I was and what we were doing, and he seemed understanding enough. I didn't think he would call the police.

Inside the room, Eddie was back between the wall and the bed, just like Wes. I ordered everyone out of the room, and pulled him out from beneath the bed. Since I'd already deprogrammed him the night before, once I had him one-on-one he was easy, and inside of a couple of hours he was out of it. But for good measure I had the girls work on him for the rest of the afternoon. I knew he was okay as soon as I saw him trying to get it on with Marcia. Then he asked for some wine, and the others came in, and they had the usual sort of high-spirited celebration that accompanies a kid's deprogramming.

I went to see Lee while the others were celebrating in Eddie's room, and talked to him for a while. All he wanted to do was go home and try to get well. He was a physical mess, and I told Dr. Roth that it would probably be best to have him visit a doctor as soon as possible. Since the evening papers and the television were filled with the story—and I knew that some reporters had already been inquiring about me at the desk—I'd made up my mind to vacate the place immediately, and so Dr. Roth said he'd take Lee home right away. I sent Marcia Carroll with them to supervise the rehabilitation, with the idea in mind that as soon as Lee was well enough to travel, they would go to her home in Cuyahoga Falls, Ohio, for a week or two.

Maria suggested that for Eddie's rehabilitation her parents' house on the lake near Toronto would be ideal. Eddie was enthusiastic about the promise of spending a couple of weeks swimming and boating and having a good time. Before we left, though, I asked Eddie if he would make a statement detailing all that had happened, giving an account of his frame of mind, attesting to the fact that he wasn't being held against his will, that he did not want to return to the Krishnas and so forth. He complied with this, and it was witnessed and notarized by the manager who happened to be a notary. The manager took some pictures of the group, and asked Eddie some questions, all of which I have on tape. Then we left.

On our way to Toronto, via Albany, Buffalo, and Niagara Falls, I had Dr. Shapiro telephone the Boston newspapers. Eddie talked to the reporters and repeated much of what he'd written in his notarized statement.

We didn't reach Toronto until Saturday. Back in Boston, on Friday, lawyers for the Krishnas were filing a suit against me and the parents, and a hearing was scheduled for the following Wednesday in the family court.

By the time I heard about this, I was in Canton, Ohio, on a deprogramming. While I was there, I was contacted by a woman in Cleveland who had a boy—Randy—in Krishna and who had learned about me from watching a television show I'd appeared on. Marcia Carroll was then back in Ohio with Lee Roth, and we all drove over to Cleveland and deprogrammed Randy Sacks in short order. He came out of it beautifully. It was Randy's mother who later became my secretary and right hand man.

While this was going on, Ed Shapiro was in Canada and had been introduced to a Professor McPherson, who taught at Guelph University outside of Toronto. Professor McPherson is, I suppose you might say, my Canadian counterpart. He has written extensively on the problem of mind control, and has deprogrammed several youngsters himself. He and Eddie hit it off well, and when they learned that Lee, Marcia, Randy, and I were going up to Montreal for a deprogramming, McPherson and Eddie asked to be in on it.

Because of bad planning on the parents' part, we never did get that boy in Montreal. Eddie, however, had himself a ball in the city. Eating, drinking, kicking up his heels, running after girls. It had been a long time without any sexual contact for him, and he was bent on making up for lost time.

Dr. Shapiro and his wife were vacationing somewhere in Canada, and returned to meet us in Toronto in time to fly to Boston for the court hearing.

I gave them careful instructions about what to do.

"Make sure that you call a news conference," I said. "Have Eddie talk to the reporters, answer all their questions. Have him tell exactly how he feels about the Krishnas now, what went on while he was inside and so forth. Let it all hang out. Once that goes on the air and in the papers, the Krishnas won't touch him again with a ten foot pole."

I like to have a deprogrammed person make a public statement like that whenever possible. It's not indispensable, and many of the kids prefer not to, and that's all right with me too. But when they do make a statement, the cult usually writes them off as traitors. They immediately issue denunciations of the boy, which, even if the boy should change his mind and want to go back, would be too embarrassing for the cult. So it's a form of insurance for the youngster.

In Boston, however, at the hearing, Dr. Shapiro's attorney had other ideas, and unfortunately Shapiro listened to him. The media was present in full force, but because it was a family court hearing the proceedings were closed to the public. Eddie got up and made a full and open disclosure of all that had happened, said that he was glad to be out and never wanted to go back. That was enough for the judge, who dismissed the case.

Then Eddie wanted to face the media. He and his father and the attorney argued heatedly about this. The attorney was dead set against Eddie's talking to the press. And his views finally won. Eddie was slipped out a back door, and they flew back to Canada, having missed a real opportunity to sew up the case tight.

He and his wife, confident that everything was all right with their son, went off on vacation to North Carolina. Eddie was staying with Professor McPherson, who took him over to the university, showed him around, introduced him to people. Apparently Ed was having a good time. He talked to reporters, addressed groups, made tapes.

A few days later, Dr. Shapiro called up and asked Ed to join him and Mrs. Shapiro in North Carolina. They sent a plane ticket, and Ed left.

He was alone for the first time since we'd snatched him. He flew to Washington, D.C. where he had a two hour layover before proceeding on to North Carolina. The Krishna people are like flies around Washington and Dulles airport is one of their favorite places to hustle. We don't really know what happened at Dulles except that some Krishnas recognized Eddie because of his still very short hair. There is speculation that he actually knew one of them. In any event, he changed his ticket, went with the Krishnas to their temple in Washington, and then flew to Boston, where he rejoined the cult.

It might sound ironic for me to say this, but I'm firmly convinced that he was bodily abducted. It would be less difficult, perhaps, for you to believe this if you'd been in the Shapiros' house in Newton that night as they were trying to break in. Still less difficult if you reflect that later, Ed made a statement that said, "The Krishna teachings offer three choices to devotees when they face blasphemy. The first is to leave the place, the second is to kill the person being blasphemous, and, if all else fails, the third is to kill yourself." And again, "Krishna teaches that violence is necessary when arguments fail."

If they didn't take Ed from Dulles bodily—if he went on his own free will—why did he fly to Washington at all? He was on his own, he had a negotiable plane ticket, he could have gone directly to Boston from Toronto.

The discrepancies in Eddie's story aimed at discrediting us are interesting too. He made it sound as though we were trying to keep him drunk and sated with sex all the time he was with us. But a week *before* he was returned to the Boston temple, assuming that they'd lost him for good and wishing to diminish the impact of the loss by discrediting Eddie, the leader of the temple said this about him: "He couldn't resist eating too much, and he was attracted to sex. It was hard for him to control his desires for sense gratification." Lee Roth was characterized as "a weak, timid person."

Another and final interesting note was struck by Eddie himself when he said, "This movement has a philosophy that he [me] can't defeat. His techniques may work on Jesus freaks and other groups because they're all nonsense anyway, but he can't deprogram us because we've already been deprogrammed by Krishna. Our eyes have been opened. Everyone in the world is hypnotized but us."

They all say that, the cults: all other cults are nonsense. And, as far as my being unable to deprogram Krishnas, in less than two weeks I deprogrammed Lee Roth, and Jim Dew, and Randy Sacks, and since then I've deprogrammed twenty or thirty more. And I also deprogrammed Eddie Shapiro, and he knows it, if he knows anything anymore.

But, you may say, what's all the fuss about? So what if a

few crazies want to shave their heads and act like fools? Every society has a certain small percentage of maniacs which any stable society can afford to tolerate. And so forth. I've heard that many times.

But Krishna is an *international* movement that is rich, powerful, and growing. It's militant and inflexible and very harsh. Some adherents believe they have divine sanction to kill when necessary. Charles Manson horrified an entire nation by his viciousness. There were only a handful of kids in that group. I believe that in Hare Krishna you have essentially another Charles Manson movement—except Krishna has many thousands of members. And gaining more every day.

As far as the numbers are concerned, numbers are a relative thing. The kidnapping of one Patty Hearst or Jimmy Hoffa electrifies the country. Hundreds, thousands of FBI agents are thrown into the case. Millions of dollars spent. SLA headquarters bombed and burned and people (black people) slain. With kidnapping, numbers are very relative.

Never mind Patty Hearst or Jimmy Hoffa or the heir to the Seagram's whiskey fortune. Imagine this instead: fourteen political kidnappings around the country each week. Just fourteen. But systematically, in a recognizable pattern. Can you see the headlines? TWO MORE KIDNAPS TODAY ON WEST COAST. KIDNAP WAVE STRIKES NEW YORK. MIAMI PREY TO KIDNAP CONSPIRACY. The Attorney General and the FBI would be turning somersaults.

Okay, what I want to say to you is that the Hare Krishna cult is kidnapping fourteen people *per day* in this country. Every day. And nobody says a word—except their parents, and nobody listens to them.

And if you persist in thinking that this is all harmless child's play, let me quote an Associated Press release of May 11, 1974:

The Hare Krishna Movement, an American derivative of Hinduism, has formed a political party aimed at achieving "God-conscious leadership."

A spokesman says that the In God We Trust Party For Purified Leaders will seek to "put God in the center of political affairs, and promote God-consciousness."

The spokesman, Stephen Royce, said the new party has named candidates for Congress in districts of New York, Pennsylvania and Georgia; for mayor of Washington D.C. and for city commissioner in Gainesville, Fla.

I don't know if they elected anybody yet. On the other hand, I don't believe Hitler got very many votes the first time around either.

CHAPTER SEVEN

Brother Julius is a fifty-one-year-old former engineer from Brooklyn, New York whose real name is Julius Schacknow. A Jew for the first twenty-two years of his life, he converted to Christianity when he was serving with the Navy on Guam in 1946. God appeared to him on that Pacific island, he later said, and informed him that it was his destiny to be a prophet. Julius took this message quite seriously and began to study the Bible obsessively. Out of the service and living with the second of his three wives, he spent every spare hour researching Sacred Scriptures. The second Mrs. Schacknow recalls, "Every night I would go down into his basement study and turn out the lights. His Bible would be across his chest and he would be asleep—always, always, always."

He worked at various jobs up and down the East Coast for twenty years, studying the Bible and getting into various sorts of trouble with women. By 1959, his wife feared for his sanity. He had told her of a complete mental breakdown he'd suffered in the Pacific, she says, and she was sure it was happening again. He refused to rest or seek psychiatric care, and the following year his wife left him.

A few years later he married for a third time and moved to

Dover, New Jersey because it was safe, according to him, from the earthquake he was predicting would devastate New York City. He had the Lord's word on this; it was supposed to strike in 1971. The day of doom has been updated several times since then. Today Julius lives in Meriden, Connecticut.

When he was living in Dover, he was already forming the nucleus of the cult he finally established in Meriden. He would get four or five couples to read the Bible with him with varying degrees of zeal and ecstasy, but then the group would collapse as soon as Julius began quoting Scriptures as justification for wife-swapping. Numerous complaints were filed against him with police departments around the East concerning alienation of affection. Uglier allegations also began to fasten onto him, but Julius denied them all.

In 1970 Julius reported that he had had a chat with God. God asked him if he had any questions he'd like answered. Julius claims that modesty almost prevented him from speaking out, but at last he pulled himself together and asked God:

"Am I Your Son, Jesus?"

"There never was another," God replied.

Told that her ex-husband was going around claiming to be Christ, Schacknow's second wife sighed and said, "I'm very sorry to hear that he's gone to that extreme."

Julius had felt that he was the reborn Christ all along, but it was good nevertheless to have this endorsement from on high.

Bursting with his freshly minted divinity, Julius rushed off to a regional convention of a fundamentalist church in Tennessee called the Church of God. By definition any Church of God was his, and he meant to have it, all 1,000 members strong. He got up before the flabbergasted assembly and preached a sermon in which he declared that he was Christ. To his dismay, nobody believed him. "I think he was very hurt," commented the head of the church afterwards.

Hurt but undaunted. The other Christ had started with twelve, after all. He would do the same. He headed for Connecticut, preaching, prophesying, and healing. Unfortunately, none of his prophecies ever came true. He prophesied the earthquake; it didn't happen. He told one of his followers that her child-bearing days were over; she got pregnant the following week. He advised another devotee that she would not perish until all the rest of his followers had been martyred in his name; in the course of the next year not one of his followers died (as a martyr or any other way) except the woman, who broke her neck in a kitchen accident. He predicted an outbreak of pneumonia in Brazil; the closest thing to it was a plague of killer bees. He foretold the discovery of Noah's ark and detailed all that would be revealed thereby; not even the rudder was unearthed.

His record of healing also left something to be desired. A man in Thomaston, Connecticut, a diabetic, stopped taking insulin because Julius assured him he was cured. Two days later he fell into a deep coma and almost died. Julius assiduously applied himself to growing a new foot on one of his followers to replace one that had been amputated. He also tried hard to raise someone from the dead.

Curiously, this string of failures did not and has not worried Brother Julius. Even more curiously, his poor record has not dented the faith of his disciples, numbering now, in Meriden, upwards of fifty. He preaches and heals and prophesies all over the state. He has been invited to speak in public schools (he seems particularly attractive to high school students). The members of his cult are fanatical in their insistence that he is the true actual living Christ.

Ted Patrick reserves a special loathing for Brother Julius. He has tangled with him several times, dating from the summer of 1973 when he dislodged and deprogrammed two of Julius's followers, and continuing through the spring of 1975 when he freed another and made an abortive attempt to spring four more.

TED PATRICK: By and large, 1974 was a good year for me. The work was being well-publicized all over the country, the cults were on the defensive, and more and more parents were learning where to turn for help and were calling me.

I had a small but effective organization (if you can call anything so loose an "organization") scattered around the country and a secretary to coordinate everything. We had any number of grateful parents offering their homes for deprogramming and rehabilitation in New York, Kansas, Connecticut, Florida, Nova Scotia, New Jersey, Pennsylvania. Wherever I was working, I wasn't far from someone who was willing to give up his home for a week or two in order to assist in the battle.

I still hadn't recovered from the financial beating I'd taken the year before in the Dan Voll case, and a legal problem in Denver was hanging over my head, but these seemed minor inconveniences in the face of what I was accomplishing. Then, at the end of the year, I received a great morale booster in the form of a judge's decision in Seattle.

The U.S. Attorney in Seattle, a man named Schwartz, had finally decided to press charges against me in the Kathy Crampton case on behalf of the Federal government. Pat Wall again agreed to defend me, and we decided to waive my right to a jury trial and have the judge hear the case.

Wall's pre-trial memorandum presented to U.S. District Judge the Honorable Walter T. McGovern did the trick. In it he detailed all the facts about Erdman's cult and spelled out the justification line of defense we'd used in New York.

On December 11, Judge McGovern, after studying the memorandum and hearing arguments from both sides, came to the following conclusions:

"It is indicated by both sides that the questions before the Court are as follows.

"One, may a parent legally justify kidnapping an adult child upon necessity grounds here alleged?

"My answer to that is in the affirmative, that there is such a common law defense and I so find.

"The next question that I consider is stated by Mr. Schwartz in his letter to the Court of December 6, item no. 3:

"Does the availability of the defense turn upon the parents' mere belief that a set of circumstances exist, or, rather, must it be demonstrated that the circumstances in fact exist?

"My answer to that question is that the availability of the defense turns upon the parents' reasonable cause to, and that they do in fact have sufficient belief to consider that the child, Kathy Crampton, was in imminent danger.

"The conclusion of the Court is, of course, that the parents did have such a belief and, in fact, I think the government does, in fact, concede that point.

"The next question is No. 3 in Mr. Schwartz's three-pronged questionnaire:

"If a parent may avail himself of such a defense, is it available to an agent of the parent?

"That is the key question in the case before us.

"Let me say this:

"The parents who would do less than what Mr. and Mrs. Crampton did for their daughter Kathy would be less than responsible, loving parents. Parents like the Cramptons here, have justifiable grounds, when they are of the reasonable belief that their child is in danger, under hypnosis or drugs, or both, and that their child is not able to make a free, voluntary, knowledgeable decision to stay within the so-called community.

"I might add that I do not find, I do not make a finding from the facts alleged by either side in their offers of proof as being true or not true.

"For the purpose of my decision, it is totally unnecessary. I am speaking only in terms of the reasonable belief in the minds of Mr. and Mrs. Crampton. Where parents are, as here, of the reasonable and intelligent belief that they were alone not physically capable of recapturing their daughter from existing, imminent danger, then the defense of necessity transfers or transposes to the constituted agent, the person who acts upon their behalf under such conditions.

"Here that agent is the Defendant."

And that defendant was me, Ted Patrick. Judge McGovern may have lacked some of Judge Wright's flair and style but the words meant the same thing to me and were worth every bit as much. Acquittal. Vindication. I was elated and spent a very happy Christmas with my family. The signs for the New Year were bright.

One of my first cases of the New Year was in Meriden, Connecticut, where I'd been requested to deprogram a man I will call John Santini from the Brother Julius cult. John had been married for ten years, and had six children. According to all accounts, he was a model father and the marriage was highly successful. John had worked at a variety of jobs. He was a mortician, a life insurance agent, studied metallurgy for a while, and was a salesman for a chemical company. Then, sometime in 1973, he and a couple of friends decided to start a magazine. John was acquainted with the Brother Julius cult because his wife Helen had a brother who belonged. John decided to run a three-part exposé of Julius and his activities in the magazine; after interviewing him several times, John himself was hooked and joined up.

Helen became aware of how serious her husband was when she would make love to him. He kept talking about Julius while they were making love, as if Julius was there in bed with them.

Shortly after he joined the cult, John moved out of the house and took an apartment with another of Julius's followers. A while later he lost his job; apparently he hadn't been doing any work—all he wanted to do was preach to his fellow employees about the Bible and Julius. For several months the wife's parents and John's brother Bob, who lives in Wallingford, Connecticut, supported her and the children. John never sent them a dime. On top of that, John sold some stocks that belonged to the children and gave the money to Julius. Even more incredibly, he then tried to sell the house out from under them, explaining that "the Lord would provide." He also told Helen around that time that if he was ever faced with a choice of denouncing Julius or letting her and the children die, he would have to let them die. But he advised her not to feel bad about that because they would all be reunited in heaven. Wisely, Helen slapped him with legal action that halted his plans to dispose of the house and turn the proceeds over to Julius.

The night Bob Santini picked me up at LaGuardia it was snowing hard and I was dead tired. He'd wired me twelve hundred dollars two weeks before and wasn't sure until he saw me that he shouldn't just kiss his money goodbye. When he did see me, in his own words, "I thought, Oh my God. What the hell is this! I was expecting some big football player type, and instead here's this little black man with horn-rimmed glasses and an attaché case. Then, in the car, he mumbles something about 'We got to have a plan,' lights a cigar and falls asleep!"

We drove to Plainville, which is about fifteen minutes by car from Julius' headquarters in Meriden, and went into Helen's house. Along with Mrs. Santini, there was her father; a cousin named Wendy; Wendy's husband Mike; and another man, who owned a restaurant in the area and seemed to have some underworld connections. I'll call him Ronald.

I wanted to go to sleep and lay out a plan of attack in the morning, but Bob was afraid he wasn't going to get his money's worth—he wanted to get down to it right away. "We'll call him up and tell him there's an emergency here—that he has to come right home," he suggested. "Ron and Mike can go over to his apartment and pick him up."

"Okay," I said. "Sounds easy enough. But first nail all the windows shut and lock the doors. Just leave the front door open. Soon as he's inside, lock that too."

The telephone call was placed, I don't remember by whom, but whoever it was sounded convincing because when Mike and Ronald got to John's apartment he was all excited and upset. He wanted to know what was wrong—whether Helen was sick or the children or what—but the two men said they didn't know, that they were only there to take him home.

He came through the front door of his wife's house with a lot of energy. "What is it?" he cried. "What's happened? What's going on?"

Nobody said anything; they just stood there looking at him. Then Bob, his brother, locked the front door. He whirled around. "What're you locking that door for?" Bob didn't reply. "Where's the kids?"

"We sent them over to Grandma's," Helen said. "We want to talk to you."

"I knew it!" he exploded. "I knew it was a trick! Let me out of here!" And he ran into the kitchen to try that door; only I was sitting there at the kitchen counter blocking his way.

"Who the hell are *you?*" he exclaimed.

"My name is Roosevelt," I smiled. (That happens to be true; my middle name is Roosevelt.)

"Roosevelt! What do you want?"

"I've come to talk to you, like your wife said."

"Talk? I don't want to talk. I want out of here!" He grabbed the wall phone and started to dial a number. Ronald reached for the receiver, took it away from him, and ripped the whole phone, box, wires, everything, right out of the wall.

"You're gonna talk to the man," he said.

"No I'm not!" John screamed, and lunged for a large ornamental knife, the size of a machete, that was hanging on the wall. Before anyone could stop him, he swung it over his head and smashed it down on the counter about an inch from my hand. He started to swing it again, but Bob and the others jumped him, disarmed him and dragged him into the living room.

"Oh, I get it, I get it," he was shouting. "You're going to deprogram me, is that it?" I'd deprogrammed three other Juliuses a year before so he knew what it was about. "What do you think I am, a computer?"

"You don't have the sense of a computer," I told him. "Brother Julius has you so messed up, you don't have the mind of a two-year-old."

This set him off and without warning he tore a huge stereo speaker from the wall and rushed at me with it. I was sitting in front of a broad expanse of picture window at the moment. As he came running at me I tensed, ready to duck and take him, when he swerved suddenly and heaved the speaker smack through the window. It sounded like a bomb had dropped.

Ronald, the restaurant owner with the underworld connections, put a bear hug on him and said, "Look, baby—you'd better cool it."

"Yeah?" John said. "What'll you do if I don't cool it?" His face was all contorted and red and his eyes were wild.

"You don't want to find out," Ronald said.

"Yes I do!" he cried, and bursting free he made a dash to

the door. Mike and Bob subdued him and then when he still wouldn't calm down, Ronald let him have it, belting him in the jaw and laying him out flat and cold.

"Get some rope," I said. "Nothing else to do but tie him up and get out of here. All the neighbors must be awake for a mile around. Sounds like a pig-sticking."

The women went to the basement and brought up some old frayed rope that wouldn't have held a dog, so we tied John with an extension cord instead and piled into our cars and drove to Wallingford where Bob Santini had a house pretty much secluded in the country.

It was just about dawn when we arrived. I was tired, but I thought time was of the essence since I knew that when John didn't return to his apartment, and when Helen's phone registered out of order, his roommate would call Julius who would call the police. So I went right to work. I couldn't make much progress, though, due to the number of phone calls that kept coming in. For one thing, Ronald had left his place of business the previous night telling his partner he'd be back in a few minutes. When he didn't return, the partner got worried and began phoning around looking for him. Julius meanwhile had gone to the police and told them that Ronald and Mike had abducted John. The Plainville police put out a warrant for their arrest. Then, they went to investigate Helen's house and —finding the smashed window, the busted speaker, the phone ripped out of the wall, chairs turned upside down, and a length of rope on the kitchen table—they concluded that John had been murdered. To help them along, Julius had a vision in which he saw John's body buried in a sand pile. Someone remembered that Helen's father was in the construction business and in his yard there was a great hill of sand, covered at the moment with the snow that continued to fall.

Therefore the police went out to interview Helen's father.

"Do you know where your daughter and her husband are?" they asked him.

"Sure," he said. "They're on a second honeymoon."

"Second honeymoon!" exclaimed one of the cops. "We were

just over at their house. The window's smashed, busted stereo, phone's off the wall, furniture tossed all around. If that's their second honeymoon, I'd hate like hell to see the first one."

"Sorry, officer, I don't know a thing about it," Helen's father said.

All of this we learned during that day as different people called with fresh information about who was saying what to whom.

I said to Bob, "Julius *has* to figure out eventually that you're in on this. The police are going to be checking every member of the family. We'd better get the hell out of here and deprogram him somewhere else."

Bob got on the phone trying to locate someplace for us to go. At last a psychiatrist friend of his offered his office in Bedford, a nearby town, on condition that we came around after hours and left early the next morning.

It was evening by the time we loaded up the cars and took off—half an hour ahead of the Wallingford police, as it happened, who arrived to find a dark and empty house.

I felt a lot of pressure to deprogram John fast, and I worked hard on him and made some progress. Ronald got on the phone and called a lieutenant he knew in the police department and said, "What's this about there being a warrant out for me?"

"That's right, Ron," the lieutenant said. "You're in trouble."

"What the hell are you talking about?" Ronald was in a bad mood because he was stuck there and couldn't go home. He'd come away from work to do a friend a favor for ten minutes, and now almost twenty-four hours later he hadn't washed, brushed his teeth, changed his clothes or slept much. "What kind of warrant? What's the charge?"

"Murder," the lieutenant told him.

"Murder! You out of your mind? Who'd I murder?"

"John Santini."

"John Santini's right here with me and his wife Helen. He's fine. He was in that damned Brother Julius cult, and he's here now with his wife and his brother and we're trying to talk some sense into his head."

"Oh," said the lieutenant. "That changes the picture."

"Bet your ass it does." They talked for a while and then the lieutenant said, "Well, we're going to close the books on this case. But be careful, Ron—the state police have begun an investigation and so have the Wallingford police. I'll keep you notified of what's going on."

I worked on John until about three, and then called a halt. I was ready to pass out with fatigue. We slept wherever we could, on the floor mostly, until seven, and then cleaned up the place and cleared out. I figured that the Wallingford police had already been to Bob's house and so it was safe to go back there and finish the deprogramming.

I went straight through with John, nonstop, at his brother's house for twelve hours and I could tell he was beginning to come out of it. We went to bed at midnight and I let him sleep till eight, and then I finished the deprogramming in a couple hours more. He came out of it very strong. He was shocked by what he'd done, almost couldn't believe it.

"How could I have deserted Helen?" he kept asking. "How is that possible? And abandon my kids. I can't believe it."

Gratefully, the others—Wendy, Mike, Ronald among them (we'd picked up a few more relatives and friends along the way)—departed, leaving Bob and Helen and John and me alone together. Bob, who likes to cook, prepared a big steak dinner in celebration that night. I remember he had candles on the table, and John and Helen were happy and affectionate. They really did look like they were on a second honeymoon.

During the meal the Wallingford police knocked on the door. Bob went to deal with them.

"We just want to know if anyone here is being held against their will," they said.

"Nobody here is being held against his will," Bob answered. "That's my brother and his wife and that's a friend. We're just having dinner, as you can see."

"Then—uh—nobody's being held against their will, is that right?"

"I don't know about anybody else," John put in. "Maybe my wife or my brother is. But I'm sure not. I'm fine."

We talked to them for a while longer, and then one of them,

looking over at John, asked again, "So then everything's okay here? You're positive?"

"Everything's just perfect," John replied with a smile. And they went away.

Later one of Brother Julius's attorneys called and asked if he could speak to John. I decided to take the chance and let him talk. We heard him saying, "Look, I'm here with my wife and I'm going to go home with her. I'm fine. I don't want an attorney, I don't need an attorney. I'm not pressing charges against anybody. Just leave me alone, will you? I'm where I want to be."

"As long as we keep the Julius people away from him," I told Bob and Helen, "there won't be any trouble. I'll take him to my house in San Diego for rehabilitation. Couple of weeks, he'll be his old self again."

John seemed so strong, in fact, that I had no objection to letting him and his wife spend the night in a motel nearby. They went off like young lovers.

"What a relief!" Bob said. "I can't tell you . . ."

"I know," I said.

We spent most of the next day just fooling around, talking, listening to music, laughing, taking it easy. Ronald had called inviting us all to dinner at his restaurant, and we were getting ready to leave when the state police came in. They said they were investigating a robbery in the neighborhood, but I knew why they were there since our friendly lieutenant had tipped us off that they were coming. So I said, "I don't know if you fellows picked it up on your radio the last few days, but there's been a report that a man was kidnapped around here. Well, this is the man."

John was seated on the couch with his arm around his wife smiling at the officers. He did not look very much like a kidnap victim, and the police seemed embarrassed. They questioned him halfheartedly for a few minutes, apologized for interrupting us, and left. And we went to have dinner with Ronald.

Ronald thought it might be a good idea to try to settle the business with all the police once and for all, so he called his friend the lieutenant and told him that we were having dinner at his place and invited him to send someone down to question John. The lieutenant called the state police, and the Wallingford police, and I think maybe even the Meriden police. A bunch of them turned up anyway, and John sat and talked with them privately for an hour or so. They were all satisfied that no crime had been committed and that John was there of his own free will. Ronald bought drinks all around and we thought that the case was officially closed.

I spent that night in Plainville with John and Helen at their house. In the morning his children were brought home from their grandmother's and John spent hours playing with them. They were overjoyed to have him back, and to see him normal again, and loving.

Around noon, though, while I was in the bathroom, the phone rang and John answered it. I never let a person use the phone until his rehabilitation is over, but I guess Helen didn't want to make a scene in front of the children. As bad luck would have it, it was one of the leaders of the cult, and immediately John began to float back in.

It's probably hard for many people to believe that a single conversation with a cult member can do so much damage to someone just deprogrammed, but it's true. A lot of confusion and fear continues to exist in the person's mind. That's why you have to watch them so carefully for a while, until they develop enough psychological strength to deal with the pressures alone.

I could see what was happening to him, and I thought, "Better get him to San Diego pronto." Helen was so happy to have her husband back that she didn't notice he was floating; she wouldn't have recognized the symptoms anyway. Not to alarm her, I didn't tell her. It wasn't really crucial, I felt, so long as we got out of there and on the plane.

"Helen, why don't you call the airlines and see what time a flight leaves LaGuardia for California today. I'd like to get a move on."

"Sure," she said. But before she could move, John was at the phone.

"I'll call them," he said. "Let me."

He dialed a number and I tried to listen to what he was saying. The children were playing and shouting and making a lot of noise so I didn't hear everything, but I heard enough to know he really wasn't talking to any airline. "Okay then, we'll be at LaGuardia at two-thirty," he said, and hung up.

"There's a flight at three-twenty," he said, coming into the dining room where we were. He was wearing a false, unconvincing smile.

"What airline?" I said.

He hesitated. "Uh—Eastern. No, I mean, United. Yeah, United."

He went through the motions of playing with the children, but I could tell his mind was a million miles away. I figured this was serious, so I drew Helen into the kitchen and said quietly, "I don't know who the hell he was talking to, but it sure wasn't any airline."

"Oh God!" she said. "What are we going to do?"

"Don't know. Have to think about this for a minute."

The phone rang again a few minutes later. It was the lieutenant. "Ted, the FBI is going to have LaGuardia staked out when you get there this afternoon. Thought you might like to know. They're going to pick you up."

That made things really tight. Obviously I couldn't go anywhere near LaGuardia now. What I wanted to do was to whisk John out of there and go to work on him again for another day or so. But there were only myself and his wife; if he put up a struggle there was no way we could handle him without help. And how to get help?

John came into the kitchen and gave us a suspicious look. "What's the matter with you two?" he asked. "You look like somebody died."

"John, who were you talking to before?" Helen blurted.

"What do you mean?"

Well, it was in the fire now, I thought. Maybe I could still reason with him.

"The FBI is staking out LaGuardia, John," I said. "You were talking to the cult and they phoned the FBI."

At this he went to pieces. Began raging and screaming and tearing around the house. The children were terrified and began to cry. "I'm getting out of here!" he shouted. "I'm leaving. I'm never coming back."

"Ted, do something," Helen cried.

But I couldn't do anything. I could hardly lower the boom on him in front of his children; if I did I'd have to tie him up. Then we'd have to put him in the car, drive through Plainville with him and the children, leave the children at the grandmother's, go someplace else. And I knew Helen wouldn't be any help at all. There was nothing I could do.

He was stuffing his arms into the sleeve of his coat yelling wild things. The children were wailing, grabbing at him, trying to stop him. He pushed them aside and ran out. Helen, the children streaming after her into the snow, ran after him, begging him to stay.

As he reached the sidewalk, a family friend came by in a truck and recognized him. John flagged him down and jumped in and they drove off.

I figured he would be going directly to the police, and after I'd comforted Helen and the children as well as I could, I jumped into my car and rushed downtown.

John was there. I told our friend the lieutenant to keep him there for a few hours at least and telephoned Bob to tell him what had happened. Anticipating that something like this might occur, Bob had had the foresight to have commitment papers drawn up in advance. He hurried to the psychiatrist, obtained the papers, and dashed over to the police department.

John was committed that afternoon.

I tried to explain to the doctors that this wasn't the sort of thing they were accustomed to dealing with. "You can't let him use the phone, and he shouldn't have any visitors except the family."

They acted like they understood, but they really didn't. It

simply isn't a psychiatric problem. Within three days John was on the phone constantly. Then the Brother Julius people began sneaking in to see him. It didn't take long before he was back in the cult as deeply as ever.

Naturally, in the weeks he was there, no evidence of psychiatric difficulty showed up in any of the tests. He was sane. I could have told them he was sane. They had to release him, and once released he went straight back to the cult and he's been there ever since.

I can still see those children chasing him out into the snow, screaming, "Daddy, Daddy, we love you! Please don't go!" And I'm determined to get him back. One way or another, I'm going to get him back, and this time Brother Julius isn't going to get near him again.

That spring I deprogrammed a lot of young people around the country from the Divine Light Mission. This cult, headed by a fat little playboy calling himself Guru Maharaj Ji, depends on a form of mind control achieved through the practice of meditation. One of the girls I deprogrammed, Marcia Carroll, who had helped in the Eddie Shapiro case, explained how it all worked:

"Meditation is an important aspect of the whole orientation, or indoctrination. That's one of the problems of understanding the cults. Most people think of meditation as really deep thinking. Actually meditation is not thinking at all. That's how they get to you. The more meditation you do, the less able you are to reason. It becomes painful to think at all. So whatever they tell you, you do.

"They taught us four meditation techniques. The first is with light. He tells you to close your eyes and then he presses on your forehead and eyes with his fingers. He tells you that you will see light and after a while you do. He's reading from the Scriptures —Biblical Scriptures—the whole time, explaining that light is a spiritual experience, the way to see God. You concentrate on nothing but the light.

"A second technique was to close off your ears, to listen to the music in your head. You cut off all the sounds of the outside world and after a while you really hear, probably caused by sensory deprivation, sometimes a roaring of waves, sometimes a single note. I really heard a lot of stuff. Sometimes I heard nothing.

"Then you would meditate on the sound of your own breathing. When you meditated hard enough you would transcend that sound and you felt a vibration, a tingle. You felt in tune with yourself. The leaders of the cult compared it to the 'breath of life that God breathed into Adam and Eve.' When you do that you feel that you're really experiencing the thing God meant you to.

"The fourth technique is called 'living waters,' or nectar. You put your tongue back into your nasal cavities and taste the fluid. It takes a lot of practice but you can do it. That's how they claimed Jesus lived in the desert for forty days and nights. They quoted the Bible's Scripture where Jesus talks about drinking the 'living waters' and thirsting no more.

"With more and more meditation you experience a sort of hypnosis, a sort of self-hypnosis. It keeps you there."

Naturally the cult is a big business. I dealt with people who had given everything they owned to the Guru. Donations of fifty thousand dollars were not uncommon. One woman I was deprogramming had signed over an inheritance of half a million dollars to the cult.

The Guru's business enterprises are extensive. There is a film production company called Shri Hans Productions specializing in marketing films about the fat teen-aged Guru. There is Shri Hans Records that puts out LP albums about the Guru. There's Shri Hans Publications which publishes a monthly magazine *And It Is Divine* with a circulation of 150,000. Divine Sales International sells secondhand goods. Divine Services will paint your house, repair your roof, fix your plumbing, do your housekeeping, cut your grass, service your car. The mission is also into travel services; there's Shri Hans Aviation, an airline; Divine Travel Services; and Divine Travel International. They market electronics equipment under the name Divine Electronics, and spread the gospel through the efforts of Divine Light Dance Ensemble and Divine Light Players of the Living Arts. Divine Light Mission owns a sixty-story skyscraper in Denver, where it makes its headquarters, and a fancy townhouse in Manhattan's Murray Hill district.

The Guru doesn't like to call attention to the cult's finances, probably because he has his eye on its tax-free, non-profit status. He's been quoted as saying that he offers his services voluntarily, "To give people peace. We are not charging any money for it." But the con man in him slips out every once in a while, and he was also quoted as saying, "It doesn't make a hell of a difference where I am. It's all the same to me. It's just one big holiday, a lot of fun." His own mother, maybe worried about the playboy existence he leads jeopardizing the profits, finally denounced him for what she called "his despicable, non-spiritual way of life."

At any rate, I deprogrammed a lot of kids from that cult the spring after the Santini business, and from Tony and Susan Alamo's Christian Foundation, and Sam Fife's Body of Christ, and a lot of others almost too numerous to mention, right on through the summer into the fall.

During that period I also mixed it up with Julius again. A New Jersey family named Goski had been seriously disrupted by Julius. Altogether six members of the family had been caught up in the cult in the past two years. Four brothers, a sister, and the sister's husband. Of this group, one of the sons, Joe, was still living at home with his parents and could properly be said to be half in and half out of the cult.

I was asked by Mr. and Mrs. Goski to come to New Jersey to deprogram their youngest son Tim, who had been on a basketball scholarship at the University of Georgia. He had abruptly quit school, severed all ties with his parents and gone to live with Julius in Meriden. The daughter, Cindy, had been the first to be attracted by Julius—through a friend named Mark, who later became her husband. After that it was a chain reaction.

The Goskis had been moved to rescue Tim when they heard that Julius was arranging a marriage for the boy; they heard

furthermore that Julius was ordering vasectomies to be performed on all his male followers. Given a Roman Catholic
family with twelve children, this last was plenty of cause for
alarm.

I went to New Jersey and deprogrammed Tim, and in the
process also deprogrammed Joe, the son who was living at
home. Since then both boys have been strong supporters of my
work and have helped me from time to time. At that point,
though, their major concern was the rescue of their other
brothers and their sister and her husband.

I felt that it might be possible to snatch all four of them
simultaneously, and we agreed to make the attempt as soon as I
could find an opening in my schedule. The opening didn't occur
until June.

The second week of June I was staying at Bob Santini's
house in Wallingford. It was a very busy time. I deprogrammed
three kids from Sun Myung Moon's Unification Church in eight
days, and was coordinating the deprogrammings of three other
kids in nearby communities. I was working overtime because I
knew I would be going into jail in a few weeks, perhaps for a
long time, and I wanted to accomplish as much as I could before
then. (I'll explain about that later.)

Since Meriden was only an hour or so by car from Wallingford, I thought now was as good a time as any to get the Goskis
and I began to lay my plans. I dubbed the attempt Operation
Big Four.

To snatch four adults was going to require a small army and
a lot of split-second timing and teamwork. So I called in my
"heavies." A great big mean-looking ex-motorcycle, Hell's Angels type named Goose. Joe Franklin, who'd helped me with
Bernie Weber. Joe Goski, who is built like a linebacker. Tim
Goski, a couple of other Goski brothers who had never been in
the cult, and assorted friends and relatives. Altogether, twenty-
two people gathered in the basement of Bob's home to discuss
strategy.

We knew that Mark and Cindy were living in an apartment
house in Meriden, and we also knew that John and Ronnie

worked nights at something called TAMPCO, or The Anointed Music and Publishing Company. This is an office in downtown Meriden where the Julius people publish various sorts of childish rubbish—religious comic books and the like that they don't sell to anybody but themselves but which they take very seriously.

Our plan was to send two cars to the apartment house with eight people, including a girl named Betty who was a former friend of Cindy's. The eight, including Goose and Joe Franklin, were supposed to split up into two teams. Betty was going to go into the house (Cindy was expecting her), up to the third floor where they lived, and tell them she had a flat tire and ask if they would come down and help fix it. If both came down, the two groups would hit them as soon as they emerged from the house. If only one came down, one group would nail whichever it was, and Goose and Joe Franklin would dash into the house, up the stairs, and nail the other one.

Across town at TAMPCO, the other fourteen would deploy themselves in a Volkswagen van and two cars. Joe Goski would go into TAMPCO and tell his brothers that he had changed his mind and wanted to join the group once more. He would lure the brothers out to the van on some pretense or other, and snatch them. Both groups would then drive to a house in the Appalachians where I would meet them for the deprogramming.

It was a good plan. Unfortunately it didn't work out quite the way I'd envisioned it. Maybe if I had been there things would have gone better, but as a result of all my legal problems, I was careful never to be present at the actual snatch of anybody. It was too dangerous. I must say, however, that it took a lot of the satisfaction out of my work for me.

What happened was that all twenty-two of them took off for Meriden and got there late at night, some time after ten. Two cars went to the apartment house and the other two plus the van went over to TAMPCO. The idea was to try to hit TAMPCO and Cindy and Mark simultaneously, at eleven. The Julius people are scattered around the city but they keep close tabs on one another via constant telephoning, especially if anything suspicious seems to be going on. My gang was well aware that as soon as anybody was snatched, everybody else would know about it immediately, so it was important to get all four of them at the same time.

The snag developed when Betty went into the apartment where Cindy and Mark lived. She simply took too long inside. I don't know if they didn't believe her story about the flat, or if she was slow in demanding help. Anyway, after about fifteen minutes, Cindy called over to TAMPCO to ask John Goski to come over and fix the tire. But by then John Goski had been grabbed and was gone.

At TAMPCO, when Joe Goski entered the building he found that only his brother John was present; Ronnie wasn't there. Joe decided to go ahead anyway, told John he'd changed his mind and wanted to come back to the group. John was apparently overjoyed, and did not hesitate to go outside when Joe told him he had some cases of soda in the van he needed help with. When he slid open the doors of the van he was confronted by four very tough and determined young men who jerked him into the van by the front of his shirt so fast he didn't have time to even yelp. They slammed the doors and drove off, heading for the mountains.

Back at the apartment, Cindy and Mark were suspicious. No one else at TAMPCO knew where John was. Outside, Goose and Joe Franklin and the others guessed that the plan was coming apart. A car pulled up to the curb and two Juliuses from TAMPCO got out. Franklin and Goose were trying to hide in the shadows on one side of the porch, but the Juliuses saw them and came over.

"What's going on?" one of them asked.

"Nothing, man," Franklin said. "We're just smoking a joint."

The Juliuses asked a few more questions, seemed doubtful and wary and went inside.

"Maybe we just better storm the place," Franklin whispered to Goose. "Kick the shit out of everybody."

Just then, however, the front door opened and Cindy and Betty appeared. But Cindy wouldn't advance more than a few steps from the door. The plan was that Goose and Franklin weren't going to move until the others did, and the others, being new to this business, hesitated and froze and lost the opportunity. In a few moments Cindy was joined by several others of the group, and as they came out the police arrived. As Franklin said, "I knew then it was all over."

The police were investigating the kidnapping at TAMPCO. The Julius people talked with them for a while and went back in, and then the police questioned Franklin.

"What you doing here?"

"Just out for an evening stroll," Joe told him.

"What do you know about what happened at TAMPCO?"

"What's TAMPCO?" Joe can look very innocent when he has to.

"Come on, come on. There was a kidnapping over there and you know it."

Joe scratched his head and looked baffled. "Kidnapping? What would I know about any kidnapping?"

"You working for Ted Patrick?"

"Ted who? Patrick? That name sounds familiar. Let me think. Oh yeah, He's that black dude that snatches kids from cults and shit like that, ain't he?"

"You working for him?"

"Hell no. Why would I be working for him? I told you. I was just out for an evening stroll."

"Look," one of the cops said, not being unfriendly. "We know the score here. We dealt with Patrick before. I hope you guys get who you're after. But I have to warn you that if you take them by force and we get a complaint we're coming after you."

"Sure wish I knew what you guys were talking about," Franklin mumbled, scratching his head again and shuffling off.

Naturally everyone was disappointed that we'd captured only one of the four, but we were delighted to have him. The next day I drove up to the mountains and spent thirty-six hours working on John and brought him out of it.

The Goskis were bent on still another attempt to secure

Ronnie, Cindy and Mark, and so was I. As a result, a week later, we had another strategy session in Bob Santini's basement. The house was in a pretty confused condition just about then because I had a boy deprogrammed from the Unification Church spending the night there along with four or five other former cult kids who'd assisted in his deprogramming. We were sending him off the next day for his rehabilitation. Bernie Weber, who I'd deprogrammed from Moon a few weeks before, was also present, along with Bob, my secretary Mrs. Sacks, and four other kids who were stopping for the night before proceeding to Boston the next day to snatch a kid from the Hare Krishna cult. So we had a mob to begin with in addition to the ten or so who had gathered for the raid on Julius's place.

One carload was going to stake out the house where we now believed Cindy and Mark were living (they'd moved out of that other apartment) and another two cars—with Tim Goski and a friend of his whose name I can't remember, Joe Goski, Goose and Joe Franklin—deploying themselves outside a big house where a lot of the cult members lived communally and where we knew Ronnie was staying.

It was a Sunday night, and there was going to be a meeting of the cult downtown somewhere. Our plan was for Franklin's team to wait outside the house until Ronnie arrived and then hit him as he was exiting from his car. The others would do the same at Cindy and Mark's.

"Now listen to me," I told them all. "If you have to go inside, forget it. It can't be done. When you go into a house you only have three minutes to do the job. You have to hit them outside. If something happens and you can't hit them outside, forget it and come on back. If we don't get them tonight we'll get them some other night. But if you go into the house and screw up, that makes it only so much harder the next time."

They all said they understood and took off, Goose in what Franklin calls his "attack gear." Goose is big, about six-foot-five, and strong as iron. He wears his hair long, with a sweatband around it. His arms are tattooed, and when he goes out on a mission he wears heavy boots, a leather vest, and black leather gloves like a strangler. I think all that is part of psyching him-self up. At heart he's really a gentle young man, but when he gets riled, he has been known to become aggressive. That night he got carried away.

The one car never did see Cindy and Mark, and returned eventually around 3:00 A.M., empty-handed. I suspect Cindy and Mark weren't really living in the house we'd staked out. For what happened at the other house—which was an old two-story stone place on a dead-end road outside of Meriden—where Ronnie was living, I'll give you Joe Franklin's account, since I wasn't there.

"We met at the Ford garage up by Bonanza around eleven. Me and Goose were in one car, and Joe, Tim and that red-headed kid were in the other car. And then we went up to the lake, turned around and came down and parked on that street. All the lights in the house were on. It was all lighted up. Full of people.

"We stayed in the next-door neighbor's driveway for about fifteen minutes waiting for Ronnie to come home. All of a sud-den Ronnie came out of the house. I guess he hadn't gone to the meeting. There was a girl in the yard taking down some clothes and he said something to her. We were just getting set to take off after him when he turned around and went back in the house.

"So then we didn't go. Joe was standing up against the house and he thought Ronnie had seen him. He came over to us and said, 'I think he saw me.' So we went up the road a little and sat down beside this curb, trying to get it together and we thought we better wait to see if the police came, figuring maybe Ronnie called the police.

"But I figured, hell, why wait for the police to come if he did call them? Let's just go—and try to do it in three minutes.

"So we went through the yard and me and Goose stood by this little shed that was in the yard, and Joe went up to the door to see if it was locked. The door was open and soon as we saw the door was open we ran up.

"It was a real skinny damn steep staircase, man, no wider

than that. A bitch. So we go running up this staircase single
file. Then at the top was a kitchen on the right, at the end of
a hall, and steps going down into it and everything. The door
to Ronnie's bedroom was at the top of the stairway. What we
didn't know was that in Ronnie's room there was a sort of
little cubbyhole. It wasn't a door, just a skinny little cubbyhole
cut into the wall connected to another bedroom where there
were three or four other guys. That cubbyhole wasn't supposed to be there and we didn't know about it.

"Well, Joe just smashed, you know, just smashed the door
down. What happened was Ronnie happened to be standing
behind the door doing something, and when he smashed the
door down he squashed Ronnie between the door and this
desk. You know, he almost knocked Ronnie out. If he had
knocked him out that would've been sweet, we'd have had it
all sweet. But it didn't quite knock him out and then he began
freaking, you know, yelling in this high-pitched squeal, like
"Eeeeeee!" So then Joe grabbed him, and Goose was following him into the room, and I was behind Goose, because we
had to go single file because everything was tight.

"But when Joe banged the door down and Ronnie started
yelling, all these guys came running from the kitchen this way,
and other guys coming up the stairs that way, and, you know,
coming from all over.

"Joe and Goose both had ahold of Ronnie and they were
bringing him, so I started on the other guys, you know, Mace-
ing them, hitting, whatever. The Mace didn't really work. I
mean it worked, but they kept fighting. What it came down to
was, we had to fight. I mean, I'd spray somebody and then they
were still kicking and I had to just kick them back.

"By this time a couple guys had crawled through the damn
cubbyhole. Joe and Goose were both holding Ronnie, and while
I was messing with the dudes on the stairway, Goose was
getting hold of Ronnie's feet when all of a sudden this big
dude come through the cubbyhole with a crutch, like—you
know—for a broken leg. And he walloped Goose with this
crutch. He hit him on the arm and shoulder. He was after his

head but Goose saw him at the last second and flung his arm up to protect himself, like this. And there was about three guys that come crawling in from every damn place. And so Goose had to fight them off. You see, they had ahold of Ronnie. I was in the hallway with two other guys so Goose had to fight by himself.

"I came back up the stairs to help Goose. But then those guys from the kitchen began to come again, and then—you know, I don't remember exactly, we was kicking, you know, you get frantic—and I went ape-shit with them for a little bit.

"So this one guy come out of the woodwork and clobbered Goose with the crutch and Goose laid him out. He was a little confused, wondering where the dude had come from, but he didn't have time to figure it out and he went for Ronnie's feet again. So then here come *another* one! Goose is thinking, 'What the hell! Where the hell they all coming from?' He *knew* they weren't coming from the hall. So he laid that one out too. And then another one. Hell, he was laying everybody out.

"So anyway, I just got done with them other guys and Joe was dragging Ronnie and it looked like everything was coming along, so I went down the stairs to clear the way and I turned around and the next thing I know this new guy is standing behind me and he says, 'Hey, what's going on?' He must have just joined, because he had short hair and no beard.

"You know, if he hadn't said nothing, he could have clobbered me. I was getting set to grab Ronnie's hands and when he said 'Hey, what's going on?' I turned around and blasted him and then hit him with the Mace.

"Then Goose sees me getting into it with this dude, and figures I'm in trouble. So he took a swan dive from the top of the stairs. Came flying right over me. He just took a swan dive, didn't touch nothing all the way down. He just went flying through the air, walloped me, and I flew up against the wall and he landed right on that guy. They tumbled a little bit and then ran outside.

"So then I ran back upstairs, where Joe was still with Ronnie, and there was guys all over, you know—feet kicking, arms, legs, everything. Joe couldn't manage him and people we'd laid out were starting to get up, so finally Joe gave up and said, 'Let's get out of here,' and went running down the stairs, and I took off behind him.

"In the meantime Goose was outside beating on that other dude that didn't have a beard. So we come running out and Joe yells, 'Let's get out of here!'

"By this time Tim Goski had driven the Buick in front of the house. The redheaded kid was—I don't know where he was, he never even came in. So everybody ran to the Buick including Goose. As he was running he tripped right over a little stone wall in the grass. You know, it was just a little wall, about this high, and he went skimming across the street, tearing up his knees. Then he crawled in the car and I ran up and got in my car and they took off and I took off. Nobody followed us. Wasn't anybody in no shape to be following us. I whizzed by the house and I didn't see anybody nowhere."

The minute Goose and Franklin and Joe Goski walked into Bob's place, Goose limping, his pants torn, bleeding from the knee, a big black-and-blue welt on his arm, Franklin's shirt torn and he was all messed up, I started waking people immediately, even before I heard their story. Julius knew about Bob's place from the incident with his brother John, and I guessed that this would be the first stop for the police if they were going to come looking for us. So I wanted the house empty—and fast!

"Come on, wake up. Up! Get dressed. Get moving! Everybody out of here," I shouted, going from room to room. We had about fifteen people staying there; they were sleeping everywhere—couches, chairs, floors, beds. It looked like a field hospital.

"Take Jim, you three, and go to the cabin in the mountains. Bill, you and Bob and Steve, take the Pinto and go on up to Boston. You guys find a motel room."

Everybody was running around, gathering up personal belongings, stuffing them into suitcases, only half awake, confused, scared.

"Goose, Joe, what the hell you doing? They'll put you away for ten years! Get the hell out!"

I swear, inside of five minutes the house was empty and there wasn't a car in the driveway. I cleaned up the place, then sat down and smoked a cigar, and did some quiet cursing of Julius Schacknow and all his tribe. I suppose I could have been damned mad at Goose and Franklin for disobeying my orders, but I felt more frustrated than angry. It seemed like unless I did everything myself, it didn't get done right. But then I put some music on the stereo and waited for the police. By dawn they hadn't arrived, and I figured they weren't going to come after all, so I got ready for bed.

Before I fell asleep, though, I was already making plans for the next attempt to rescue Ronnie and his sister and brother-in-law.

I promise, I'll do it yet.

CHAPTER EIGHT

Patrick's critics are forever challenging his credibility by referring to him as a high school dropout. While he was still working for Governor Reagan and trying to force the Attorney General to investigate the Children of God, a bureaucrat in Sacramento demanded scornfully, "Who the hell are you to be taking things like this into your own hands? What makes you think you're qualified to be doing this kind of work?"

It's a question a lot of people have asked since then. Who the hell is Patrick? What does make him think he's qualified for this peculiar profession?

TED PATRICK: I was raised in a red-light district in Chattanooga. We were so poor even the rats boycotted our house. That was a rough, tough place to grow up. I remember one of the streets in our neighborhood was so bad it was called Death Alley. There was everything going on there, you name it. If we didn't have it, it didn't exist. Thieves, prostitutes, murderers, pimps. From the time I was old enough to remember, I saw people being killed, shot up, cut up, beat up. The place was so bad even the police didn't want to come in there.

Downstairs in the building where we lived, there was a moonshine liquor operation. It was fifty cents a half and a dollar a pint. Fifteen cents for a shot, and a quarter for a double. A lot of people depended on that moonshine to get through the day. A lot of them were alcoholics, and they'd fight out on the streets under the window where I slept at night, and slash each other with knives and razors.

When my mother had to leave us alone occasionally, someone might come and stay with us for a few hours, and it might be a prostitute or a crook or for that matter somebody wanted for murder. Thieves, con-artists, racketeers, smugglers, black marketeers—they were your neighbors, your relatives, and your best friends.

From the very beginning I had a speech impediment that set me apart from the other kids, and probably had a lot to do with making me somewhat of a loner as an adult. Until I was sixteen, nobody could understand what I was saying. It was like being locked into an invisible prison. There was this wall between me and everybody else—a communication barrier, and it kept me shy and backwards and miserable and embarrassed for most of my childhood.

We were Methodists and we were black which meant that our community was constantly being infested with prophets and faith healers, witch doctors and fortune tellers and self-proclaimed Messiahs peddling salvation and snake oil. You know, that was the era of Father Divine and Sweet Daddy Grace, powerful and hypnotic religious con-artists and their success spawned thousands of third-rate imitators all across the nation. There wasn't any television in those days, and we couldn't afford radios or the movies, so going on a Saturday night to tent meetings, revivals, and things like that was a form of entertainment and psychological relief from the misery of people's everyday lives.

I remember Sweet Daddy Grace used to come to Chattanooga

a couple times a year. One of his angles was to lie down in a casket and pretend to go into a trance. I had a job at the funeral home that used to provide the caskets, so I always had a ringside seat. Sweet Daddy would crawl into the casket and close his eyes and then pretend that he was communicating with the spirits of the dead.

"I got a man named Jones!" his voice would come booming out of the casket.

Since there was always somebody in the crowd named Jones, someone would begin to scream, "That's Henry, that's my Henry!"

And Sweet Daddy, imitating another ghostly voice, would cry out, "Give this man a token of your faith in him so I can talk to you."

More often than not the poor woman would half break her neck to pour her life's savings into the casket on top of Sweet Daddy who would then tell her what was on Henry's mind.

Once, a feeble imitation of Sweet Daddy Grace came to town, by the name of Prophet Brooks. He was also into the casket scene, only he went Sweet Daddy one better. He advertised that he would actually die for half an hour or so and have communion with the saints. He'd get in the casket and we'd close the lid. He had some tiny holes in the lid to let air in, but one time something happened to the holes, they got blocked up, and when we opened the casket finally, there was Prophet Brooks turning blue. "What the hell you tryin' to do?" he gasped and sputtered at us. "Kill me?"

Whenever some new prophet or faith healer would come to town, which was often, my mother would pack me up and carry me to him hoping to have me cured of my speech impediment. I went to fortune-tellers who, for twenty-five cents, assured my mother that I would be cured in two weeks. Two weeks later I still couldn't talk, and my mother would carry me to a palm reader, who would say it was only a matter of time before God restored my tongue. But God never did restore my tongue and I would begin to feel guilty—guilty about the money my mother was spending, guilty that I couldn't speak, as though it was all my fault. I thought I'd done something terrible and God was punishing me and I didn't know why or for what. I went to phrenologists who felt the bumps on my head. I went to voodoo types. Nothing worked. A faith healer would come to town and my mother would drag me to him and we'd all pray and he'd lay his hands on me and proclaim me cured and everyone would weep tears of joy. Only I wasn't cured and I felt guilty about not being able to pray hard enough. It never occurred to me that the faith healer was at fault; I just naturally assumed the fault was mine. I went to Holy Roller meetings where everybody spent whole nights shouting and babbling and praying over me with absolutely no success. I just couldn't pronounce the words.

The result was that I developed a deep fear of words. I think I can honestly say that the only thing I've ever really been afraid of in my life was words. After a while I stopped even trying to speak, it was so painful and humiliating.

Not so surprisingly, I found an escape: I buried myself in the Bible. Bible studies were a very important part of our schooling in those days—probably the most important part. In time I knew the Bible inside out and backwards. I suppose the sense of guilt I felt about my responsibility for my speech impediment made me a more fanatical Bible student than my schoolmates were; maybe I thought the answer to my unique evil could be found there, and if the answer, possibly the cure.

It wasn't long before all I could think of was hellfire and damnation, and in this I was encouraged by my teachers, who probably also thought the speech impediment was God's punishment for some terrible sins I'd committed even before I was born. My Bible class would go on what schools now call field trips, to visit jails mostly, and the state prison now and then, to bring the word of God to the convicts. I think I must have made another connection as a result of those trips between criminal behavior, Holy Scripture, and my accursed speech impediment. Which only drove me deeper into the Bible. I guess, given the way my mind was working, I could have been a preacher myself—except, of course, that I couldn't make myself undertsood. I could read, and I liked to read, but because I couldn't express myself, I was miserable, and things went on like that till I was in my teens.

Then I just got tired of it all. Somehow I woke up one day and realized how tired I was of not being able to communicate, how inconvenient it was, and how unnecessary. Since everybody had been praying for God to give me normal speech from the time I was old enough to know, I had assumed that a cure was strictly in God's hands, and that if I wasn't cured it was God's will. But that day it occurred to me to say to myself, "Look, everybody's praying to God and begging God and asking God to cure me. But what is it I'm doing for myself?" I wanted to be like the other guys, I wanted to be able to talk to pretty girls like everybody else. So I made up my mind that I had to get off my rear end, stop feeling sorry for myself, and learn how to speak. I began to work on it, work on it hard, and finally, when I was sixteen or so, I'd gotten to the place where at least I could get my point across, where at least I could make people understand me.

It was about that time also that I began to emerge from my Bible-obsession and to see that book in a larger context. Once I began to lead a more normal life, I could judge, looking back, how abnormal and even morbid I'd been in my religious thinking.

I'm sure that realization had a lot to do with my feelings about the cults some thirty years later. I had been programmed too; in fact I'd programmed myself, and I knew firsthand how miserable and stunted that kind of life could be.

I suppose it was also inevitable that the employment I would choose for the rest of my life would depend upon talking. I had sixteen years of silence to make up for. Another result of that speech impediment was that it made me an activist. If you can't talk you have to express yourself through actions, and all my life I've been the sort of person who's impatient with sitting around jawing a problem to death. As soon as I see what needs to be done I like to get moving.

By the time I'd conquered the speech difficulty I realized I'd never be college material. Besides we were poor and needed money so I dropped out of school and went to work after the tenth grade. The media doesn't miss too many opportunities to mention the fact that I'm a tenth grade dropout. But, just as I worked hard to overcome my speech handicap, I've worked hard over the years to educate myself. And I'm proud of how I've made my way.

None of it was ever easy. I've done just about everything when it comes to making a living. One of the first jobs I had was driving around Chattanooga's ghetto when I was twelve, helping my father who ran a numbers racket. In those days rackets were a matter of survival for blacks (and in many places still are today) and everybody supported them, including the churches. So there wasn't any particular shame attached to what my father did. It was a job; it helped feed his family.

Since then I've swept floors, been a chef, a waiter, a chauffeur, a masseur, worked for an undertaker draining the blood out of cadavers, was in the printing business, did construction work, was a barber, drove a truck. Whatever was available wherever I was.

At one point I managed to save a few dollars and went into business with a cousin of mine. We opened a nightclub in Chattanooga called the Cadillac Club and did pretty well. Eventually I had the opportunity to go into business for myself and sold my share of the club to my cousin and leased an empty restaurant and cocktail lounge from a friend of my mother's. Even then, however, I wasn't awfully careful about the technicalities of business dealings. I felt a man's word and his handshake were good enough. I still tend to feel that way, in spite of being burned on account of that attitude many times. With the restaurant and cocktail lounge—after I'd redone the place, and stocked it, and booked two big bands from Atlanta for the opening—two days before I was set to open, political enemies of mine made trouble for me and I never did open. Lost most of my money too.

From an early age, I'd sensed that government and politics were the quickest paths to success for black people, and I was always political, always interested in organizing, bringing pressure groups to bear. Even as a kid, during World War II, I made myself the leader of something called the Junior Commandoes who used to go around collecting scrap iron for the war effort. We won some national award, as a matter of fact. Later, about the time I went into business with my cousin, I was cochairman of the Nineteenth Ward in Chattanooga, and, naturally—as always happens in politics—I made enemies, and they did me in when I tried to open my own club.

I was twenty-five then, I'd been in and out of the service and I was married, with an infant son, and dead broke. A buddy of mine was going to California to work and asked me to go along. I had an uncle living in San Diego I could stay with, so I went, leaving Ruth Ann and the baby with my parents.

I got a job the second day I was in San Diego, working for a company that sold supplies and uniforms to schools and hospitals. Then I got a job as a maintenance man with Convair, driving a truck. That job opened my eyes to the extent of racial discrimination in California. There were few blacks employed by Convair, and those that were employed had the most menial jobs. I saw men with Master's degrees sweeping floors. This wasn't right and I decided to do something about it.

Using the political experience I'd gained in the Nineteenth Ward in Chattanooga, I organized the blacks and we began filing complaints with the appropriate federal authorities. I aimed our complaints at the federal government because at the time the government accounted for about ninety percent of Convair's contracts. My organization was frankly political— most of the blacks in San Diego didn't vote and I knew the only way we were going to get anywhere was through the political process. We called ourselves the Chollas Democratic Club, and, in the beginning, we had twenty-one members. In a month we had over 100. Shortly, Convair was hiring blacks.

As soon as I'd saved enough money I sent for my wife and baby. Since then I've brought my whole family to California, including my parents.

And I expanded the scope of the Chollas Democratic Club's

concerns. We began to picket supermarkets in the black neighborhoods. You would have a situation where the neighborhood was 90 to 95 per cent black, and there wouldn't be a single black person employed in the supermarket. They didn't even have any blacks sweeping the floors. It was worse than Chattanooga.

I never went to the managers of these places in the spirit of negotiation. I always went to lay down demands. I'd go into a place, introduce myself, and tell the manager, "We had a meeting of the Chollas Democratic Club last Sunday and we voted to picket your store starting Thursday. We're going to maintain the picket line indefinitely if we have to, until you start hiring some black people here." Usually, they buckled immediately and gave in to our demands.

We hit Kresge's and Woolworth's downtown and we got a lot of publicity. Our membership ranks swelled. Then we systematically went on to hit a supermarket and a liquor store each week. Not only were blacks being hired, but as a result of the publicity, other minorities were joining the club in droves. It wasn't long before we had a racially mixed membership of over 900—blacks, whites, Mexicans—and all of them were working to get people registered to vote as well as picketing and laying plans for more pressure-group action on other merchants.

I remember we hit a very large chain of supermarkets called Mayfair Market. I talked to the general manager and told him he was next. He pleaded with me, "You mean you're going to throw up a picket line just like that?"

"Just like that," I said.

"Give me a chance."

"Give you a chance?" I said. "You've had a hundred years. How much time do you want?"

We picketed that chain for twenty-three weeks before they gave in, and along the way they were forced to close down one store entirely.

The Chollas Democratic Club wasn't my only interest. I organized something called the Logan Heights Businessmen's Association to promote the welfare of black businessmen in the area. And I organized the Junior Government of Southeast San Diego, another civic-action group.

I also took on the public school system. My wife was a teacher—biology and home economics—but when she got to San Diego she couldn't get a job. There were almost no blacks in the system. Now, when I'd been working for that company supplying schools and hospitals with uniforms and things, I got to know a lot of people around the city who were influential in school affairs. With their assistance I filed a complaint with the state and threatened to picket, using the same tactics that had been successful on the supermarkets. They were also successful with the school system; they finally began hiring blacks in some numbers, but my wife never did get a teaching job until I went to work for Governor Reagan.

That job was an outgrowth of yet another group I formed, the Volunteer Parents Organization. The principal purpose of the VPO was to assist in keeping the lid on racial disturbances in the schools. When the Watts riots broke out in Los Angeles, about 500 demonstrators drove down to stir up trouble in the black sections of San Diego, and the Volunteer Parents Organization went in in force and were instrumental in preventing a similar explosion there. I won a Freedom Foundation Award for my efforts during that crisis, and it brought me to the attention of the Governor's office and led ultimately to my job as Special Assistant for Community Affairs.

That was a big, responsible job. I represented the Governor's office in two large and populous counties, San Diego and Imperial. Originally, not much was expected or demanded of me. A couple hours work a day. I turned it into a fifty or sixty hour a week job and had the satisfaction of knowing that I helped many people who otherwise wouldn't have been helped at all. All the clubs and organizations I've been president or founder of have been service-oriented, aiming at benefiting the people. It's how I view my work as a deprogrammer: I'm performing a service, a public service, which no one else is willing to perform.

I feel that up till now my life has been more successful than anyone had a right to hope for when I was, say, ten years old. In the past few years I have spoken on college campuses all over the country, from Boston to California, and I can't help thinking at times, when I'm addressing a history class, or a sociology class, or participating in a seminar with PhD's, that for a black man from Chattanooga, a tenth grade dropout, whose parents and relatives and friends once despaired of my ever being able to utter an intelligible sentence, everything considered I haven't done too badly with my life. I don't feel that I owe anyone an apology.

CHAPTER NINE

The Holy Spirit Association for Unification of World Christianity, a/k/a Unification Church, Sun Myung Moon, Founder, was sponsoring an international scientific conference at the Waldorf Astoria Hotel in New York City in November, 1975. The conference was billed as the Fourth International Conference on the Unity of the Sciences, and the church's publicity listed a host of eminent scientists around the world as chairmen and advisers. In July of that year, the newspapers began to run stories to the effect that most of the advisers and chairmen so listed had never been made aware of Moon's connection with the event and still others were not even aware that such a conference was taking place.

Amitai Etzioni, Professor of Sociology at Columbia University, complained that the conference sponsors "have tried to inject Moon into everything and of course we do not share his views. They are starting to try to use the conference to legitimize a supporter of President Park of South Korea and someone who wants to turn the United States into another South Korea."

Other prominent men whose names were used in the church-sponsored advertising without their knowledge and/or permission—and who said they would not attend the conference—were: Norman Cousins; Professor Oscar Handlin of Harvard; Ernest Boyer, Chancellor of the State University of New York;

Zbigniew Brzezinski, Professor of government at Columbia; and Warren Bennis, President of the University of Cincinnati.

Sun Myung Moon is a former Korean industrialist turned evangelist. The cult that he heads is a theological-political instrument, combining elements of Manicheism, Nazi-style anti-Semitism, Calvinism, and the most discredited aspects of pre-Reformation Roman Catholicism, including the selling of blessings and indulgences and a doctrine of "indemnification" for the sins of one's ancestors.

While his followers contend in public that Moon never claims to be the Messiah, that he merely leaves the possibility open, it is a fact that in the training sessions of the converts, which escalate from 3-day sessions to 3-week sessions to 40-day sessions to 120-day sesssions, Moon is repeatedly referred to, in no uncertain terms, as the Messiah and the Lord of the Second Advent.

The 120-day training manual is a thick blue loose-leaf binder containing 402 pages of text and several appendices. On page 160 of the manual, under the heading of "Family Problems," which discusses how kids should deal with their parents' opposition to their membership in Unification Church, they are told: "But sooner or later they [parents] also can understand what Divine Principle is because this movement will cover America. Then how do you think they will feel? Then they can understand that Rev. Moon is Messiah, Lord of the Second Advent."

On page 96: "Between the Lord of the Second Advent and Syngman Rhee were mediators: two ministers. The two ministers were representatives of Christianity. They betrayed Father. Therefore Syngman Rhee started to persecute the Lord of the Second Advent after he became President of the country."

Similar references to Moon as the Messiah are sprinkled liberally throughout the manual.

The intellectual level of the training can be illustrated by the following passage, which occurs on page 322:

When will the Messiah come again? Let's investigate to find

the answer. In order to find when he can come, let's investigate the history of Israel and the history of Christianity. Then you can explain historical parallels. You don't have to start with Adam. Just introduce the history of the Israelites. First Jacob came and went into slavery in Egypt 400 years. Then Moses appeared (400 years). Then captivity and return (210 years). And then after 400 years the Messiah came.

Then this pattern will be repeated. You have only to show the facts. Four hundred years of persecution by the Roman Empire, then 400 years under the patriarchs, 120 years of the Christian Kingdom starting with Charlemagne, 400 years of the divided kingdoms of East and West, 210 years of papal activity and return, and then the Messiah must come after a 400 year period.

The text goes on to demonstrate how the Bible prophesies that the next Messiah will come from Korea—by an amazing coincidence, he was to be born around the time of Sun Myung Moon's birth.

The anti-Semitism of the cult is expressed in this passage (page 302 of the manual): "Karl Marx was born in Germany and was Jewish. Jesus was Jewish and Karl Marx was Jewish, both . . . His works were summarized into three books called *Das Kapital* . . . The main theory of *Das Kapital* is the theory of exploitation, or theory of surplus value. His understanding was silly and foolish, but still it worked for a while. Simply speaking, Marx says he is rich and we are poor, let's take what he has . . . Communism is the philosophy of hatred."

Communism is the offspring of Karl Marx, who was Jewish. Jesus was Jewish. Ergo, Jesus is also a philosopher of hatred, as are all the Jews.

And for all the Unification Church complaints about Patrick's kidnappings, there is this passage on page 159:

Adam, son of God—Satan took him and God shed tears of grief. Therefore, because of restoration, God will take back his own Adam from Satan's side. Your physical parents are not Satan, but behind them is the Cain position which represents the Satanic position. Therefore, when children are taken by God, the parents feel the same feeling that God felt when he lost his children. This way there is restoration, an idemnity condition. Therefore the parents must have shed tears when the Unification Church kidnapped their daughter and their son because Satan kidnapped God's daughter and son. But the purpose of kidnapping is not kidnapping itself. The purpose is to save, to give eternal life, to give eternal joy and happiness.

To Patrick, Sun Myung Moon is public enemy number one as far as the cults are concerned.

TED PATRICK: Moon calls himself a Christian, but his movement has been denounced by Christian churches the world over. He used to be a Presbyterian in Korea, but they threw him out for heresy.

He claims that when he was sixteen he had a vision and God told him he was supposed to finish the work Christ failed to accomplish. He established the Unification Church around 1954, and now he has chapters on college campuses in just about every state of the Union.

I've deprogrammed a lot of kids from Moon's group and I know his operation inside out. Just like Hitler did, he tells you what he's after. He's said over and over again that he wants to rule the world. And he's got an entire foreign government backing him in the attempt.

He and the South Korean dictator Park are old buddies. I don't have to remind you that the term "brainwashing" came from Korea during the Korean War when many of our prisoners of war were subjected to intensive political indoctrination, using the same methods so many of the cults—and especially the Unification Church—employ today, namely fatigue, psychological fear, isolation, repetition of political dogma, and so forth.

If you're not inclined to take my word for Moon's connection with dictator Park, maybe you'll take the word of the Boston *Globe,* which on July 12, 1974 did an article on Moon.

"Moon's chief aide," the article stated, "and leader in the

United States, Col. B. Hi Pak, was a member of the Korean
Central Intelligence Agency, which has operated in this country.
The Unification Church has prospered in drawing money and
members [in Korea] and some observers have pointed out that
its good fortune has coincided with the increasingly dictatorial
regime of President Park. In an interview, an official of the
National Council of Churches, who returned from South Korea
last May, said: 'A number of people who have investigated the
Unification Church have been struck by the money available
to them.' He said that 'it is widely rumored here and abroad
that the Korean government is giving them support' and that
'A linkage is widely assumed.'

"A U.S. State Dept. official in Washington said, 'The fact
that Moon and his nutty religion can exist in Korea and find
money to come to the United States when legitimate religious
organizations are being repressed leads people to wonder if
there is an intelligence connection.' He said that it was his 'suspicion that Moon is no real intelligence officer, but since he is
involved with the collection and development of funds, they
may be funneled back to Korea for various purposes.' "

The article also quoted J. Hung Lee, a former cultural attaché
and information director for the South Korean embassy in
Washington, as saying that, "Moon started from scratch and
accumulated his wealth under the Park regime, not before."
He went on to say that under the Park government, "You can't
operate a sizable industrial and commercial enterprise without
having political ties or at least personal favor with the Park
regime. Park is in need of support from anybody. He is very
unpopular, so he will take advantage of anyone helping him.
When Park wants a show of public support, he can get mobiliza-
tion of Moon's followers for anything."

The paper adds, "The critics also say that Park wants a better
image for Korea (and for himself) abroad and this allows the
Unification Church to send help to its organization in the United
States so it can hold rallies such as the one in Boston."

What kind of threat is this to the average American citizen?
(Aside from the threat of losing his child to the cult.) Well,

remember that in the spring of 1974, Moon took a calculated gamble that President Nixon would escape impeachment. He organized massive demonstrations in Washington in Nixon's behalf, and took out large advertisements in newspapers all over the country in support of the ex-President. After that Nixon had him to the White House and they were photographed embracing. Moon is after power. Moon is political. He's mainly political.

You see pictures of him with the Mayor of New Orleans, and with Strom Thurmond. He's in the White House. He sucks up to Park. He puts his kids out into the streets to support specific political candidates, looking for returns on the investment later. The Providence *Evening Bulletin* of October 25, 1974, carried a story in which it said, "Last summer Moon followers worked in the successful senatorial campaign of Rep. Louis Wyman, R., N.H. . . . Paul Dietterle, Wyman's campaign manager, confirmed that about 20 Moon followers helped distribute Wyman bumper stickers." Ann Gordon, a girl I deprogrammed from Moon, confirmed Dietterle, saying that church centers in all fifty states are into political campaign work.

But most politicians being what they are, they'd accept campaign help from a pack of vampires if they offered it, and Moon knows this, and with this well-disciplined and indoctrinated army he can have an impact on any campaign he sets his mind to influencing. He could put hundreds of volunteers into any state overnight to work for a particular candidate. That's a very attractive proposition to some polecat running for office, especially when he can soothe his conscience by telling himself he's being aided by a religious group. And it's not likely to occur to him that he's conspiring to assist a dictator of a foreign government to influence a U.S. election.

Moon's bible is a book he claims to have written that he calls *Divine Principle*. It is crammed with pseudo-scientific nonsense to make it look respectable and deep. There are all kinds of charts and illustrations; graphs of one sort or another; charts; terms like "Individual Truth Body, and the Inner and Outer Quarduple Bases," relating concepts of God and Man to things like molecules, protons, and electrons. On the surface, the sort of stuff a student in college is likely to see on a classroom blackboard in a physics class or an engineering course.

As Shelley Turner, another ex-Moonie, commented, "They'll put two plus two equals five on a blackboard and if they can prove it on two other blackboards, most college kids are going to believe them. All their life they've been taught that what goes up on the blackboard goes down in their notebooks as the truth."

Maybe that explains the success Moon has recruiting disciples on college campuses. His recruiting arm on the campuses is something called the Collegiate Association for Research of Principle, or CARP, as they call themselves.

In March of 1975 a controversy over the role of CARP on the campus of Kansas State University boiled over, and for a week or two the Kansas State *Collegian* ran a number of editorials, articles, and letters to the editor about the Unification Church and its methods and goals that show how Moon operates.

In an editorial of March 7, 1975 entitled "Beware of CARP," the paper stated its reason for the editorial: "The recent alarm over the activity and purposes of the Collegiate Association for the Research of Principle (CARP) operating in Manhattan [the name of the town the school is in] has made one thing clear: K-State students MUST be made totally aware of what CARP represents and what it has been doing. . . .

"FACT: CARP is a student arm of an international sect headed by a Korean industrialist, Sun Myung Moon, who professes to be finishing the work of Jesus Christ. That work is said to be the breeding of 'the ideal race.' CARP and the other 'Unified' sects do not state this association (with Rev. Moon) in any of their promotional material, lectures or initial 'discussion' sessions."

This last is an important point, and one I made when I was talking about infiltrating the Children of God at Santee. Students are not advised in advance what it is they're going into. When they ask specific questions they are lied to. Often several days pass before Moon's name is even mentioned. By that time enough indoctrination has occurred that they are unable to make a truly free choice of whether they want to join or not.

After a few more facts, the editorial concludes by addressing the large question of religious liberty. "Freedom of religious belief is essential. But what is equally essential is that we are protected from elements which, by deception or false pretense, will alter or diminish one's ability to distinguish and choose between alternative responses and beliefs."

Incidentally, CARP is not the only Unification Church front organization. There are others, among them: Project Unity; One World Crusade; International Federation for Victory Over Communism; Freedom Leadership Foundation; American Youth for a Just Peace; The Little Angels of Korea; the Professors Academy for World Peace; and the Committee for Responsible Dialogue. For all of them, Moon's headquarters in Barrytown, New York calls the shots.

It doesn't take a rare genius to wonder why a "Christian" group would have to resort to deception and lying and the use of front organizations to recruit members. The conclusion should be obvious: unless the Unification Church employed such methods, nobody in his right mind would join.

The reason for all this secrecy, of course, is that Moon doesn't have anything to do with religion. It's a big business operation, plain and simple. In addition to the munitions factory in Korea he owns factories that produce ginseng tea, titanium products, pharmaceuticals, air rifles, and lots of other things. But that's only a part of his fortune. The bulk of it in America comes from the unpaid labor of the kids he has out on the streets. How much does he make annually? Well, by the church's own estimate, the yearly budget is around fifteen million dollars.

One of the boys I deprogrammed, John Colaluca of Fort Lauderdale, Florida, turned over his Mercedes-Benz to the group. That's standard. They give whatever they own—cars, bank accounts, securities, whatever. Colaluca said that in the New Orleans center there were approximately twenty "Moonies," all of whom were earning roughly two hundred to five hundred dollars a day per person by hustling in the streets. Moon has three expensive pieces of real estate in upstate New York, owns two yachts, and has recently suggested that he was interested in purchasing the Empire State Building. He also has plans for establishing a university in New York State—a prospect that when you think about it makes the blood run cold. He has enough money (along with the backing of the South Korean government) to open a tuition-free school and probably get it accredited. Thousands of families who are deceived by the church's promotional literature would no doubt find it attractive. And Moon would have a captive audience for his indoctrination.

The cult tries to dismiss attacks against its fund-raising practices with some strange arguments. Joseph Tully, director and president of the church in New York State, had this to say about their financial affairs:

"Reverend Moon's beginning is the same as Christ's. His country (Korea) was ruined just as Israel was ravished by Rome. But we're not stopping where we began 2,000 years ago. Christ too would have needed greater resources. I would have hoped the Son of God would have been given something nicer than a mud hut."

This Tully doesn't seem to know his Bible very well. He forgets that the Son of God could have had anything He wanted. He *chose* a mud hut, and deliberately chose a life of poverty for Himself, to set an example, to stress that heaven did not look kindly on the luxury-sucking types like Sun Myung Moon.

John Colaluca had been a premed student at Tulane. After joining the Unification Church he dropped out of school. Robbie Meripol, his fiancée, joined to be with him. She dropped out also, giving up an honors scholarship in English literature. She gave the cult her seven-hundred-dollar tuition plus a thousand dollars she'd borrowed from a friend.

It took both Robbie and John a long time to get over the psychological fear that had been instilled in them. Robbie said later that after she was deprogrammed she still was worried on her flight to John's home in Fort Lauderdale. "Even on the plane I had moments of fright when I thought the plane would crash to punish me for leaving the Moonies," she said.

The psychological damage the group inflicts on its people can't be overestimated. On an NBC special in May of 1975, a Barrytown doctor testified that kids coming to the emergency ward of the hospital from the Barrytown center displayed all the classic symptoms of extreme paranoia. He said they were disoriented, incoherent, profoundly confused. Other former members were quoted on that show as feeling at times that they were locked up in an insane asylum at the center in Barrytown. They provided vivid descriptions of kids freaking out, screaming, having visions of the devil "just like in *The Exorcist.*"

I have a notarized statement in my possession that was made by a college student I deprogrammed—written at his own suggestion, with no pressure to do so from me or his parents or anyone else—explaining in more detail what life was like for him in the cult. At this writing he has been out for four months, has a summer job as a clerk in a bookstore, plans to return to school part time and live with his parents for a semester or two, feeling that to return to school full time might result in his returning to "the same old intellectual ruts" that got him into the cult in the first place. He has an unusually high I.Q. and comes from a stable, loving, closely knit family. Both parents are well-educated. The boy is one of those who felt school was not the answer to what he wanted out of life. He was searching for some deeper meaning, and in the process experimented first with drugs, and then with "meditation." He now says that meditation is a very dangerous thing to fool around with since it makes a person vulnerable to mind-control groups such as Moon's. Here are the essentials of his statement.

TO WHOM IT MAY CONCERN: Here are, to the best of my memory, the facts concerning my indoctrination into and subsequent period of membership in the cult which calls itself: Unification Church. I hope that this may help others become more aware of the potentials of mind manipulation and its threat to self-determination.

I have used quotes around those passages which are paraphrased from what I heard and learned in the cult for the past ten months, although they may not be direct quotations.

In May of 1974 I decided to leave school after two years of study [name of the school as well as his name withheld at the boy's request]. That same summer I began a hitchhiking journey across the country.

On July 20 I arrived in the San Francisco Bay area, State University of California at Berkeley. A girl approached me within minutes of my arriving on the campus. After several words of small talk she asked me in a heavy accent if I was religious, then invited me to visit an international religious movement. As we walked to their center I asked questions about the nature of the religion. She only said, "Wait and see," and hummed songs to herself.

At the center there were several others in quiet discussions. I was offered tea and cookies. We looked at some picture books and listened to classical music. Still I could get no direct answers to any questions. However, I was invited to attend the weekend workshop starting that night in the San Francisco center where "everything would be explained."

During the workshop we were allowed no more than six hours sleep, ate fairly well (our meals were never well balanced), and never had a free moment. We slept on the floor, about ten in a room. Most of the two days were spent listening to long lectures explaining the philosophy and religion: The Divine Principles. Other activities included much singing of specially written or selected songs, group games, and the sharing of the "testimony" of how an older member was "led" to the Unification Church.

Sunday night I was invited to travel with several other "trainees" to Pasadena for a five-day training session for further study of the Divine Principle philosophy. The next morning we drove to the training center, a mansion where the regional director lived, and Mr. Moon stayed when he visited. I never got to see the regional director there, and we were not allowed inside the mansion. Instead we all slept on the floor of a small cottage.

"Studying" consisted of our reading out loud the entire *Divine Principle Study Guide* which outlines the complete *D.P.* book. This was supervised by the "director" of California. The day's schedule of activities repeated that of the workshop.

On the fourth day of our training we were taken to learn fund-raising. In a van we drove to shopping center parking lots where each was left individually with several cartons of candy boxes. We were told that it didn't matter what we said to the people. "Look straight into their eyes, and don't waste too much time with one person. Keep running from one to the next." It was a terribly draining day, mentally confusing, emotionally upsetting.

After returning to San Francisco I was told to "witness" downtown for more recruits. Five days later they transferred me to a mobile fund-raising team (MFT). We traveled around California to raise money for the Berkeley center which was apparently deeply in debt. There was little time for any more "studying." We woke at about 6 A.M. and began selling between 8:30 and 9:30, after a cereal and sandwich breakfast. Lunch was another sandwich or two on the parking lot. We returned for dinner around 10 or 11 P.M. . . .

The philosophy teaches that your time, your life, is not rightly your own, but belongs to God who works through Moon who works through the hierarchy of the cult. You have no "free" time because every moment must be given to God through your immediate superior. You must give up your *self* completely. . . .

Satan will try to pull your thoughts away from Master and Divine Principle in many ways. He will *use* your "old world" friends and family to lure you away. You must resist this "temptation" and cut off from them. You must fight Satan. You must never stop thinking of "Master." Every thought that is not "centered" must be suppressed. Every doubt is a foundation for Satan. Sing their songs, pray deeper, work harder!

How is it then, that so many people could become ensnared by this mind manipulation? When presented as a philosophy, it is a convincing system to someone open to new possibilities. More important, however, are the group pressures encountered.

One evening a girl had decided to leave the "Movement." About twenty people sat in a circle. The regional director was present. He proceeded to alternately tease, rebuke and belittle her. We all obediently laughed, and encouraged her to stay. She finally broke.

From the initial encounter there is an unceasing bombardment by intense physical and mental pressures forcing conversion and absolute adherence to doctrinal discipline. There is constant snubbing of all past religion and philosophy for misleading people by half-truth and not having the same "ultimate" salvation. Mentally it is overwhelming. During the workshops and training programs Divine Principle "study" occupies most of the day. Eight or ten hours of listening to lectures, repetitive and with manipulative wording, not being used to the reduced sleeping time, left my mind in a daze.

I was pushed as quickly as possible to give myself totally by accepting it all as the "complete truth.". . .

There will be times when you must do things with which you disagree. They may go against all of your previous upbringing. You might be told to sacrifice yourself, or to kill people, even those once close to you. Because you cannot fully understand you must not stop to think or question, but your faith must carry you through the mission. God (or Satan) is testing this faith, and you must prove true. Not only your own "salvation" rests upon this, but also the salvation of the entire world.

To exercise and develop this obedient faith a leader might give you a "condition," for example, a condition for prayer for one half hour every morning. These can be imposed to regulate any aspect of your life: eating, sleeping, talking, singing, etc. Once I was told to hit myself repeatedly, harder each time.

"Every doubt is a foundation for Satan." Through this idea the mind control is maintained. There is no release, because it is a perfectly closed system, absolute and total. There is no room for compromise. All escapes are methodically destroyed. "You are either controlled by God (i.e. Moon) or by Satan (all else)."

"Physical parents are often used by Satan, and must be dealt with carefully. They are not your true parents (Moon and his wife are), but must eventually become your spiritual children." In general, members are encouraged to write short notes to parents expressing great positivity toward their present involvement, and a feeling of love for them greater than ever. However, I was told (along with others) that I was too attached to my parents, and that this was hindering my spiritual growth. If I sincerely wanted to do what was best for them, as well as for myself, I would have to cut off from them completely for several months.

"Your decisions and actions not only affect your own eternal life, but that of your friends and family, and even ancestors who are already dead. You are held responsible. If you leave the Unification Church you are lower than Satan." Guilt and doubts battle each other, to be conquered and subdued by self-enforced mind control. "In order to grow spiritually you must learn to do the things you like the least."

How can anyone be happy living this kind of life? They teach how to program oneself through mind control, using song, prayer and hard work, to be happy and positive in any situation.

Deep prayer is a powerful tool for reinforcement of the mind manipulation through sincere repetition of the doctrines. When done in a group, each person is shouting, praying differently, in unison. Often this intense, repetitious praying leads to "the experience of God's heart." These are cathartic moments, similar to many "conversion experiences," which are heavily stressed as direct break-throughs to God, and seen as signs of increased "spirituality." These experiences serve as constant reinforcement for the long days of hard, draining work. Dreams are also often interpreted as supportive of "Master," Divine Principle and strengthened faith.

Here I would like to conclude that had it not been for the strong action of my parents in actually forcing me to be "deprogrammed" from this "brainwashed" state I would still be a totally dedicated member. There was little way for me to break the bonds of their control on my own, and I would have continued to sacrifice myself, ready to lie, cheat, steal and kill for the cause of the cult. I am thankful that after ten months of blind submission I am now free of this system and its manipulation. I am deeply grateful to those people who worked behind my back and in spite of my protest to accomplish this. Because of this direct experience I feel a great sympathy for all those who remain enslaved by mind control systems, and I seek to help in any way possible to make people aware of the reality and danger of the situation.

I want to add that this boy's interest in "finding deeper meanings" to life has not diminished very much. He is still searching, and still idealistic, and still holds a view of the world and its problems and the solutions to those problems that I disagree with strongly. But that's fine with me. What he has learned is that the cults are no answer to what he's looking for, and that's all I'm in this to demonstrate.

Another girl I deprogrammed, Winnie Swope, offers still more information about what goes on inside the Unification Church.

Winnie is a short, slight, very vivacious and fun-loving girl. Her father is a psychology professor at a community college in Westchester County, New York. At the time she joined the Unification Church she was a sophomore at the University of New Hampshire. "I'd never been happier in all my life," she said. "I was really interested in school, I was making real good grades, I didn't have any problems to speak of. I most definitely was not out to save the world or find transcendental truths about anything. I had been experimenting with drugs, but I'd quit those and was straight again and happy. I had some close good friends, and I had established a really solid relationship with my boyfriend. Things couldn't have been better."

Near Christmas of 1974, Winnie was studying for her final exams in the Student Union when she was approached by a girl she'd never seen before asking for directions to the art building. She said she was new on campus and was supposed to meet someone there. Winnie told the girl that she was going in that direction, and if she'd wait while she finished her coffee she would take her there. The other girl sat down, ordered coffee for herself, and began to talk.

"She wanted to know if I was interested in world problems.

Naturally I told her I was. We got to talking about starvation in underdeveloped countries, the population explosion, birth control, things like that. Religion never once came up. We talked for maybe an hour. Then she told me that she had a group of friends who had a sort of discussion group where they discussed the kind of thing we'd been conversing about. She asked if I'd care to sit in on a session. I don't know why, but I was suspicious right off the bat and I said, 'This isn't any sort of religious group or anything, is it?' She said, no, absolutely not. World affairs was their bag. So I thought: Why not? I'm always interested in trying new things, and there was always the outside chance that this would be worthwhile. So I accepted her invitation to meet her friends and we left the Student Union. It never occurred to me to wonder about what had happened to her appointment with her other friend at the art building, which she never mentioned again after she sat down with me."

Well, of course the "new girl on campus" was a recruiter for the Unification Church, but in that first encounter Winnie had with those people, the name of the church was not mentioned. There were about fifteen other kids present, some of whom Winnie knew by sight. And while most of them were clean-cut, a few had long hair and beards.

"I thought if those freaks were there, it couldn't be all bad, so even though I was immediately turned off by all those haircuts and all that friendliness and all those smiles, I decided out of politeness to stay and listen to what they had to say. I figured I didn't have anything to lose but an hour or so.

"The regional director, a man named Michael Smith, did most of the talking, and his eyes never left mine through the whole thing. It was weird. At first the discussion was general, but gradually Smith worked it around till they were talking about God as the solution to all the world's ills. Then he went into a long involved philosophical kind of thing, putting all sorts of illustrations on the blackboard that looked vaguely scientific, trying to prove the existence of God. I didn't have the slightest idea what he was talking about and I didn't care. I was bored and I wanted to go home.

"Afterwards, the girl from the Student Union and a few others asked me what I thought of everything. Again, wanting to be polite, I told them I thought it was 'interesting'; but also wanting to be truthful, I told them I really didn't understand very much of what they were driving at.

" 'Well we're having a weekend workshop,' the girl said. 'If you'll come, everything will be a lot clearer then.' It was very strange: I didn't like them, I didn't want to see any of them again, I certainly didn't want to waste a whole weekend with them or anyone else for that matter except my boyfriend (I wanted to study for finals) and yet I heard myself accepting their invitation! It was a funny kind of psychological pressure they put on me; I mean I felt *obligated* to go with them on the weekend. They were all so eager for me to come, maybe I was just flattered. I don't have a really good explanation for why I went. I just told them that I would.

"As soon as I was alone, I was furious with myself. I went over to my boyfriend's and told him what I'd done. 'I don't want to go,' I said. 'Well then, don't go,' he told me. 'No problem. Just don't go.'

"That was Tuesday, I think. I brooded about it all week, and somehow couldn't find it in myself not to go. I had a date with my boyfriend Friday and I called him and told him I was going to break it to go to the workshop. He was very upset and unhappy. I remember him begging me not to go, and me feeling helpless to do anything else."

The cult took Winnie and about twenty or thirty other kids off in a bus that Friday night. They took the group about fifty miles from the campus to what had been a private school off in the boondocks somewhere in the mountains. They were completely isolated, with no means of transportation back to the campus. In effect, they were prisoners for the weekend. What's especially worth noting here is that throughout these initial encounters her attitude was negative and defensive. She tried consciously to withstand them at every turn.

"That first night, Friday, they got right into the lectures. The lectures were more openly religious in nature, and I thought to myself, 'Oh my God, I'm in with a bunch of Jesus freaks!' I immediately began to try to tune them out. But there wasn't anywhere else to go, nothing else to do but sit there and listen. From the beginning I was a rebel. They segregated us according to sex and I didn't like that so I went and sat with the boys, which the leaders didn't like. A few times I got up and tried to leave the room, but two or three of them would come up to me looking hurt and concerned, as though they'd let me down, as though they were taking my wanting to leave as a personal insult. So I would stay because I didn't want to hurt their feelings. But I was bored, and I kept thinking what a fool I'd been to come, and wishing I'd listened to my boyfriend.

"That was a major part of their strategy for the weekend, never to give you a second alone with your own thoughts. The next few days we did a lot of game-playing and exercising as breaks from the lectures. I didn't like the games and a few times I tried to slip away to my room and read a book. Right away there were two or three of them all over me asking, 'What's wrong, Winnie, don't you *like* us?' I always ended up playing the stupid games.

"They were into singing a lot too. One of the songs was called 'The Generation of Righteousness.' It went something like, 'As the day comes out of the night, a Generation will come forth, a Generation of righteousness.' Once the subject of Moon was introduced (on Saturday), the songs were frankly in celebration of him. One, called 'Song for Father' had a verse that went:

> I will never leave you anymore
> For I have found in your bright eye
> A river of love, a heart of gold
> A peaceful mind, a hand to hold.

I blush now just remembering. I blushed then too, as a matter of fact. I was majoring in psychology and Russian, after all. And there I was singing nonsense that would embarrass a child.

"The lectures and discussion sessions were endless. I was

sleepy a lot because they kept us up late Friday and Saturday
night and woke us up early, but when I'd begin to doze off,
someone would tell me that 'sleepy spirits were sitting on my
shoulders.' That was the intellectual level. Sleepy spirits.

"To keep my sanity, I took a notebook and drew a line down
the middle of the page. On the left side I would write down the
arguments of the lecturers, and on the right side I would carefully write down my refutations of what they said. After a while,
without my really noticing that it was happening, the column on
the left side began to outweigh the column on the right. Soon,
I wasn't putting anything at all down in the right column, I was
just filling up the left with things they were saying that consciously I did not believe."

Winnie tried various mental tricks to keep herself rational
during that long weekend, and thought she'd made it when on
Sunday night everyone was driven back to campus. They arrived
so late, however, that Winnie decided to spend Sunday night at
the center—she lived off campus, did not have a car, or money
for a taxi.

"I don't know what happened then," she says. "I went to
sleep Sunday night really, really confused. My head was spinning. I kept telling myself over and over that these people were
nuts. Then, Monday morning—I simply *don't know* how or
why I did this—I woke up and went to the leader and begged
him to let me join."

Prior to that Winnie dressed like most college kids, her hair
long, jeans, sandals. Two days after joining, she turned up in
her boyfriend's room wearing a skirt and a blouse, the skirt
below her knees, and with her hair cut. "He was just stunned,"
she recalls. "I told him what I'd done, and that I was quitting
school to go to Portland, Maine for a twenty-one-day training
program. I told him I'd given my life to the Lord. He couldn't
believe it. He cried. Then I went around to all my professors
and informed them I was not going to take the final exams,
trying to arrange for incompletes that I might make up at a
later date. They were all disturbed by my decision, but went
along. Only one guy didn't. 'Did you join that Unification

Church?' he asked me. I told him I had. 'Those rotten sons of bitches!' he swore. 'Young lady, you're nuts!' And he flunked me.''

The cult sent her to Portland where she underwent a rigorous three week "training" program. During the program, after she was already well-indoctrinated, the leaders let her call her father to announce that she had quit school. "He almost went up through the roof. He begged me to at least finish the semester, but I wouldn't budge. I remember I made the call from the office of one of the leaders, and while I was talking he kept showing me pictures of Moon. We were programmed to pictures of him. After you'd stared at him long enough you really believed that he loved you, and that you loved him and how privileged you were to enjoy that relationship."

Winnie describes her three weeks at Portland this way: "We had lectures all day long, and discussion groups where we discussed the lectures, and discussion groups where we discussed the discussion groups. I never did read *Divine Principle*. Sometimes I would try to get into it and it would take me an hour to read two sentences."

She had loved to ski, but when she looked out the window at the snow and thought how much she would like to go skiing, she would remember that it was probably Satan tempting her and she would turn away from the window. "Literally everything you liked to do was considered a temptation of Satan. Not just sex or things. If you liked to sing hymns in church, that was evil too."

As a break from the pressures of all the study sessions, they would go outside a few times a day to play games. "We played Messiah Tag and Spirit World Dodge Ball. In Messiah Tag one person was the Messiah and he would chase others trying to tag them. As soon as he tagged somebody, that person would become his disciple and they would hold hands and run after somebody else. Before you were caught you would run around the field yelling things like, 'False Prophet! Heresy! Heathen! Communists!' Then they'd catch you and all of a sudden you were supposed to be all full of love and wanting to help all the other people. The last person out was Satan, and then they'd tag Satan and he would be restored and everybody in the world would be restored. By that time in my training I took this game very seriously, and Spirit World Dodge Ball too.

"In Spirit World Dodge Ball, they throw a ball at you and when you are hit you leave the group and go behind the lines so that eventually the last couple of people left are surrounded and bombarded by the other people, and that's like the spirit world bombarding you and coming at you from all sides. At Barrytown we also had our morning cheer. We'd make a circle and someone in the middle would yell 'Heavenly Father!' And we'd all put our fists into the circle like cheerleaders and shout in unison, 'Father!' 'We're going to have victory for you today, Father!' And we'd respond, 'Yes, Father!' 'We're going to crush Satan for you today!' 'Yes, Father!' 'We're going to raise money for our Father today!' 'Yes, Father!' 'We're going to take money away from Satan!' 'Yes, Father!' It was just fanatical. We'd finish by chanting '*A-A-A-O*' three times. That's Japanese for something. And then the guy in the middle would yell '*Abaji!*' That means Father. And we would raise our arms above our heads and yell '*Mansei!*' Which means ten thousand years. The whole thing was supposed to mean Victory for Father for ten thousand years. We'd yell that three times."

While she was in Portland she began to have trouble with her eyes, experiencing a blurring of her vision. Her leaders told her that the Devil was trying to interfere with her seeing the blackboards and advised her to pray harder. Another time she was told that her problems with her vision probably had to do with one of her ancestors who had been a peeping Tom and now she was paying indemnity for his sins.

Finishing the twenty-one day program at Portland, Winnie was then sent to the center in Barrytown for a forty-day training program. There her eyesight began to deteriorate rapidly and she got very worried. "But when I asked to be allowed to see a doctor, they kept stalling and putting me off. They wouldn't arrange the transportation for me. 'Are you sure it's more important than these lectures?' the leaders would ask me.

'This is God's word. Is the fact that your eyesight is a little blurry more important than hearing God's word?' They put a lot of that kind of pressure on me and I would feel guilty and then convince myself that it probably was Satan trying to invade me, and I would work harder and pray harder.

"Then we went on a prolonged fund-raising campaign. I don't know. I was in terrible physical shape, I was going forty-eight, sixty hours at a time without sleep. I remember one night in New York City we were supposed to be witnessing, lecturing. I'd been out on this corner for eighteen hours. It was freezing cold. We had this blackboard set up and were giving Principle lectures, at three in the morning! You can imagine how many listeners we had at three in the morning. But we kept lecturing anyway, to the parked cars, the lampposts, the fire hydrants. Finally after about a week of that, and fund-raising all over New England, I just couldn't take it anymore, and I ran away, hitchhiking to the Boston center where I pleaded with them not to send me back to Barrytown. They finally agreed, and they let me make an appointment with an eye doctor in Boston."

The doctor informed Winnie that she had a detached retina. He said it was one of the worst cases he'd ever seen. If she had waited two more weeks, the doctor claimed she would have lost the sight completely in that eye. "And the people at Barrytown were pressuring me to stay just for a couple more weeks." The doctor was amazed that she could have delayed obtaining medical assistance for so long. Naturally Winnie couldn't explain why she'd delayed.

She underwent an operation, and it was successful. She recuperated for a while in the Boston center, and then returned to Barrytown to complete that phase of her training.

"I was there a couple weeks and had an appointment with the doctor in Boston to check my eye. But they didn't want to let me go. They tried to get me to visit a doctor near Barrytown, and they were pretty mad at me when I wouldn't agree. They finally gave me just enough money to get to Boston and

I left. But I miscalculated my money and spent my last eighteen cents on a candy bar, so when I arrived in Boston I didn't even have a dime to call the center to ask for a ride. I had to go to the police station and use their phone. I spent that night at the center and the next day went to the doctor's office. As I was coming out of the office my brother and a friend grabbed me on the stairway.

"We'd been told about Ted Patrick. He was described to us in lurid terms. We were told that he strapped you to a bed, beat you, tortured you, raped you, wouldn't let you eat or sleep. So when my brother grabbed me, I knew immediately that I was going to be deprogrammed, and I was scared. I screamed bloody murder. I held on to the bannister, and bit and kicked. But they got me into the car.

"When Ted first walked into the room, and instead of this big black gorilla in tight leather pants he was a funny looking little man with glasses, I almost laughed with relief. He looked so comical. But I still didn't trust them. I figured he had assistants and *they* would be the ones who would beat me and rape me and make me lose my mind so I'd be invaded by Satan. We'd been told that if we were ever kidnapped we shouldn't say a word. But one of the leaders in Boston had been complaining about that tactic—he said he was sick and tired of kids not standing up for what they believed in. So I made up my mind to defend my beliefs."

She was tough. Winnie has a very strong mind and she talked like hell. I never heard a girl talk so much, so fast. But in about twenty-four hours I had her deprogrammed. And it wasn't two weeks after her rehabilitation that she was helping deprogram other Moon kids in Connecticut and New York. She has also made speaking appearances and given interviews. She's been reconciled with her boyfriend and plans to return to school. About her involvement with the cult and the future, she has said, "There are some kids still inside whom I really love, and I would really like to get them out. And when Moon falls, I'm going to really enjoy that. But let's face it, I have my own life to lead. I can't be spending the rest of my life trying to deprogram people." Which is about the healthiest and most welcome attitude a person can have once he's out of a cult.

And Moon is going to fall. Already investigations into his activities are under way in several states, and what he's been doing just can't stand up to full, open public disclosures. Moon knows it too. Although he has big plans to fill Yankee Stadium in 1976 and organize a mass rally at the Washington Monument, one of the boys we rescued told me that the word is circulating through the centers that *if* America isn't saved by 1978, the Unification Church is going to have to concentrate on Europe and abandon the poor old United States to Satan. Moon is already packing his bags, it sounds like to me. I'll be very happy to escort him to his plane when he leaves.

I want to conclude this chapter with a quote from a rabbi, who says what needs to be said as well as anyone can put it. Rabbi Maurice Davis, of White Plains, New York, is a brave, eloquent man. On May 24, 1975, he preached a sermon to his congregation about the evils of Unification Church. Rabbi Davis had done an extensive investigation into the workings of the cult. After detailing the history of the movement and the way it works and the havoc it wreaks wherever it goes, he quoted a letter from a Christian minister in Louisville who had witnessed some of Moon's goons roughing up his wife and another woman who were distributing anti-Moon literature outside of a Unification rally in Indianapolis.

Then Rabbi Davis said:

"In that regard—and only in passing—I received a phone call from a member of our congregation relating to me what might, or might not, have been a threat against my speaking on this subject tonight.

"Following that, however, I received a letter which was a dimly veiled threat, and then two phone calls, rather specific, that I had better be very careful what I say tonight.

"Well, I am very careful of what I say. And very carefully

I say it. I hold this movement to be evil and dangerous. I hold Reverend Sun Myung Moon to be a charlatan and a manipulator of people. I hold his inner henchmen to be devious, unscrupulous, and false. And I hold the kids that are caught up in this to be the innocent victims of their own weaknesses, the innocent victims of their own dreams, the innocent victims of their own needs. But most of all the innocent victims of Reverend Moon.

"Now, I cannot say it any more carefully than that."

CHAPTER TEN

If Patrick's biggest problem is, as he's said repeatedly, educating the ignorant public about the cults and their activities, it's also been one of his most frustrating tasks. Governmental indifference to his pleas and warnings, media resistance, the reluctance of organized religion to take a firm stand in support of his work and against the cults, have all left him angry but not discouraged. A central truth about him is that he does not discourage easily.

TED PATRICK: What I'd like to see is a law passed that removes the tax exemptions from all churches. Let's say a law that taxes all religious organizations just 1 per cent of their income. There isn't a legitimate church in the country that can't afford 1 per cent, and it would allow the Internal Revenue Service to at least get a foot in the door of some of these cults to see what's going on inside. Many of the cults flourish partly because they are not accountable for their money; they are immune to any governmental checks and balances.

In most churches there's an element of democracy. Pastors don't have a license to spend the money any way they see fit. In my church, the congregation has voting rights, and if we're dissatisfied with the way our minister is handling the finances, we can kick him out. Moon and Maharaj Ji and Hannah Lowe and Paul Erdman and Brother Julius, however, aren't responsible to anybody. They are totalitarians, and they're protected by the First Amendment to the Constitution.

As things stand, no one has even tried to define the difference between a legitimate religion and a tax-dodging racket. The fact remains that certain behavior on the part of individuals who adhere to no particular creed is punishable by jail, when the same behavior, done in the name of a tax-exempt church, goes not only unpunished but largely uninvestigated. Some religious sects, for example, don't believe in medical care, blood transfusions, and the like. It wasn't until recently that the courts began to intervene, when children were involved, in cases where certain churches forbade blood transfusions. If you or I, however, were to refuse a transfusion for a child who was dying, without religious grounds to back us up, and the child died, we'd go to jail for second degree murder or manslaughter. If we let two of our own children die from sniffing Teluene, we'd be imprisoned for child abuse. But when Paul Erdman does it, in the name of Love Israel and the Church of Armaggedon, the authorities in Seattle are so intimidated by his claim to be a religious leader that not only is nobody held responsible, but the authorities don't even conduct an autopsy for three days while Erdman tries to bring them back from the dead! If you or I kept a young man locked up in our house, worked him for twenty hours a day without pay, fed him one meal, prevented him from having any contact with the outside world, stole his money, took his car, and taught him to work for the overthrow of the government, they'd throw the book at us in court. If you're Sun Myung Moon doing all these things, you get an invitation to the White House!

Now I've been accused of taking the law into my own hands. "What if everybody took the law into his own hands when he disagreed with it? Where would we be then? What would we have?" I've heard that argument a million times. What we'd have would be anarchy, obviously. But generally speaking, it's hard to find other areas of the law where there aren't perfectly feasible alternatives to taking the law into your own hands.

A friend of mine who lives in Connecticut and is an atheist complained to me about the Connecticut law that closes the liquor stores on Good Friday. He feels he is the victim of religious discrimination. He asked me if he would be justified, in my view, in smashing down the doors of a liquor store on Good Friday and taking a bottle of Scotch.

But he has an alternative. The problems are obvious to everyone, the issues are clear-cut. He can get up a petition, he can try to force a referendum on this issue, he has resort to the courts, he can organize a lobby in the state capitol. If he does all this, and loses, well, in a democracy he has to abide by the majority's ruling. But he has avenues of appeal that he can use to seek redress without taking the law into his own hands.

In the case of the cults, there were no such avenues. I would prefer to go the legislative route. Anybody who thinks I enjoy all these legal battles, the convictions, the jail sentence, must be crazy. But the only way to develop blueprints for legislation to govern the cults was to produce evidence about what was happening inside them. No law enforcement agencies would launch an investigation because of the First Amendment. A dog won't run from the smell of a skunk the way a politician will put his tail between his legs and take off at even a hint of controversy in the religious area. Believe me, before I started taking kids out bodily, we tried everything. First through my connections with the governor's office in California, then in Washington, the Congress, the Attorney General, the Speaker of the House, the President. All we ever got in reply were sympathy cards.

In November of 1973 I wrote a long letter to the Speaker of the House of Representatives, Carl Albert. I detailed what was going on in the cults, and concluded with these words: "At this point, I am not asking you to believe what I am saying, but to give me an opportunity to produce proof of my allegations. Since Congress and law enforcement agencies refuse to have an investigation of these cults, I hereby, Mr. Speaker, request that you form a committee to have a Congressional investigation of me, Ted Patrick. I feel the people of the United

States deserve to know the truth and be protected from this movement that is sweeping the nation and destroying the minds of our youth."

I thought that was clear enough. I wasn't afraid of an investigation. Could the cults say the same?

I never got an answer from Albert.

So I made an appointment to talk to him. When I got there he wouldn't see me. I talked to three of his aides instead. They referred the matter to the Rules Committee, which was like throwing it into the garbage can.

So I was blocked at every turn. "Show us some hard evidence," they kept saying. "Then we can do something." Well, the only way to obtain the evidence was to get some kids out and have them testify. And there wasn't any legal way to do that. So I had to break the law. Then when we presented the authorities with the evidence, they still didn't do anything.

There should also be some laws governing fraudulent business practices in the name of religion. If you or I bought an hour's time on television and advertised for money to help starving refugees in Bangladesh, and then when the money came pouring in, we spent it instead on a yacht, a mansion and other personal luxuries, and did not send a penny of it to Bangladesh we would be in jail so fast we wouldn't know what hit us. But when Sun Myung Moon sends legions of kids into the streets asking for money for prison reform and drug rehabilitation centers when there are no programs in either area, when all the money goes straight into his pocket, and when he justifies it by saying they're taking money from Satan—nobody does anything about it. If it were only rumored that Moon and the other cultists were doing this, that would be one thing; but we have sworn testimony of former members. If in a murder trial I produced the sort of eyewitness testimony we can produce about Moon's fraudulent business practices, the jury would hang him in five minutes. But that same sort of testimony, when it's presented in a trial dealing with a religious figure, won't buy you a cup of coffee. Hell, you can't even get the thing to trial.

So I've had to do what I've done in order to secure the evidence I needed to define the issues with the hope that corrective legislation might follow. I had to take the law into my own hands.

But even that sounds overly dramatic. One thing I have learned in the past few years is how relative the term "law" really is. Most people tend to think of law as an absolute. It's anything but. What's lawful in California may not be lawful in Colorado or New York. What is illegal in one set of circumstances becomes legal in another set. A police officer in Seattle may turn his back on a rescue and say it's not a kidnapping. He may even assist me by holding the car door open while I dump a Kathy Crampton into the back seat. Or a police department in Boston may refuse to accept a man's complaint that he was forcibly restrained, saying it's a family matter. But in New York, that same act, that same set of circumstances, may produce an entirely different reaction on the part of the police.

So in many cases the police decide what the law is and isn't. Which is important when you're talking about taking the law into your own hands. Now I've heard a lot of pious and hypocritical people complaining about the police taking on themselves the burden of responsibility in these areas. Police are not popular in certain intellectual circles around the nation. However, the same people who denounce the police for looking the other way when I "take the law into my own hands," are the first to applaud when the cops look the other way in Central Park in New York, when five hundred thousand kids are all getting stoned on marijuana at a peace rally. The outrage of liberals, the liberal conscience, is a very selective thing.

My point is that the law is constantly being taken into the hands of somebody, and when a strong measure of common sense seems to suggest that the law is outmoded, or impossible to enforce, sensible people gradually set out to modify it. In the area of religious freedom, though, fear overcomes common sense; there is this mania about tampering with any syllable of the provisions guaranteeing religious freedom, even though intelligent people realize what I say about the cults is the truth.

My hope has always been that if enough of the public learned the facts, remedies might follow. That is still my hope, and it's mainly why I wanted to tell my story in this book. A politician is only as good as you make him, and as bad as you let him be. He will only respond, and then very reluctantly and grudgingly, to the massive pressure of public opinion.

But it's not only the apathy of politicians that protects the cults. The churches of America have to shoulder their part of the blame. A lot of clergymen of various faiths have sat in on deprogrammings. They've seen firsthand what's going on. Yet most of them refuse to take a stand and come out publicly in support of what I'm doing, or even to denounce publicly what the cults are doing. I can't understand what they're afraid of. There is a moral vacuum in some churches of this country, and I think it's that vacuum that the cults are rushing in to fill. You would think that at the very least the legitimate, organized churches in the U.S. would want to initiate their own investigations of the cults in order to warn their congregations of the dangers to their children. But the Rabbi Davises are very few and far between.

Well, I'm sorry about that, and I'm disappointed and disillusioned to some degree. But I have no intention of backing off. I'm going to keep at them all—politicians and clergymen alike—until I make them understand, or until I drop dead trying, one or the other.

CHAPTER ELEVEN

Patrick's pugnacity notwithstanding, it's been a lonely battle. Nevertheless, there were moments when it appeared that he was getting his message through the barricades of apathy, suspicion and outright hostility. The acquittal in New York was one; the verdict in Seattle was another. However, in the spring of 1975, in California, all the elements of society he rages against and despises combined against him.

TED PATRICK: Towards the end of October, 1974, I'd been away from home for more than a month, traveling around the country, deprogramming. I was eager to get back to San Diego to spend some time with my family. There was also the business of having to prepare for my trial in Seattle. I had to go to Los Angeles and discuss some things with Mr. and Mrs. Crampton.

For some weeks prior to that, my secretary, Mrs. Sondra Sacks, had been in communication with a Mr. and Mrs. Rogin in Buena Park, California, which is a suburb of Los Angeles. The Rogins had a girl, Joanne, in the Hare Krishna cult and wanted me to help. Joanne was coming home for a visit to see a favorite aunt, and they wanted to retain me to deprogram her. Mrs. Sacks told them that I wasn't expected to be back on the Coast for a few more weeks, and that I certainly wouldn't be there on the date the Rogins said Joanne would be at home.

But Mrs. Sacks's son, Randy, had also been a Hare Krishna and when Mrs. Rogin found that out, she asked Mrs. Sacks if she and Randy would be willing to drive to Buena Park and try to talk to their daughter. Mrs. Sacks agreed.

Then, as it happened, I returned to San Diego a week or so before I'd planned to. Sondra explained the situation to me and said she and Randy were driving up the following day to Buena Park.

I told her, "Sondra, I don't want to get involved with those people. I don't have the time for one thing. I have to get ready for the trial and I haven't seen Ruth and the kids for weeks. I'm tired. I'm going to L.A. tomorrow to see the Cramptons, and then I want to come back here and take it easy for a few days. If I begin deprogramming this girl, it could take three, four days. I just can't do it."

She understood, but said she was going anyway, and as long as I had to go to L.A. we might as well all drive up together; she would talk to Joanne and then wait while I took care of my business with the Cramptons, and then we could all drive back to San Diego together. I said I didn't know how long I'd be with the Cramptons.

"However long it is, Randy and I will wait until you're ready to come back."

So the next day we went. When we arrived at the Rogins' house the mother was naturally surprised to see me. I hastened to explain that I couldn't get involved with deprogramming her daughter, and gave her my reasons. She was disappointed, but was pleased that Randy and Sondra were there at least.

"I'll just wait out here in the car until you're finished," I said. "I'll take a nap. Then we'll go into L.A."

But it was a hot day, and the Rogins had a swimming pool in the backyard, and Mrs. Rogin invited me to wait back there, in the shade, with a glass of iced tea. So I sat by the pool chatting with a grandmother while Randy and Sondra went inside.

It was around three-thirty in the afternoon when we got there, and I waited outside for two, maybe two and a half hours. Then Sondra came out, and said, "She's calmed down now. I think maybe she'd listen to you if you'd come in and talk to her."

"Sondra, I told you, I don't want to get involved in this. You can't ever tell where it's going to lead."

"Just for a few minutes. Just see if you can do anything with her. Then we'll go."

I sighed. "Okay, but I'm not going to stay."

The girl was in the bathroom, sitting on the floor. She was wearing a blouse and a long white slip. She had her knees drawn up and her face against her knees. I never did see that girl's face. If I'd met her on the street the next day I wouldn't have recognized her.

Her father was standing by the bathroom door. We shook hands and then I went in and sat down on the toilet.

"My name's Ted Patrick," I said. There was no response from the girl. "What's your name?" She didn't say a word. "Do you believe in Krishna?" You couldn't tell if she even heard me. "Do you mind if I talk to you for a while?" Still nothing.

I opened my briefcase and took out a picture of Prabhupada, the Krishna leader. When I deprogrammed Randy he'd given me a lot of their literature, books and pamphlets and things, and whenever I travel the trunk of the car is always filled with cult stuff. I said to the girl, "Look, Joanne, I know what you're going through. I've dealt with lots of kids in the Krishna cult. I know the sort of psychological fear you're undergoing. See this? This is a picture of Prabhupada." She didn't look, didn't even raise her head. "I know they told you that if you ever showed disrespect to this picture, terrible things would happen to you—demons would come out of the wall, and devils, and all sorts of things. Well, look." I ripped the picture into little pieces. "See? I just tore the picture to bits. You see any demons coming out of the wall? Anything terrible happening to you?"

There was a long silence, and then she said, "Mother, can I have a glass of water, please?"

Her mother poured her some water from the bathroom tap and handed her the glass. She took it, raised her head, and flung it in my face. There were a few moments of commotion. Someone handed me a towel, and then all of a sudden, taking advantage of the confusion, she jumped to her feet and was out the door like a shot. As soon as I realized she was gone, I went outside, got into the car and drove away. All told I wasn't in that house for fifteen minutes.

While I was driving around town, Joanne had sprinted to a neighbor's house and banged on the door, yelling bloody murder. They let her in, but before she could call the police, the parents and Randy Sacks arrived. They got hold of her and carried her away, explaining to the neighbors what was going on. Those people didn't call the police, but some other neighbors who were watching from their windows did. Forty-five minutes later, when I drove up to the house again, the police were there.

At that time no charges were filed. Joanne told the police that she wanted to be taken to the police department, and when she got there she telephoned her husband, who was also in the cult, and asked him to pick her up.

In any event, I didn't think anything else about it. I went on to Los Angeles, talked to the Cramptons, and then went home.

A week later I got a call from the Buena Park police saying there was a warrant out for my arrest. They were charging me with malicious mischief and false imprisonment. Warrants were also out for Sondra and Randy as well as the parents.

I still wasn't much worried. The way I travel around it takes a long time before anyone catches up with me to serve papers. As it turned out I would have been a lot smarter simply never to go back to Buena Park. But eventually I did, and the case came to trial with me and Sondra and the Rogins as defendants. Randy was tried separately in juvenile court.

The pre-trial memorandum my attorneys put together, out-lining what we intended our defense to be, was comprehensive and persuasive. It was essentially the same line of defense that we used in Seattle.

We began by quoting the definition of necessity as a defense, which is the same defense we used in New York. The gist of it was based on the decision in a 1969 case in California (*People vs. Richards*) that said the defense of necessity prevents a person from being punished when his otherwise illegal acts avert greater evil than they cause.

Then we took up the question of justification's precedents in common law. Here I'm quoting from the brief:

> Blackstone asserts that no crime has been committed: "When a man has his choice of two evils set before him, and being under necessity of choosing one, he chooses the least pernicious of the two."

And we cited many examples of justification by necessity.

Then we stated the provisions of section 3.02 in the Model Penal Code drafted in 1962 which says the following:

Section 3.02 Justification Generally: Choice of Evils

1. Conduct which the actor believes to be necessary to avoid a harm or evil to himself or to another is justifiable, pro-vided that:

   a) the harm or evil sought to be avoided by such conduct

is greater than that sought to be prevented by the law
defining the offense charges; and

b) Neither the code nor other law defining the offense
provides exceptions or defenses dealing with the specific
situation involved; and

c) a legislative purpose to exclude the justification claimed
does not otherwise plainly appear.

We went on to argue that, "Many states have adopted the
Model Penal Code 'Choice of Evils' statute or a variation
thereof. Other states have statutes stating that conduct lacking
'evil design or intention' is non-culpable (e.g. Idaho, Montana).
Still other states have provided by statute that all common law
justification defenses are available (e.g. New Hampshire). The
following states have expressly, through statute, established
justification as a valid defense: Colorado, Connecticut, Georgia,
Hawaii, Idaho, Illinois, Kentucky, Louisiana, Montana, Nevada,
New Hampshire, New York, Oregon, Pennsylvania, Texas,
Utah, and Wisconsin. Other states have proposed criminal codes
including justification by necessity as a defense which are pending legislative approval."

We pointed out further that the proposed Criminal Code for
the state of California drafted by the Joint Legislative Committee for Revision of the Penal Code recognized justification
as a defense. We went on to argue:

The principle of necessity . . . states that conduct otherwise
illegal, may be justified if the actor "can show" that it was done
in order to avoid consequences which could not otherwise
be avoided. That the actor "can show" the justifiability of his
conduct suggests that the actor must demonstrate substan-
tiating facts that are within his particular knowledge—facts
upon which the actor subjectively relied in executing his
avoidance-of-evil course of action. The Model Penal Code,
also proposes a subjective standard—"conduct which the actor
believes to be necessary to avoid a harm or evil."

In order to back up our argument that the parents did have

reasonable fears for the health and welfare of their child, we laid out the evidence at some length:

We propose to show that Mr. and Mrs. Rogin became aware of increasingly alarming information commencing from the time of Joanne's initiation into the Hare Krishna cult up to and through the time of the acts alleged in the complaints herein. The information known to the parents consisted of: 1) Personal observations; 2) Observations and experiences of former Hare Krishna cult members recounted to the Rogins; 3) Information from other persons, including parents familiar with the Hare Krishna cult and/or similar cults; and 4) Television, newspaper, and magazine reports. The information caused them to reasonably believe that Joanne's physical and mental welfare were in serious danger by virtue of her association with the cult, and that the only way to save her from serious harm was to attempt to keep her from returning to the cult environment by convincing her of the imminent physical and mental harm she faced.

Mr. and Mrs. Rogin observed a drastic change in their daughter Joanne's personality and physical and mental state after her entry into the Hare Krishna cult:

1. After graduating from high school at seventeen years of age, Joanne ceased to live at home and moved in with the cult at their "temple." Her appearance, dress, the way she spoke, and the new subject area of her conversation suddenly became very strange. Her total attention focused on the divine "Lord Krishna," a Hindu sub-deity, and how to serve his directives as communicated by Prabhupada, a Bengali businessman who came to the United States in 1965. She deserted her entire religious upbringing and worshiped idols consisting of the blue-colored boy-god Krishna and his consorts, offering food and gifts before their graven images and changing the idols' clothing (including a set of pajamas) three times daily.

2. The Rogins continuously found their daughter out on the street by a shopping center near their Buena Park home peddling cult pamphlets, books, and incense, as well as dancing and chanting loudly. Even when it was raining and

cold, the Rogins saw their daughter had no footwear other than unmatched shower clogs and no rain gear or jacket to wear. They were distressed to see her alone, confronting strangers, and asking them for money.

3. Although Joanne wouldn't live at home, was devoting her entire energies to the cult activity, and had even been married to another cult member, she still had to return to her parents' home for such essentials as soap, toothpaste, vitamins, and other household items. Furthermore, she often asked them for money, which they never refused her, although they could ill afford to make such contributions.

4. During their visits on Sunday at the "temple" the Rogins saw how their daughter lived. She slept on the floor, the rooms were cold, and there was no heating source. She had no warm clothing and existed on a nutritionally insufficient diet. She had to rise at 3:00 A.M. every morning and take a cold shower to stifle "evil lusts", then chant the Hare Krishna mantra for at least two hours. She told her parents she got very little sleep and the parents observed that she was exhausted and slept ten to twelve hours each time she returned home to get money and other necessities.

5. Her parents learned that Joanne was ordered to sell books and incense, other cult members would drop her off alone daily on various street corners. Often she called her parents (collect) to come and take her home so that she could eat and rest. But the Rogins had to be certain to get her back to the location where she had been selling the books before the other cult members returned to get her so that they wouldn't know she had been home. (When the cult members finally learned of Joanne's trips home, she was no longer stationed near her home.) One time Joanne was so exhausted from her required peddling and begging that she passed out while waiting to be picked up by her parents.

6. The Rogins discovered that the cult leaders had "assigned" a husband to their daughter. They learned that her name had been placed on a list and the cult leaders "picked" her for marriage. They learned from their daughter that, even in marriage, sexual relations were forbidden except when the leaders permitted, which was once a month and only for the purpose of procreation because the sex act was "vulgar" and

"strength-draining." The husband lived with the men and she lived with the women in the "temple." In telephone conversations, their daughter complained bitterly about her unusual marital arrangement as well as treatment she received from her "husband," who was solely dedicated to Krishna.

7. Their daughter told them that if she ever had a baby the cult would send it to Dallas where a national "school" for cult indoctrination was located. They were also shocked by their daughter's description and their own observance of infant and child care at the cult "temple." They observed a complete absence of any emotional involvement with the children.

8. Their daughter often called her parents "murderers" because they ate meat. She told Mrs. Rogin that she was only her "sixth mother" because there were five "spiritual mothers" ahead of her.

9. When her parents expressed concern over her physical appearance and condition, she told them her body was just "stool and urine" and meant nothing.

10. When Mrs. Rogin took her daughter shopping, her daughter would often stop in the middle of the store or street and loudly commence chanting, causing difficult and embarrassing scenes. When they tried to engage their daughter in discussions about the cult, she would begin chanting endlessly so that they were unable to talk to her.

11. Joanne displayed an unusual affinity toward cows, which the Rogins learned were worshiped by the cult. On several occasions when the Rogins drove their daughter back to the "temple" she had them stop at a farm where there were cows. In disbelief they saw her on several occasions go into the field, pet, hug, rub, and kiss the cows. After a while her parents would practically have to drag her away despite her protestations. The Rogins believed the cows were treated better than the cult women and children.

12. Aside from Joanne's strange behavior and diminished health, the Rogins believed that the cult was engaged in an extensive economic deception and that their daughter was a victim of this deception. They saw that their daughter and other devotees, through begging and peddling, were collecting hundreds of dollars a day, yet their stark living conditions revealed little in return for their efforts. They observed that all

of their daughter's personal belongings were appropriated by the cult leaders, including all her cash, jewelry, and clothing.

Mr. and Mrs. Rogin had spoken personally with a former member of the Hare Krishna cult who had been rescued by her parents from the cult. Among other things, the Rogins learned of the following facts from Miss Sue Thompson on September 11, 1974:

1. That she had been subjected to mind control by the Hare Krishna leaders and instructed not to use her mind or think of herself because it was "of the devil" to do so, and, therefore, "evil."

2. That she was assigned to Kennedy airport for the purpose of begging and soliciting for the cult every day for twelve to fifteen hours per day. She would bring from two hundred to five hundred dollars to the temple after each mission.

3. That the cult leaders told her to hate her parents and other people in the "outside world" (not in Hare Krishna) because they were "murderers" since they ate meat and "demons" since they did not worship Lord Krishna.

4. That the girls in the group were treated in an inferior manner. They were only supposed to work and serve the male members of the group, never speaking to them unless it was "crucial."

Miss Thompson emphasized to the Rogins that she and others involved with the cult were not happy as individuals, but were participants only by virtue of fear and mind control. She urged the Rogins to get their daughter out as soon as possible if they cared about her safety.

The Rogins heard Mr. and Mrs. Kurt Crampton on a radio talk show discussing the plight of their daughter who had been victimized by a New Testamental Cult called the Church of Armaggedon a/k/a Love Family. Mrs. Rogin contacted Mrs. Crampton by letter and was referred by Mrs. Crampton to other parents who had been helped by Ted Patrick in rescuing their children from the influence of cults.

Mr. and Mrs. Rogin talked with Mrs. Sondra Sacks, mother of Randall (Randy) J. Sacks, who was a Hare Krishna cult member who had been rescued by his mother with the assistance of Mr. Patrick. In the course of several conversations with Mrs. Sacks the Rogins learned:

1. Mrs. Sacks said that her son felt that he had been "ripped off" for the two-and-one-half years while he was a cult member; that, although he had been told he was working for God (Krishna), he discovered that his entire effort had been for the cult leaders' financial benefit.

2. Mrs. Sacks told the Rogins that Randy not only signed over all his material possessions, but that he relinquished his personality, his thinking, and virtually his entire life to the cult. Mr. and Mrs. Rogin strongly identified with her when she told them that Randy only came home when he wanted something, or some money, and that he acted like a "zombie" most of the time.

3. Finally, the Rogins learned that Randy, after his release from the influence of the cult, was willing to assist anyone who wanted to help their children escape cult domination, just as he had been helped.

The brief concluded, "For the foregoing reasons, we submit that the defense of justification by necessity is a proper one, that the evidence we have, in part, set forth as an offer of proof is admissible in support of this defense, that the merits of the proposed defense in this particular case are a question for the jury under proper instruction, and that it is the prosecutor's burden to disprove the defense of necessity beyond a reasonable doubt."

I thought we had an airtight case. The verdict in New York in the Dan Voll trial had seemed to me to be confirmed by the Seattle case. The defense of necessity had worked twice, and I was confident that those precedents would carry the day in California.

It was especially important for me to win this one, furthermore, inasmuch as I was still on probation as the result of a conviction the previous summer in Denver. I had tried to help five Greek-American families recover their daughters from a quasi-religious group. We had succeeded in snatching two of the girls, whom I deprogrammed. Before their rehabilitation was done, however, the cult members, encouraged by the District

Attorney in Denver, got to them and eventually the girls were persuaded to bring charges against me and the parents.

The parents copped a plea and got off with a fine. I refused to cop a plea or to make a deal with the prosecutor, and I stood trial. The trial was very confusing, and, to make a long story short, though I was acquitted on the charges of kidnapping and unlawful conspiracy, I was found guilty of unlawful imprisonment.

That verdict was still under appeal. I was still on probation. I knew that if I was now convicted in California, it would amount to a violation of my probation in Denver, and I might very well end up in jail.

As I said, it seemed like an airtight defense. In fact I believe it *was* an airtight defense. The only problem was, the judge refused to let us present it. "This is a matter of religious liberty, plain and simple," he said. And he restricted our defense and all testimony to the "facts" of what happened that Sunday afternoon in the Rogins' home.

Well, it boiled down to Joanne's story against the stories of Mrs. Sacks and Mr. Rogin and Randy. Interestingly enough, earlier, Randy had been found not guilty by the judge in the juvenile court, characterizing Joanne's testimony there as "less than truthful." That was putting it mildly as far as Joanne's testimony was concerned. She lied like hell.

She had Sondra screaming at her non-stop for four hours, beating her, wrestling with her, sitting on top of her to hold her down. The same with Randy and the Rogins. If we'd done half the things to her she claimed we did, she would have had to come to court in a stretcher. As far as I was concerned, the main point was the time she claimed I spent in the house. In fact, it was somewhat less than fifteen minutes; Joanne had me there for almost two hours.

That the jury did not believe her completely was indicated by the fact that Sondra was acquitted on the charge of assault and battery although Joanne's strongest allegations had to do with being beaten by her. However, they found her guilty of false imprisonment; they found me guilty of false imprisonment also, though they acquitted me of the charge of malicious mischief.

A few weeks later at the sentencing, the parents, who were also found guilty of false imprisonment, were fined a nominal amount of money and placed on probation. The probation officer, whose duty it is to make recommendations to the court as to the severity of the sentence, thought a fair sentence for me would be a three hundred dollar fine and probation. Normally, the judge hands down a sentence far more lenient than what the probation official recommends. Not in Orange County. The judge gave me a year, all suspended but sixty days, and placed me under probation for three years.

The seriousness of the sentence (which we immediately announced our intention of appealing, so that I was released on my own recognizance) went far beyond the sixty days. I realized at once that I was going to have trouble back in Denver. Sure enough, at the beginning of June my lawyer called from Denver and said I had to appear for a hearing on June 26 to review the question of whether I'd violated the conditions of my probation. That it would be something less than a balanced, objective hearing was suggested by my attorney's closing words: "The judge said you'd better bring your toothbrush."

Still, I thought I had reason to hope that I'd avoid going to jail. For one thing, the Denver conviction was under appeal. So was the one in California. But most importantly, I felt I had not violated the conditions of my probation. The judge had told me that deprogramming was not against the law, and that, at the invitation of the parents, I was free to talk to their children. However, as soon as I understood that the person was being held against his will I was supposed to get up and leave. Technically speaking, in California I'd done that. When the girl made her break, I left. She herself testified that I'd never touched her. She lied, however, in testifying that she'd made repeated attempts to break out and had been restrained while I was present.

Anyway, I thought the wisest course of action was to hope for the best while expecting the worst. So I prepared my family for the prospect that I would be in jail for a while (eight months was the minimum I could expect to be behind bars) and was pleased at the understanding of my children. They have witnessed numerous deprogrammings in my home; they know what the kids look like when they arrive and how improved they are when they leave. They were therefore able to appreciate the fact that I wasn't facing a jail term because I'd done anything wrong. And that was a comfort.

On Thursday, the twenty-sixth of June, at eight-thirty in the morning, I was in the offices of my attorneys in Denver. They were not optimistic about my avoiding jail. After all, two and a half weeks before the hearing, Judge Zita Weinshienk had announced to my attorneys that she was sending me to jail. The hearing, then, promised to be an empty exercise.

It was a bright, hot, sunny day. The sidewalks around the courthouse were jammed with reporters and cameras. We pushed through the crowd and went inside. The courtroom was also packed.

While we were waiting for the judge to appear a woman approached me and introduced herself. She said she'd come a long way for the opportunity to ask me to deprogram her child, who was caught up in the Unification Church.

"Let's see what happens here," I said. "If I can, I'll talk to you when this is over."

The court reporter arrived, sat down at his machine and nodded a greeting to me. I smiled back at him and waved. He had lost his brother to a cult, and his mother and father too; the brother had gone berserk and murdered them. He knew.

Then the judge came in and the D.A. stood up and recommended that my probation be revoked and that I be sent to jail.

He was followed by my attorney who requested a stay of execution, making the point that in fact I had not violated the conditions of my probation. The judge denied the motion.

Then I took the stand and for the first time told my side of what happened with Joanne Rogin in Buena Park. My attorney asked me, "While you were in the house did you remember the conditions of your probation here?"

"Yes, I did."

"Please explain those conditions."

"If I was talking to a person eighteen or over, the minute I realized he or she was being held against their will, I was to get up and leave."

"Have you violated those conditions?"

"No."

The prosecutor examined me next, and asked if I had had a chance to tell my story at the trial in California.

The judge denied that she had ever said that the conditions of my probation were what I claimed they were. But transcripts of the proceedings bear me out.

After I was finished on the stand, Mrs. Sacks testified in my behalf, and then the judge gave her verdict. I was sentenced to eight months in jail, to begin immediately, and my bail was set at twenty-five thousand dollars.

The amount of the bail made everyone gasp. My attorney went through the roof. He had argued very powerfully that I had never had bail imposed on me in the Voll case, the Kathy Crampton case or, for that matter, in the Rogin case. I was always released on my own recognizance. He pointed out that I had come to Denver to reply to the original warrant in this case of my own free will; because it was a misdemeanor, I wouldn't have had to stand trial at all. I had demonstrated time and again that I was a responsible citizen, and that when the courts asked me to appear I appeared.

But the judge wasn't having any of it. Her mind was made up. The bail was twenty-five thousand—a sum far in excess, I might add, of the bail set for rapists, bank robbers, child-abusers and other felons under that court's jurisdiction.

The sheriff came over to me and said, "Let's go, Mr. Patrick." I shook hands with my attorneys. In the turmoil that had followed the departure of the judge I caught a glimpse of the woman whose child was in the Unification Church. She was talking agitatedly with Mrs. Sacks. Later Sondra told me that the woman said, "The minute Mr. Patrick gets out of jail, I want him to come and deprogram our child."

The sheriff led me through the crowd and down a hallway to an elevator. The press was running along with us peppering me with questions. Then I was inside the elevator and the doors slid closed.

We went to the sheriff's office first, where an inventory was made of the few personal belongings I'd brought with me, and then I was taken downstairs and put in a police bus with about twenty other convicts, some in leg irons, some in handcuffs, and we set out for the county jail.

As we drove through the sunny streets of Denver, I sat looking out the windows at scenes I would not see again for a long time, and thought about all that had happened since that other fateful bus ride I had taken three years before from Mission Beach to the commune of the Children of God in Santee. The Collinses, the Lockwoods, Dan Voll and Judge Wright, the Cramptons, the Shapiros, Bernie Weber, Winnie Swope, the Santinis and the Goskis. All the fights and the hassles and the public speaking, and the snatches and the deprogrammings— all the bizarre things that I'd taken part in, and the terrible people I'd met, and the wonderful, kind and generous people too. Pat Wall and Professor Duke at Yale, Professor McPherson in Canada, that sheriff in Kelso, Washington, and many more. I thought about them all during that ride, and concluded that, on balance, I had nothing to regret, no reason to feel sorry for myself. If I had to do it over again, I would do it the same way.

And I decided I would put my time in jail to good use, laying out plans for further campaigns against Sun Myung Moon and Prabhupada and the Guru Maharaj Ji and all the rest of them. Because if the cults thought they had derailed me they were mistaken. I'd only been detoured. I would be back, and when I got back, the cults would be the first ones to know about it.

POSTSCRIPT

It would have been pleasant, Ted Patrick's secretary was thinking, if they'd sent a limousine to meet them at the airport. Mrs. Sacks had amused herself during the flight from San Diego with vague daydreams of a liveried driver bowing them into the back seat, butlers announcing them, servants bringing them things to eat and drink, baronial splendors of one sort or another out of *Citizen Kane*. Not that any of this was even a distant possibility, of course. The visit was purely exploratory, and while no one was pledged to secrecy, exactly, there was a tacit understanding that discretion should prevail.

The three of them—Patrick, Sondra Sacks, and a man whose son had been deprogrammed from the Unification Church— rented a green Duster from a Budget Rent-a-car at the airport and drove themselves to Nob Hill. Mrs. Sacks was nervous. How could she not be nervous? What did you wear on such an occasion? She had debated a long time that morning before selecting a white pants suit. She'd spent extra time on her hair and her cosmetics.

It was a beautiful late afternoon in summer, and the city was lovely. She was fond of San Francisco, and had often been there with Ted on business. But never to Nob Hill; never on business like this.

Well, she reasoned, in the last analysis the lady was a mother, just as she was. Mothers were mothers, whether they lived on Nob Hill or in Cleveland. Mrs. Sacks would meet with her on that common ground. If she'd learned anything in these long months of traveling around the country with Ted, it was how to deal with mothers whose children were lost. And on the phone the lady had sounded gracious, kind, dignified, very considerate. Still, a person could be excused some nervousness.

Ted was not nervous. He never was. He sat there smoking a cigar and humming along with the music on the radio, his head moving up and down rhythmically in time to the strong soul beat he loved so much. He could be going to a reception for the Queen of England, and it wouldn't phase him; he would be just as composed—a little withdrawn, a little removed from his surroundings, using the time spent traveling to cat-nap, absorbing some of the sleep that was forever in such short supply.

They parked the car across from the Mark Hopkins and stood looking up for a moment at the mellow old apartment building that faced the glamorous hotel. A uniformed doorman admitted them. Yes, they were expected. They took the old European-style elevator up to the tenth floor. No one spoke on the ride up.

They stepped out of the elevator into a kind of foyer with a marble floor, and a door opposite. Before they could knock, the door opened and the woman—prettier, more youthful than she appeared to be on television, and softer too—smiled and extended her hand and said, "Hello, how nice to see you." Then Mrs. Hearst stepped back into the apartment to let them enter.

A year ago, Ted had taken a group of deprogrammed youngsters to the offices of the San Francisco *Examiner* to try to persuade an editor that what had happened to Patricia Hearst was identical to what was happening all over the country to young followers of Sun Myung Moon, Guru Maharaj Ji, David Berg, Hannah Lowe, and all the others. Ted had been certain of this the first time he heard one of the tapes of the captive Patty's voice. He'd declared then, unequivocally, "Let me get my hands on her and I'll deprogram her in no time flat."

Impressed, the editor had contacted Patricia's parents, and an appointment to meet had been set up through Mrs. Sacks. But schedules had conflicted and the first appointment was postponed, and then so was another one, and time passed, and there was the bank robbery in between, where Patty appeared holding a machine gun, and the shoot-out and fire bombing in Los Angeles and Patrick's legal problems.

Now, three weeks after Patrick's release on bail from the Denver jail, they were finally together, introducing each other, Randolph A. Hearst, in slacks and shirt-sleeves, leading the way into the spacious living room. He was serious, slow-speaking—an important man and conscious of it, but cordial and solicitous. Mrs. Sacks, who had come to give the Hearsts a sense of her own experience as mother of a former cult victim, felt she'd been right. They were just parents, and she warmed to them accordingly.

The living room was not exactly out of *Citizen Kane,* but it was very elegant. Mrs. Sacks looked about, appreciating the expensive rugs, the antiques, the paintings, and the view of San Francisco spread out below in the twilight. Hearst was pleased at her admiration, and directed her attention to points of interest in the panorama, while Patrick, who was not there to admire landscapes, addressed himself at once to the purpose of their visit.

"This man," he explained, gesturing toward his companion, "had a son in the Unification Church who I deprogrammed. I want you to hear his story so you'll see how it compares with what happened to your daughter."

As they ate cheese and crackers laid out on a coffee table, the man whose son Patrick had rescued began to talk about Sun Myung Moon and draw parallels between the mind-control techniques of the Unification Church and the Symbionese Liberation Army. Obviously none of this was news to the Hearsts. Mrs. Sacks realized that they wouldn't be in this apartment if the Hearsts had not done extensive amounts of homework on both Patrick and his profession. Nor would they be here if the Hearsts weren't already hopeful that Patrick could help them.

At some point another of the Hearst daughters came into the room with a young man, said hello, and went off to another part of the house.

Patrick brought out a tape recorder and some casettes. "The girl on this tape was in the Hare Krishna cult. I'd like you to hear how she sounded before she was deprogrammed. See how much the sound of her voice is like Patty's on those tapes. And how she says the same things, calling her parents pigs, agents of the Devil. Like somebody had written a script for her and she was reading it. Listen."

He snapped on the machine. Mrs. Hearst bent forward from the waist, frowning slightly with concentration. The voice that came into the room was frail, empty, hollow, and without expression.

"That's just how your daughter sounds," Patrick said.

Indeed, except for the references to religion, the voice might well have been that of Patricia Hearst. The husband and wife exchanged a glance, and Mrs. Hearst nodded.

It began to get dark outside, the tall windows turning into mirrors of the scene. Patrick played several more tapes. While they were playing, Hearst got up, announcing that he was hungry. "Would you like something to eat?" he asked the guests. They declined, and Hearst went into the kitchen to fix something for himself. If any butlers or servants were on the premises, they didn't show themselves. Mrs. Hearst remained seated, listening hard to the tapes.

"But this isn't a religious thing specifically," she said after a while. "Would your methods still work with Patty?"

"She's programmed," Patrick replied, putting his casettes and his player into his briefcase and locking it. "Doesn't matter what someone's programmed *to*. It can be the Bible, it can be a telephone book. Mind control is being exercised. There's a book you ought to read called *Battle for the Mind* by a man named Sargant, William Sargant. I think he lives in England. Best book I know on the subject. It explains the whole technique. The Korean POWs weren't programmed to religion either."

"Maybe we could talk to this Sargant, Randolph," Mrs. Hearst suggested to her husband, who had returned from his snack by then. "What do you think?"

"We'll see," he said.

"The thing is," Patrick emphasized, "if you don't have her deprogrammed, she's never going to come out of it. There's a woman I know of who left a cult in New York on her own, but because she didn't have anyone to deprogram her she almost went out of her mind. Tried to kill herself. Went through mental hell for more than a year. The fear and confusion is very strong and someone who knows what he's doing has to deal with it."

"And you'd be willing to try once we find her?"

"You let me know, and I'll drop everything and come running," Patrick promised.

"All right," Mrs. Hearst said finally. "If anything happens we'll be in contact with you."

"You'd better let me give you our phone number here," Hearst said, "so you can get through directly to me. I'll give you my private number at the office too."

The meeting had taken four and a half hours. Mrs. Sacks took in the view of San Francisco at night one more time before everyone shook hands and said goodbye.

The day that Patty Hearst was apprehended by the FBI, Patrick talked on the telephone with Mrs. Hearst. Mrs. Hearst was profoundly relieved that her daughter was in custody, upset that the authorities were for the moment refusing to let her see her daughter, but confident that as a matter of course Patty would soon be out on bail. "When we have her home I'll get in touch with you," she said.

As of this writing, two months have passed and Patricia Hearst remains in custody. Patrick made another visit to the Hearst apartment on November 11, 1975. They had further discussions. When they were over, Hearst told Patrick that as soon as something broke in the case they would be in touch. Friendly and solicitous as before, he offered Patrick the use of his chauffeured limousine while he was in San Francisco. Patrick, always consistent, refused the offer.

But after this meeting, Patrick was not optimistic. Batteries of psychiatrists and lawyers had intervened in the case, and his opinion of psychiatrists and lawyers in general is not high. For him, the alternatives are categorical: either Patricia Hearst will be deprogrammed or she will be a psychological vegetable for the rest of her life.

"She just can't be held responsible for anything she did

after the SLA brainwashed her," he argues. "That wasn't Patty Hearst doing those things—it was a zombie. It's the same thing with Squeaky Fromme," he goes on, alluding to the young would-be assassin of President Ford. "Squeaky Fromme is just what I'm talking about. Manson went to jail and those girls were not deprogrammed. They're still programmed to what he told them.

"Even if they plead not guilty because of insanity with Patty, she's lost. Might as well plead guilty. Either way she's never going to be herself again. They can send her to every psychiatrist in the country, it won't do any good. No psychiatrist can cure what's wrong with her. I know it. They've taken her mind away. Why don't people understand?"